THE
MASS MEDIA
ELECTION

*Sponsored by the Committee on
Mass Communications and Political Behavior
of the Social Science Research Council*

American Political Parties and Elections
general editor: Gerald M. Pomper

*Copublished with the
Eagleton Institute of Politics,
Rutgers University*

THE MASS MEDIA ELECTION

How Americans Choose Their President

Thomas E. Patterson

PRAEGER

PRAEGER SPECIAL STUDIES • PRAEGER SCIENTIFIC

Library of Congress Cataloging in Publication Data

Patterson, Thomas E
  The mass media election.

  (American political parties and elections)
  "Copublished with the Eagleton Institute of
Politics, Rutgers University."
  Bibliography: p.
  Includes index.
  1. Presidents--United States--Election--1976.
2. Mass media--Political aspects--United States.
I. Social Science Research Council. Committee on
Mass Communications and Political Behavior. II. Title.
III. Series.
JK526 1976.P37   324.7'3'0973   80-15986
ISBN 0-03-057729-2
ISBN 0-03-057728-4 (pbk.)

Published in 1980 by Praeger Publishers
CBS Educational and Professional Publishing
A Division of CBS, Inc.
521 Fifth Avenue, New York, New York 10017 U.S.A.

Printed in the United States of America

to Ellie

PREFACE

The impact of the mass media has not been a major topic in voting studies of the past 25 years. Until the last decade, in fact, the news media were not regarded as an influential force in U.S. politics. Writing in 1961, V. O. Key characterized the press as "a common carrier" of the messages of the political elite, while others likened it to a mirror held up to society.[1] Because the role of the media was seen essentially as a passive one, it was not a high research priority.[2]

Supporting this belief was the failure of earlier voting studies to show that the media did influence the public. Conducted in the 1940s, this research was expected to reveal such an influence. The apparent impact of scientific mass propaganda in totalitarian Europe in the 1930s and of Franklin Roosevelt's radio broadcasts in the same period suggested to many observers that the mass media's influence was hypodermic—if messages were communicated often enough and well enough, they seemed to be absorbed largely intact by mass audiences.[3] At least for presidential campaigns, however, this assumption was dispelled by the work of Paul Lazarsfeld and Bernard Berelson. Conducting panel surveys during the elections of 1940 and 1948, they discovered that media exposure seldom changed people's minds. They concluded that voters' opinions were molded by their party and social allegiances—allegiances that undermined the media's ability to change attitudes.[4]

This research settled for most scholars the question of the media's impact on the electorate. Some election analysts asserted that the media were powerless; most simply concluded that the media's effects were of secondary importance and concentrated on factors that might better explain the vote.[5] Beginning in the 1950s, the impact of party loyalty and issue attitudes on candidate choice became the focus of election research. The two major voting studies of the period—Angus Campbell et al.'s *The American Voter* (1960) and Norman Nie et al.'s *The Changing American Voter* (1976)—make almost no mention of the mass media or their impact.[6]

An issue-party-vote perspective still dominates the study of electoral behavior.[7] In recent years, however, there has been renewed interest in the influence that the campaign and particularly the media have on voters. The increased number of primaries, the decline in party loyalty, and the emergence of media-based campaigns have rendered what happens in the campaign more important to its outcome, prompting questions that go beyond the way in which people's attitudes relate to their vote. How involved do citizens become in the media campaigns of today? Are their images of the candidates influenced substantially by the media? How well informed are the voters via the mass media? What influence does campaign communication have on their candidate choices? Which of the political system's needs are met by the media campaign of today?

In the past decade researchers have begun to answer these questions. Several fairly comprehensive studies were conducted during the 1972 presidential campaign;[8] considerable research has been done since 1970 in schools of mass communication;[9] and there were literally scores of small research projects on the media's impact on voters during the 1976 campaign.[10] Altogether, the findings of the research of the past ten years provide considerable information about the influence of mass communication.

A major problem facing researchers has been the available data. Although the Lazarsfeld-Berelson studies used panel surveys, most of the surveys conducted since 1950 have involved single interviews with the respondents. Entirely adequate for researching the effects of party loyalty and issue attitudes, since these do not change greatly during the campaign, such surveys are inadequate for the study of the change that occurs during the campaign. This type of analysis properly requires repeated interviews with the same respondents, which is the procedure involved in panel surveys. Although several panel surveys have been conducted in the past few years, each of them has had major limitations. The panel survey that Robert McClure and I directed in 1972, for example, spanned only the general election. Ideally, it would have covered the entire election year so as to facilitate examination of the media's impact during the primaries as well.

This book has the benefit of what is likely the most comprehensive panel survey ever conducted for the study of change during a presidential campaign. Beginning in February 1976 before the primaries began and ending in November after election day, the 1200 respondents in the panel were interviewed as many as seven times each. These interviews provide a remarkable chronicle of how people's thoughts changed as the campaign progressed and permit a precise analysis of the media's impact on their thinking.

This book also relies on an extensive content analysis of the mass media's campaign coverage in 1976. An analysis of the news content of network television, daily newspapers, and weekly news magazines reveals how the news media covered the campaign, the candidates, and the issues.

The support for my research was provided by the Markle Foundation. A nonpartisan private foundation, Markle has contributed significantly to communication research by concentrating its grants in the area. The uses of the data obtained through this particular grant will not end here. I am turning the panel data over to a research archive where they will be available to interested scholars; the data can answer many more questions about the media, campaign, and voters than are addressed by my work.

ACKNOWLEDGMENTS

A grant from the John and Mary R. Markle Foundation provided the support for the research on which this book is based. I am grateful to the Markle Foundation and I particularly wish to thank Dr. Lloyd Morrisett, president of Markle, and Jean Firstenberg of the Markle staff for their assistance during the research project. I am also deeply indebted to Forrest Chisman, who was with Markle when I first inquired about support for a 1976 election project. Our first correspondence occurred early in 1974 and, for the next 18 months, Forrest worked to make the project a reality, a selfless effort for which I will always be grateful.

I am indebted to the Social Science Research Council (SSRC) for its help in several phases of the project. During the formative stage of the project, I had considerable assistance from Eleanor Sheldon (then president of the SSRC) and Ronald Abeles. Later, Kenneth Prewitt (current president of the SSRC) and Robert Gates provided their help.

A special debt is owed the members of the SSRC's Committee on Mass Communication and Political Behavior. It was during meetings of this committee in 1975 that a number of the ideas underlying this research were developed. The members of the committee, in addition to Eleanor Sheldon, Forrest Chisman, and myself, were editor-author-scholar Ben Bagdikian; Leo Bogart of the Newspaper Advertising Bureau; Richard Brody, political scientist from Stanford University; Steve Chaffee, mass communications professor from the University of Wisconsin; Philip Converse, political scientist from the University of Michigan; Herb Hyman, sociologist from Wesleyan University; Gerald Kline, then with the journalism department at the University of Michigan and now department head at the University of Minnesota; and Ithiel de Sola Pool, political scientist from the Massachusetts Institute of Technology.

The survey fieldwork for the project was conducted by Response Analysis Corporation of Princeton, New Jersey. I am grateful to Response Analysis for its assistance and particularly want to thank Robert Steen, the project officer, for his persistent efforts. I also thank the staff of about 100 interviewers who visited the homes of the survey respondents. Their skill in administering a series of challenging questionnaires was the first step toward the data for this book.

I am grateful to Robert McClure, my colleague at Syracuse University. The study that he and I jointly directed in 1972 was a forerunner of this study. Although Bob did not involve himself in this project, his ideas had a continuing influence.

I also want to thank two other Syracuse University colleagues—Ron McDonald, chairman of the political science department, and Guthrie Birkhead, dean of the Maxwell School of Citizenship and Public Affairs—who saw that I had the time necessary to conduct this research.

Most of all, I want to thank those who helped me prepare the survey and media content data for analysis and aided in the preparation of the manuscript. Unless one has been involved in a project like this, it is almost impossible to imagine the amount of effort involved in coding some 6,000 interviews, in content analyzing several thousand news stories, and in analyzing the resulting data. For these tasks, I had the good fortune of having a capable staff that performed with utmost care and cheerfulness. James Campbell, my graduate research assistant; Jill Alexander and Monona Wali, two of my coders; and Suzanne Ratzlaff, my editorial assistant, worked with me over a long period of time and gave me more help than ever could have been demanded by their pay and working conditions. I also want to express my heartfelt thanks to Lisa Bagdonas, Donald Beaver, Karen Beckwith, Daniel Bloom, Maureen Bonaduce, Maurice Boucher, Peter Brereton, John Carey, Stephanie Cherny, Cheryl Cohen, William Cole, Audrey Davidson, Robert Dziok, John George, Brian Gifford, Richard Godfrey, Matthew Kevin Greene, Anne Hamer, Karen Holohan, John Kelly, Julie Leidig, Joan Levy, Gerald Lourie, Barbara Mydosh, Patty Narciso, Marion Noble, Randy Parsons, Deborah Pela, David Phillips, Grace Potter, Richard Robbins, Maria Sambuco, Della Shupe, Elaine Swift, Barbara Thompson, Kathleen Tomlinson, Roberta Toner, Gloria Tripolone, Achala Wali, Maureen Walsh, Olive Ward, Nancy Wyrough, and Sandra Young.

Finally, I want to thank June Dumas, Maria Taylor, and James Bilodeau for typing draft after draft of the manuscript. Their patience and good cheer helped ease a difficult time.

CONTENTS

LIST OF TABLES

PART I
INTRODUCTION

1

A BRIEF ON THE MASS MEDIA ELECTION

Today's presidential campaign is essentially a mass media campaign. It is not that the mass media entirely determine what happens in the campaign, for that is far from true. But it is no exaggeration to say that, for the large majority of voters, the campaign has little reality apart from its media version. Without the benefit of direct campaign contact, citizens must rely on the media for nearly all of their election information. Moreover, the media are now without question the basis for the candidates' organizations. Presidential aspirants primarily direct their activities toward getting their messages through the media as often as possible.

ORIGINS OF THE MEDIA CAMPAIGN

That the media have an important role in the campaign is not new, but due to rather recent developments, their role is now especially prominent. At one time the nominating process was largely under the control of party leaders. As V. O. Key noted, the introduction of the direct primary in 1904 was a threat to that control,[1] but it was not until the 1950s and 1960s that the leadership's authority was regularly challenged in the primaries. Even then, as was demonstrated by the rejected candidacies of Estes Kefauver and Eugene McCarthy in 1952 and 1968, party leaders still had the power to deny nomination to a candidate not of their liking.[2] That is much less true today. The sweeping reforms of the nominating process that followed the 1968 campaign have effectively shifted control to the voting public.

From 1916 through 1968, only about 30 percent of the national convention delegates were selected through direct primaries; the rest were chosen in state conventions where the delegates selection rules gave advantage to the party leaders. The nomination of primary noncontestant Hubert Humphrey in 1968, however, created demands that led to greater voter participation in delegate selection. In 1972 just over 50 percent of the delegates were chosen in 23 state primaries. In 1976 roughly 70 percent were selected in 30 state primaries.[3]

Richard Rubin suggests that through their intense coverage of the primaries during the 1960s, the news media helped legitimize primaries "as *the* democratic way to make nomination choices."[4] Whatever their contribution to the change, the media, as a result, have become the focus of the candidates' nominating campaigns. It is now almost imperative for the serious candidate to seek nomination through the primaries, and the media are the only means of frequent contact with voters in the key states and in the nation. Instead of seeking meetings with the party leadership, the candidate now spends most of his time going from one media market to the next, seeking coverage through local news organizations and the national reporters accompanying him on the campaign trail.[5]

Second, the media's increased importance owes to changes in communication and the parties. In presidential campaigns the party was never the powerful organization implied by the stereotype of the turn-of-the-century machine. For every locale that had an organization capable of delivering the vote, there were, as Frank Sorauf notes, a hundred more where the party consisted of a mere handful of mostly inactive committeemen.[6] Nonetheless, the party was the principal link between presidential candidates and voters in the early decades of the 1900s. To be sure, signs of what historian Richard Jensen calls the advertising campaign style (one that emphasizes mass communication and the individual candidate) were already apparent, but this had not yet supplanted the earlier militaristic style that stressed canvassing and party loyalty.[7] Party organizations were still the best intermediaries then available to the candidates.

Even as late as the 1940s and 1950s the candidates' general election campaigns assigned to the party a role nearly as important as that of the media. This strategy reflected the residual strength of the party as well as the difficulty of organizing the campaign completely around the media. The print media, consisting of a large number of locally based dailies, did not provide an especially suitable foundation for a national campaign. Nor was television able in its early years to provide much coverage. Like the radio, television's newscasts were brief, allowing candidates little more than passing reference on the nightly news.[8] As well, the networks in the 1950s did not have the impressive news-gathering operations they have today. They made less use of pictures and depended heavily on news reports gathered by print organizations, reports that placed more emphasis on news events than on newsmakers.[9]

In the early 1960s, however, television newscasting underwent a basic change. Newly committed to gathering their own news material, the networks lengthened their evening newscasts in 1963 to the present 30 minutes. Transmitting their news through a visual medium to national audiences, they focused primarily on national politics and personalities, thus becoming, as Michael Robinson has noted, almost ideally suited to the publicity needs of presidential aspirants.[10]   Since 1964, in fact, the networks' evening news programs have been the major target of the candidates' campaign activities. To a great extent, candidates have scheduled their appearances around the deadlines of the evening newscasts and formed their strategies around assumptions about how the networks operate.[11]

As for newspapers, the number and dispersion of dailies still act as obstacles to their fuller use. But other changes in newspaper reporting have contributed to the making of media-based campaigns. Increasingly, newspapers have assigned reporters to the campaign trail, thus assuring the candidates of heavier coverage in locations distant from where they are campaigning. Moreover, the proportion of newspapers owned by corporate chains has grown from about 30 percent in 1960 to over 60 percent, many of them heavily dependent on election news gathered by their parent organizations.[12] Thus it is increasingly possible for a candidate to receive widespread newspaper coverage through contact with a few well-placed reporters.

These changes in mass communication, as David Broder points out, have reduced the candidates' need for revitalized party organizations.[13] In the past, the emphasis on face-to-face campaigning was based on the presumption that it was required if the voters were to be reached and persuaded. Most candidates believe that the media can now perform this task adequately, perhaps best exemplified by the heavy use of televised political advertising. During the 1960s candidates fully recognized the advantages of advertising as a means of voter contact.[14] Since then advertising has become the most costly activity of the campaign, demanding funds that previously would have been invested in the candidates' grass-roots efforts.

Third, the media have gained importance because the voters have come to depend more heavily on the information they provide. One of the most dramatic political changes in recent times has been the erosion of the voters' partisan loyalties. From the earliest Gallup polls in the mid-1930s until the early 1960s, surveys indicated that 80 percent or more of the adult public identified with either the Republican or Democratic party. About half of these described themselves as strong partisans.[15] Presently, however, party identifiers account for only about 60 percent of Americans, most of whom say they are weak partisans.[16]

Although some of this decline may be attributed to the changes in the electorate's information environment,[17] Walter Dean Burnham's historical analysis of voting trends indicates that the parties' hold on the electorate was already weakening in the early years of the twentieth century. It is Burnham's belief that the Depression and resulting New Deal only delayed a trend that has reemerged in recent years.[18]   Some decline in partisanship also could have been expected, as James Sundquist notes, when new issues created conflicts within the party divisions molded during the Depression.[19]

Whatever its exact causes, declining partisanship has made more important the role of communication in the campaign. Party loyalty is what Phillip Converse has called a long-term influence on the vote, since votes cast by party are largely unaffected by the issues and candidates specific to an election.[20] When party loyalties were stronger, the large majority of votes to be cast usually could be predicted in advance of the election; certainly, once the parties' national conventions were over, as polls conducted during past elections confirm, there was seldom much fluctuation in the candidates' support.[21]

Today, however, because of the weakening of partisanship, the vote is less predictable and more volatile. It also is more sensitive to short-term influences, such as an election's issues and personalities, which are transmitted largely by the media. Voters' evaluations of the candidates are now based more heavily on what they learn through the media during the campaign. Correspondingly, the candidates' fates depend more heavily on their media coverage.

THE EXPANDED ROLE OF THE PRESS

A significant result of today's media-based campaign is the influence gained by major news organizations. In earlier elections the press acted basically as a conduit for the candidates' messages. Although, as Walter Lippmann emphasized, the news is necessarily subjective,[22] the press once left its choices largely to the candidates. The formulas of objective journalism dictated that news coverage treat the candidates of the two major parties equally and that it be based on the facts.[23] Once nominated, the two candidates were thus assured of roughly equal exposure and, since the facts usually were defined by the contents of the candidates' prepared speeches and news releases, the agenda was essentially theirs to determine.[24]

Objective journalism continues to provide the candidates with some control over what is reported. With rare exception, every important new statement coming from a major candidate in the present campaign is reported by the press.[25] As Timothy Crouse observes, there is even much that the candidates say that is unimportant, or even downright trivial, that the press dutifully conveys to the public.[26]

Journalistic concern with what Lippmann called "the overt phases of events" also enhances the candidate's control by making what he says and does the major source of election news.[27] Since a candidate has some control over what topics he addresses and where his schedule takes him, he frequently can direct the press's attention toward what he wants it to see. Most of what the candidates do, in fact, falls under Daniel Boorstin's definition of pseudo events—happenings that are not spontaneous, but created simply to attract the press's attention.[28]

Nevertheless, objective journalism is now a less ready guide for the press in its coverage of the candidates. For one thing, the primaries present a different reporting situation than does the general election. In the primaries there are many candidates to cover, and the press must decide how much coverage to give each one. Allocation of coverage can make a difference. The press can ignore a candidate it considers unimportant, thus making his campaign almost certainly futile. To a large extent, as William Keech and Donald Matthews have noted, the press now performs the party's traditional role of screening the potential nominees for the presidency. [29]

The reporting situation also has been altered by the lengthening of today's campaign. Perhaps the most useful generalization about the press's influence is that the longer and more open-ended an event, the greater the press's discretion in reporting it. The shorter campaigns of the past, involving fewer candidate appearances and smaller press entourages, worked to maintain the candidates' control of the agenda—less was said by them and less was observed by the press. There are, however, 300-odd days to the present campaign, and on each of them news organizations report on the campaign. It is all but impossible for the candidate to control the news for a year. Major policy statements and guaranteed publicity ploys, after all, are limited in number. The lengthening of the campaign has created new opportunities for the press to base news selections on its own values, and only coincidentally will its decisions accord with the preferences of the candidates. Candidates are seeking coverage that will promote their campaigns. Reporters, says James David Barber, are looking for good stories. [30]

Finally, the strength of objective journalism as a guide to the nation's press has been weakening. During the past decade a new journalism has emerged that asserts that the press, in Paul Weaver's words, is obliged "to discover truth, not merely facts." [31] Although not all journalists embrace this new formula, its advocates feel the press must take a leading role in determining national debate. [32] In the campaign, the result can be seen in news reports that dig behind the scenes for information about the candidates' organizations and finances, purport to say just who the candidates are, and question whether the candidates are being completely honest with the voters. The effect has been to extend the press's influence on the campaign's content. "Traditionally in our democracy," writes Max Kampelman, "the nation's political agenda was the prerogative of the politician seeking and elected to public office. Now the media are [also] assuming that role." [33]

THE BOOK'S PURPOSE

This book looks closely at the mass media election of today. It studies ways in which the voters respond to it—how much attention they give it, what they learn from it, how they are influenced by it—and examines election coverage—how the press reports the campaign, the candidates, and the issues. Thus most of the pages are given to describing and explaining the nature and impact of the media campaign. The book's major purpose is to provide a body of knowledge that will contribute to an understanding of election coverage and the American voter.

Underlying this work, however, is a concern with what today's campaign implies for democratic government. Presidential elections are, perhaps, the mass citizenry's best opportunity to influence the direction of the nation's politics. Certainly, U.S. history cannot be understood without an accounting of the times when the electorate altered the party in power and, with that, the direction of government. The compelling question is whether the present campaign has better enabled the electorate to exercise its influence, a matter that the final chapter of this book will address.

2

TOPICS AND
EVIDENCE

Voters depend on the mass media for their access to a presidential campaign. What they see is not the real campaign but the media's version of it.
Election news results from a series of decisions made by news organizations
about what to observe, what to report, and what emphasis to place on various
parts of the coverage. Writes Colin Seymour-Ure:

> Indeed it is no exaggeration to claim that "the campaign" exists only
> as a construct of the media: they give to the disconnected though
> more or less coordinated activities of the participants a kind of
> scrap-book tidiness, laying out the pieces in patterns, with prom-
> inence to some while others are tucked away at the back.[1]

It is not the case that the public adopts the media's version of the campaign
in its entirety. It is in fact limited by the voters themselves. With considerable
control over the amount of election news they absorb, the voters help to govern
its impact. They also provide a conditioning influence, receiving the media's
messages after they have been filtered through and modified by individual needs,
prejudices, attitudes, beliefs, and stored information about politics. Thus, just
as the media provide an inexact portrayal of the actual campaign, the voters'
mental images are necessarily refracted impressions of the media's version.

These straightforward observations define the boundaries of inquiry in this
study. This book attempts to describe the election news, the audience for it,
and how this audience and this news combine to create the public's response to

9

today's campaign.

Part Two examines the press and its reporting of a presidential campaign, beginning in Chapter 3 with a look at the general focus of election news. What are the major themes of election coverage? Do television and the print media differ in what each emphasizes? Are the primary, convention, and general election periods reported in significantly different ways? Issues are the focus of Chapter 4. Which issues are emphasized by the press? Does the press have a bias for clear-cut issues that divide the candidates and provoke controversy? Chapter 5 then narrows in on candidate coverage in an attempt to discern what accounts for differences in what is communicated about the candidates. Is it their political pasts, their campaign successes, contrasts in style and personality? Are there differences in the ways that television and the print media present the candidates?

In Part Three the focus shifts to the audience for election news. To a large extent, voters control the amount and impact of the political information that reaches them. An important step in understanding the media campaign is to gain awareness of its audience. This analysis begins in Chapter 6 with a look at the attention people give to national news. Of particular concern is whether network television news significantly enlarges the attentive news audience beyond that of the newspaper. Is network news so invasive and broadly appealing that political information now effectively penetrates all levels of society? In Chapter 7 the analysis centers on the attention people pay to the campaign. How does their level of attention change as the campaign proceeds through the primaries, the conventions, and the general election? What role does news coverage play in this? Part Three closes with a reexamination in Chapter 8 of the conclusion of 1940s election research that people surround themselves with supportive information. Has the recent weakening of party loyalty made voters receptive to the messages of both parties? Has television greatly diminished the ease with which people can avoid one side's appeals?

Parts Two and Three are the descriptive sections of the book. Part Four is the analytical section. It attempts to show how the nature of election news and its audience combine to influence people's perceptions of the campaign, focusing first in Chapter 9 on voters' judgments about the campaign's most important aspects. The purpose will be to discover the images that voters have of the campaign, the extent to which these impressions are shared, and whether they are affected by the medium through which they are acquired. In Chapter 10 the media's impact on the voters' awareness of the candidates is studied. Are voters aware of every candidate in the running or only a select few? How does a candidate's news coverage relate to the familiarity of his candidacy? Chapter 11 addresses the press's impact on the voters' views of the candidates' chances of winning nomination and election, and whether this influence creates bandwagon effects. The analysis shifts in Chapter 12 to the public's perceptions of the issues. Do the media's messages substantially increase the voters' issue awareness? Are television and newspapers equally informative? Chapter 13 looks at people's images of the candidates. How accurate is the claim that the media's greatest power is the ability to create candidate's images? What part do the voters' political biases play in image formation?

The last section, Part Five, summarizes the findings and suggests that the present campaign places unreasonable demands on the press and the public, demands that might be alleviated by changes in election policy.

ELECTION NEWS CONTENT

The evidence for this book derives from two sources. One is a content analysis of the news media's coverage of the 1976 presidential election based on a study of nine news outlets—the evening newscasts of the three major television networks, ABC, CBS, and NBC; two newsmagazines, *Time* and *Newsweek*; and four daily newspapers. The newspapers were the *Los Angeles Times*, a morning newspaper generally ranked among the nation's five best dailies; the *Los Angeles Herald-Examiner*, an evening newspaper that is part of the Hearst chain; and the *Erie News* and *Erie Times*, Erie, Pennsylvania's morning and evening papers that, though jointly owned, have separate editorial staffs and use different wire services, the *Times* using UPI and the *News* AP.

By random selection, 6,567 political news stories appearing in these nine outlets between January 1, 1976, and November 2, 1976 (election day) were chosen for analysis. A code was given each of these stories to indicate the date it appeared in the outlet, whether it was accompanied by a newsphoto or film, its length, and its position (for example, whether a newspaper story appeared on the front page or a back page). Each story also was identified by its principal subject and actor, and whether it reflected favorably or unfavorably on this actor. The following story from the *Erie News* of May 7, 1976, illustrates the use of this code:

> Reagan Now Believes in First Ballot Victory
>
> New Orleans (AP)—Ronald Reagan said Thursday that he now believes he can win a first-ballot victory at the Republican National Convention. He also refined his position on the Panama Canal. He said that when he began his campaign, he counted on a core of delegates pledged to him, plus an eventual gathering of uncommitted delegates as the convention wore on. "For the first time, today I said to the people what I have come to believe in my own heart. I happen to believe now that I can go to the convention with enough delegates to win on the first ballot," the former California governor said. Reagan's first announcement of his hopes for a quick knockout came in Shreveport—the start of his delegate-hunting trip through Louisiana.

The principal actor in this story was Reagan, the principal subject was the delegate race, and the story was judged to reflect favorably on Reagan. Table 2.1 indicates how many news stories in each outlet were analyzed using the political story code.*

These data provide answers to a number of questions addressed in this book—which news themes and newsmakers dominated coverage, whether certain news subjects were consistently positioned more prominently in the news than others, whether certain newsmakers consistently received more favorable news coverage than others, and so on.

These data do not, however, provide a very precise indication of what was reported about the presidential candidates. Consequently, each story about the campaign was further analyzed for references to the candidates' personal and leadership qualities, styles, backgrounds, issue stands, values, campaign progress, and similar things. This segment from the NBC "Evening News" of September 22, 1976, will illustrate what was done:

> Reporter: This is a busy time for Carter's peanut processing plant because it's the middle of the fall harvest. The Democratic nominee was up early for an inspection. It was familiar territory, something Carter welcomed after a few of the roughest days he's been through since the campaign began. This morning, reporters were still asking him about the controversial interview in *Playboy* magazine. He said he wasn't sorry he'd done it and didn't think it would hurt his campaign. . . . He did get some good news last night. His latest polls show he is hanging onto his 20-point lead in the South and is running well ahead of Mr. Ford in one third of the traditionally Republican midwestern states. After Carter finished his tour [of the farm] he spent the rest of the day reading and studying to prepare for tomorrow's debate, which press secretary Jody Powell said Carter is relaxed about. Powell says Carter doesn't plan to challenge Mr. Ford with what he called "a finger in the chest approach," but he said Carter certainly will, in his words, "raise questions of his own." Powell said so much has been made about Carter being vague on the issues that the debate will be a great opportunity to prove to the voters that's not true. . . .

From this segment, the following references to Carter were coded: Carter is a farmer, Carter did a *Playboy* interview, Carter is leading in the polls, Carter has a restrained style, and Carter is clear in his issue stands. Table 2.1 indicates how many news stories were analyzed using this candidate story code.

Altogether, about 15,000 specific references to the candidates were

---

*The content analysis was done by trained, full-time employees working with copies of the newspaper and newsmagazine stories and tapes of the television stories. Reliability tests were conducted and, for the political story code, the reliability exceeded +.90. For the more difficult candidate story code (discussed below), the reliability exceeded +.80.

TABLE 2.1 NUMBER OF NEWS STORIES ANALYZED

Type of Code	ABC News	CBS News	NBC News	Erie Times	Erie News	L.A. Times	L.A. Herald	Time	Newsweek
Political story	1,137	1,254	1,074	633	653	580	245	502	489
Candidate story	351	329	308	166	216	361	232	58	56

Note: Description of code types are in text. News days were randomly selected for analysis. For these days all appropriate network evening news and newsmagazine stories were coded using the two codes. For newspapers the political story code was applied only to front-page stories and stories on the first page of the inside section. The candidate story code, however, was applied to all newspaper stories about the campaign, regardless of where they were located in the newspaper.

identified through this analysis, revealing rather exactly how each candidate was presented to the public. For example, the references indicate not only how much and what was said about each candidate's issue stands, but also how this compared with references to his personality or to his position in the race.

THE PANEL SURVEY

The second source of evidence is a panel survey in which the same individuals were interviewed repeatedly to make possible the study of changes in their thinking during the 1976 presidential campaign. In the panel, 1,236 eligible voters were questioned as many as seven times in the course of the 1976 campaign about their media use, their impressions of the candidates and the campaign, their awareness of the election's issues, their interest in the campaign, and similar topics (see Table 2.2).

TABLE 2.2 Number of Respondents Interviewed Each Time

Month of Interview	February	April	June	August	October
February	1,002				
April	772	897			
June	720	748	907		
August	660	699	756	823	
October	650	675	736	730	799

Note: The numbers indicate how many respondents were interviewed in each wave and each pair of waves. For example, the February-February entry indicates that 1,002 were interviewed in the February wave and the February-April entry indicated that 772 of those interviewed in February also were interviewed in April. For each wave, approximately 90 percent of the interviews were completed within a two-and-one-half-week period. Finally although only 1,002 respondents were interviewed in February, an additional 234 respondents were added to the panel in April and June, bringing the total number of respondents to 1,236. In addition to these five waves of personal interviews, there were two waves of telephone interviews.[2]

In all, over 6,000 interviews were conducted. Five of the seven panel waves involved personal interviews of about an hour in length. The first wave was conducted in February, before the first primary was held in New Hampshire. Its purpose was to determine what people were thinking before the campaign got under way, and the other waves were timed to bracket each of the important intervals in the campaign—the early primaries (April interviews), the late primaries (June interviews), the conventions (August interviews), and the general election (October interviews). Additionally, the respondents were contacted by telephone after the first and second presidential debates to obtain their reactions, and again when the election was over to discover whether they had voted, and, if so, for whom.*

Since many of the same questions were asked in each interview, people's responses from one interview to the next provide an accurate indicator of how their thinking changed during the campaign. To estimate the role of the mass media in this process, these changes were related to what people saw, heard, and read during the campaign.

The value of a panel survey is apparent when compared with what is called a cross-sectional survey, one involving a single interview with each respondent. If the media's influence is to be assessed from a single interview, people must be able to recall how their thinking has changed, but recall is greatly affected by memory loss and rationalization. Also, many people are not conscious of gradual changes in their thinking. Most would not have been aware, for example, that their images of the candidates systematically changed as the campaign progressed. There is another problem with cross-sectional data—what people think at any given time is the result of many factors. Much of the information and many of the opinions that voters have are acquired before the campaign and reflect the influence of nonmedia factors, such as people's educations, family and occupational situations, and so on. It is exceedingly difficult to determine from cross-sectional data how much is attributable to the campaign.

The problem is less imposing with panel data, since initial interviews in such a survey provide a baseline of what people know and think. In this study the initial interviews were conducted in February, before the campaign began. Subsequent interviews then indicate the changes that have occurred in people's thinking during the campaign, changes that can be studied in relation to their exposure to election news.†

TWO VERY DIFFERENT COMMUNITIES

Panel election studies such as this traditionally have been based on a sample of voters in a single community, as were the noted Lazarsfeld and Berelson studies in the 1940s.[3] The object of confining the survey to a single community

---

*The interviewing was conducted by paid, experienced interviewers employed by Response Analysis Corporation of Princeton, New Jersey. The questionnaires were prepared by the author.

†There is, however a special problem associated with panel surveys—namely, reinterviewing can sensitize people and, by itself, lead them to change their behavior. Past research on this problem indicates that reinterview-sensitization is not a significant factor in studies such as this one. Nevertheless, control groups (new respondents) were added to the panel in the second and third interviews, and their responses were compared to those of respondents who had been interviewed previously. No significant differences were found between these groups, indicating that reinterview-sensitization was insubstantial.

is to make possible the measurement of the respondents' media environment. A national survey, in comparison, would require the analysis of the election year news coverage of several hundred daily newspapers, a nearly impossible undertaking.

On the other hand, a single community study raises the question of whether what is found in that community applies elsewhere. In the past the presumption has been that the results can be generalized. The Lazarsfeld-Berelson studies, for example, were the basis for most axioms about the media's campaign impact in the two decades following their publication, partly because their analysis controlled for relevant population characteristics such as income and education levels, which differ between locations and that might interact with media effects.[4] Primarily, though, the acceptance of their feelings reflected the belief that the media's impact is similar in different locales. Nevertheless, in a single community study there remains the question of wider applicability.

In response to the possibility of similar problems, it was decided that surveys would be conducted in two communities. To provide a test of media effects under contrasting conditions and therefore increase the applicability of common findings, the communities were to have substantially different populations and media. One community was to include mostly blue-collar families, the other mostly white-collar families. One was to be media rich—that is, to have an abundance of news outlets—and the other was to be media poor—that is, to have only a few news outlets. Ideally, the communities would be located in different regions of the country and, since the media's impact on primary elections was of special concern, in states holding presidential primaries.

Based on these criteria, the two communities selected were Erie, Pennsylvania, and Los Angeles, California (see Table 2.3). Erie's relatively homogeneous population of 270,000 is a rather sharp contrast to the highly diverse population that makes Los Angeles the nation's second largest metropolis. In the industrial city of Erie, over 60 percent of the families make their livelihoods in blue-collar occupations. It is a heavily Catholic area whose residents are mostly of German, Italian, or Polish extraction. In Los Angeles, on the other hand, there is a broad economic base that includes slightly more white-collar than blue-collar workers. Except for its large Mexican-American population, no ethnic groups predominate.

As would be expected, the media market in Los Angeles is much more diverse than Erie's. In addition to the *Times* and *Herald-Examiner*, Los Angeles has several suburban daily newspapers, as well as seven VHF television stations—including affiliates of the three networks, a prominent independent (METRO), and an educational channel—and a large number of UHF stations. Erie, in contrast, has only two newspapers, the *Times* and the *News*, which average only 48 pages each day and print joint editions on Saturday and Sunday. Erie has four television stations, but only one on a VHF channel—the NBC affiliate. The CBS and ABC affiliates and an educational channel are all UHF stations. Nevertheless, the city of Erie did not have cable television in 1976, and less than 5

TABLE 2.3 Number of Respondents Interviewed in Each Community

Month of Interviews	Erie	Los Angeles
February	527	475
April	495	402
June	513	394
August	483	340
October	462	337
Total	2,480	1,948

Note: The smaller number of interviews in Los Angeles reflects, first, the elimination of a larger number of selected individuals because they were noncitizens or non-English speaking, and second, the fact that those in Los Angeles were less frequently at home when the interviewers called. The samples were matched against census data to determine how well they represented the population in each location. The samples generally conformed with the populations. There was, however, a slight oversampling of women in Erie and of higher educated persons in Los Angeles. For the analysis, the samples were weighted to remove these possible sources of bias.

percent of its residents received outside television stations and newspapers.

Residents of both Erie and Los Angeles had the opportunity to participate in a presidential primary in 1976. Pennsylvania's primary, the ninth of 30 primaries held in 1976, was April 28. California's primary was held on June 6, the last day of the 1976 primaries. At the time of each primary, interviews were conducted in both locations to provide evidence about primary effects on those living outside of as well as in a primary state.

In each location respondents were selected randomly, but with known probability, through the common method of block-household-individual random selection. Adults chosen through this technique were interviewed if they were English-speaking U.S. citizens. The Erie and Los Angeles samples were drawn from the metropolitan areas rather than from the cities alone. For example, the Los Angeles sample includes residents of communities like Glendale and Burbank, as well as Los Angeles proper.

PART II

THE NEWS
ENVIRONMENT

3

PRESS COVERAGE OF THE CAMPAIGN

In its coverage of a presidential campaign, the press concentrates on the strategic game played by the candidates in their pursuit of the presidency, thereby de-emphasizing questions of national policy and leadership.

In part, this reflects the tradition in journalism that news is to be found in activity rather than in the underlying causes of that activity. "The function of news," wrote Walter Lippmann, "is to signalize events." He used the example of a labor strike to illustrate his point. If you look at the headlines, he wrote, you will seldom find mention of the issues involved in the strike and you may barely find reference to them in the leading paragraphs. The strike itself—the fact that people had walked off their jobs—would be the focus of the news story. Lippmann gave a number of reasons why reporters follow this procedure: they tend naturally to note the most salient facts about events, they are faced with insufficient space in which to deal with the more complicated causes of events, and they recognize the need to report events in terms familiar to the audience. These lead the reporter, said Lippmann, to prefer "the indisputable fact and the easy interest."[1]

So it is with election coverage also. Election activity and vote returns constitute the most visible aspects of the campaign and therefore are most likely to be used by the press as election news. Heavily emphasized are the simple mechanics of campaigning—the candidates' travels here and there, their organizational efforts, their strategies—as well as voting projections and returns, likely convention scenarios, and so on. One effect of this is that a large portion of election coverage is devoted to the campaign's contestual aspects and says little

21

about which candidate would make the better president.

Campaign activity itself provides a source of news about what the candidates represent. To the degree that the campaign is reported as a policy debate, in fact, it takes place largely through claims made by the candidates at their rallies, at press conferences, and in other forums. Similarly, most of what is said about the candidates' leadership comes from the participants' claims.

These claims, however, often are of secondary interest to the press. Although journalists consider the campaign to have more than ritual significance, they tend not to view it primarily as a battle over the directions of national policy and leadership. It is seen mainly as a power struggle between the candidates. Paul Weaver wrote in describing this journalistic paradigm:

> The game is a competitive one and the players' principal activities are those of calculating and pursuing strategies designed to defeat competitors and to achieve their goals (usually election to public office). Of course, the game takes place against a backdrop of governmental institutions, public problems, policy debates, and the like, but these are noteworthy only insofar as they affect, or are used by, players in pursuit of the game's rewards.[2]

This conception traces back to the press's focus on campaign activity. Were reporters oriented instead to the political, social, and economic undercurrents of elections, a different paradigm might predominate. But their search for news focuses on the candidates, whose actions most certainly are motivated in part by the desire to win office. Many reporters also believe that the candidates' ability to play the game is the main factor in their success. It is the game and not the larger forces at work in the society that decide the final tally. "Reporters like to concentrate on campaign tactics and devices," writes the *New York Times's* Tom Wicker. "In their usual foot-race or game perspective on politics, they and their editors see these as being more critical to the election results than most issues."[3]

SUBSTANCE AND THE GAME

The press's game perspective of the election is encompassing in its scope, reaching even into those reporting situations ostensibly programmed as forums for the discussion of leadership and policy questions. During the 1976 campaign, when candidates appeared on "Meet the Press," "Face the Nation," and "Issues and Answers," they were questioned as frequently about their strategies and chances as they were about their leadership and policy views. Similarly, newspaper columnists devoted much of their space in 1976 to analyses of the candidates' prospects and game plans.[4]

The press's concern with the game, however, is most evident in its day-to-day coverage. Reporters tend to focus on the campaign's competitive aspects, typified by the coverage of Jimmy Carter's campaign swing through upstate New York on October 14, 1976. Speaking at a street rally in Rochester, Carter sought to dispel his opponent's claim that he planned to raise the taxes of middle-income Americans. He flatly stated for the first time in his campaign that only the wealthy need fear a tax increase if he were elected. Later in Syracuse, Carter delivered his standard speech about his plans to deal with joblessness and inflation.

Carter's trip to upstate New York was covered extensively by the press, but his issue statements were nearly ignored. His tax announcement, in fact, was not mentioned at all on that evening's network newscasts or in the Associated Press story that appeared in the next morning's *Erie News*. On television, the most attention given Carter's economic speech was its dismissal by ABC "Evening News" as "old familiar lines."

The news about Carter's upstate trip was that it represented a change in his campaign style. For several days preceding the trip, Carter had been harshly critical of Ford. But on this day Carter tempered his attack, seen by the press as a tactical move. With a lead in the polls and only a short time left in the campaign, Carter was said to be growing cautious, anxious to avoid a slip of the tongue that might threaten his front-running position. The following is the text of the report that appeared on that evening's news on CBS:

> Walter Cronkite: With just two and a half weeks until the voting, Carter appears to be making an adjustment in his campaign style, and Ed Bradley has that story.
>
> Ed Bradley: Carter's campaign winged toward New York State with a sharply reduced schedule that will keep the candidate on the road less often, just two or three days at a time. Carter senses he now has the momentum and President Ford the problems, so he has sharply reduced the acidity of his attacks, but still reminds voters of the President's statements on Eastern Europe and the Arab boycott. As for attacks against him, Jimmy Carter delights in telling his audience he knows what the Republicans have to say.
>
> Carter: Don't believe all the stories that you hear from our Republican administration, from my Republican opposition. If I believed everything I heard said about me, I wouldn't vote for myself. You help me, I help you, and we'll have a great country once again. Thank you very much, and God bless all of you.
>
> Bradley: A number of polls, both public and private, show Carter with a comfortable and growing lead in several key states as well as nationwide. Carter's strategists feel the cutback in the schedule will reduce the possibility that their candidate will make a serious mistake that could reverse the trend in the polls. Still, it will keep him on the road often enough to provide a contrast with the Ford campaign. Ed Bradley, CBS News, with the Carter campaign in Syracuse.

Systematic evidence of the press's concern with the game is provided in Table 3.1. The figures there are based on an analysis of television and newspaper

TABLE 3.1 Content of Presidential Election News (percent)

Subject of Coverage	Network Evening Newscasts	Erie Times/ News	L.A. Herald Examiner	L.A. Times	Time/ Newsweek
Game					
Winning and losing	24	26	25	20	23
Strategy, logistics	17	19	18	19	22
Appearences, hoopla	17	14	14	12	9
Subtotal	58	59	57	51	54
Substance					
Issues, policies	18	19	18	21	17
Traits, records	7	6	5	8	11
Endorsements	4	4	5	6	4
Subtotal	29	29	28	35	32
Other	13	12	15	14	14
Total	100	100	100	100	100

Note: Table based on a random sample of the election news coverage provided by each news source. The network figures are the combined average for the ABC, NBC, and CBS evening news programs. The figures for the *Erie Times* and *Erie News* and those in *Time* and *Newsweek* also have been combined because the separate figures were substantially the same.[5]

election reports appearing between January 1 and November 2, 1976. Half or more of the election coverage in each of the news sources dealt with the competition between the candidates. Winning and losing, strategy and logistics, appearances and hoopla were the dominant themes of election news, emphasized most strongly by the television networks, the two Erie newspapers, and the *Los Angeles Herald-Examiner*; in each of these sources, almost 60 percent of the election coverage was about the game. This dimension of the election received slightly less emphasis, about 55 percent of total election coverage, in *Time* and *Newsweek*. Of all the news outlets, the *Los Angeles Times* placed the least emphasis on the contest; still, this aspect of the campaign received 51 percent of its total election coverage.

The election's substance, on the other hand, received only half as much coverage as was accorded the game. The press did not heavily stress the candidates' policy positions, their personal and leadership characteristics, their private and public histories, background information on the election's issues, or group commitments for and by the candidates. In the *Los Angeles Times* these subjects totaled 35 percent of its election coverage. In *Time* and *Newsweek* they accounted for 32 percent of the total. In the other sources these substantive topics accounted for less than 30 percent of the election news.*

In a way, these figures underestimate the news media's emphasis on the game because they represent all campaign stories; they are based on articles taken from the back as well as front pages of the newspaper, on stories appearing at the end as well as the beginning of the evening news. When only those stories placed at the top of the news are considered, an even more complete preference for game-related stories becomes apparent. In every outlet except the *Los Angeles Times*, the game accounted for a larger proportion of lead stories than of total election coverage. *Time* and *Newsweek* appeared especially concerned with placing the game at the top of the news, giving it 66 percent of their lead space, compared with 54 percent of their total coverage.

STYLES OF REPORTING AND THEIR EFFECT

The game is made prominent by all media, but it acquires greater prominence on television and in the newsmagazines than in the newspapers. This is attributable to a difference between the typical form of television and magazine stories and the form of most newspaper stories.

In the newspapers, most political reports are simply descriptions of events. They certainly are not without logic; they are, as James David Barber puts it, "not just one thing after another, bumping down the inverted pyramid."[6] Nevertheless, these reports usually do not have a tight story line. The typical newspaper story is probably best described as a string of related facts that an editor can cut almost anywhere in order to fit the story into the available news space, illustrated by the following news story from the *Los Angeles Times*:

> DES MOINES. Jimmy Carter, speaking to enthusiastic Iowans, sharply attacked President Ford Wednesday in a bid for the Midwestern grain belt votes that Ford needs if he is to win the November election.
>
> His coat off and his sleeves rolled up, Carter spoke to a crowd that overflowed a large plaza at the Iowa State Fair. There was no official estimate of its size, but an aide to Sen. Dick Clark (D-Iowa) said he

---

*The campaign coverage not accounted for in the above figures, amounting to about 15 percent in each outlet, included news material that did not properly fit in either the game or substance categories, such as news about the election's calendar (such as the schedule of primaries) and election procedures (such as the rules governing delegate selection).

thought it was about 5,000 persons.

Carter pledged to stop embargoes on U.S. grain shipments to the Soviet Union "once and for all" and accused Ford of allowing corruption to continue in the inspection of grain shipped overseas.

After driving past the fair's red brick exhibit halls filled with Iowa cattle, hogs and sheep, past booths selling everything from apple cider to "Fred Dowie's Famous Elephant Ear Sandwich," Carter pointed out that he had been here before. That was at last year's state fair, when Carter was a little known ex-Georgia governor and peanut farmer, running for President. . . .

Television and magazine reports, on the other hand, tend to be interpretive in form (see Table 3.2). As the CBS story on Carter's New York trip illustrates,

TABLE 3.2 Form of Election News Stories on Television and in Newspapers and Newsmagazines (percent)

Form of Reports	Newspaper Stories	Television Stories	Magazine Stories
Descriptive	71	31	23
Descriptive/Interpretive	15	12	24
Interpretive	14	57	53
Total	100	100	100

Note: Definitions of the descriptive and interpretive forms are provided in the text. Those classified as descriptive/interpretive are stories containing substantial amounts of both types of reporting. Table based only on regular news stories; news briefs, news summaries, editorials, and opinion commentary are not included.

television places greater emphasis on the why than on the what, attempting to explain rather than to describe. Television's emphasis on interpretation derives from its need for tightly structured stories. In a medium that depends on the spoken word, stories that are to be understood readily by the listening audience must be given a clear focus; they cannot be allowed to trail off as a newspaper story does. The average television news story, furthermore, is only 90-seconds long, not long enough for the reporter to tell the news through the words of public officials or with a listing of the facts of an event, as is typically done in the newspaper. The television reporter must assume a more active role, sharply defining and limiting the story so that it can be told in 100 to 200 words.

For these reasons, most television news stories are built around themes. Television's "principle need," says Weaver, "is for a clear, continuous narrative line sustained throughout the story—something with a beginning, a middle, and an end." Quite unlike the newspaper, television's primary concern is not the facts of an event; it is the theme. Indeed, notes Weaver, on television the facts become "the materials with which the chosen theme is illustrated."[7] Description gives way to interpretation.

The newsmagazine depends heavily on interpretation for different reasons. As a weekly rather than a daily news source, its stories often must deal with several related events rather than a single event. A sequential description of all these events would require considerable news space and probably would not result in the lively presentations that *Time* and *Newsweek* strive to attain. Also, these newsmagazines stress news analysis and prediction, presumably to set themselves apart from the daily news outlets. Consequently, *Time* and *Newsweek*, like the television networks, develop their news stories along narrative lines so that themes, rather than facts, are the most prominent part of their news. *Newsweek's* story on Frank Church's primary victory in Nebraska is an example:

> It was an unlikely game plan for a Presidential hopeful and, with the possible exception of Church himself, no one placed much faith in the Idaho senator's "late-late strategy." His entry delayed by his chairmanship of the Senate select committee on intelligence, Church now hopes to gain momentum by winning a handful of the later primaries, acquiring a respectable 150 to 200 delegates and surviving a first-ballot effort by Jimmy Carter at the convention. Even though few major politicians take that scenario seriously, some welcome his candidacy. . . .
>
> His Nebraska campaign was very nearly a mom-and-pop show—Church crossed the state by campaign bus, while his 27-year-old son, Forrest, a Unitarian minister, minded the store—but it was also shrewdly professional. He one-upped peanut-farmer Carter, noting that agriculturally "Idaho and Nebraska are so much alike." He came out against grain-export embargoes and Federal gun control. While dissociating himself from the "Washington Establishment," he noted that the White House was no place for "on-the-job training." He pointed up Carter's "campaign of generalities" with a primary-eve TV half hour in which he answered phoned-in questions. He spent ten days in Nebraska—almost long enough to vote for himself, an Omaha newspaper observed wryly—and outspent Carter 3 to 1 with $125,000.
>
> One day after his Nebraska triumph, Church was stumping Portland with his wife and four staffers. With its May 25 primary, Oregon is the next of Church's target states—a carefully chosen battleground in his own Northwest territory—and it is crucial to his candidacy. . . . But then California's Brown announced that he would campaign there for write-in votes. That added a new twist to the race—and made it increasingly uncertain whether Frank Church would be able to work another miracle.

There is no one aspect of the campaign around which television and magazine journalists must build their themes, and almost every aspect of the campaign contributes at one time or another. Consistent with the general tendency of journalists to see the election primarily as a game, however, the dominant themes of television and magazines are the status of the race and the candidates' strategies. This tendency insures that what is said about the election's substance will not stand out as much in these media as it does in the newspaper. Facts about what the candidates represent are placed here and there in television and magazine reports but frequently serve only a supportive role, acting as background, transitional, or illustrative material.

By comparison, since the newspaper relies less on a central theme and more on events themselves, its substantive content is more likely to have an independent role. This content is often surrounded by and less substantial than information about the game and cannot be regarded as the focus of newspaper coverage. But items of policy and leadership are likely to be separate from the other links in the chain of facts that constitute the newspaper's election news, giving them greater prominence than they have on television or in the newsmagazine.

ELECTION NEWS THEN AND NOW

Every presidential campaign is somewhat Janusian—certainly a game of strategy whose score is tallied in votes and whose prize is the presidency, but also a time for the candidates to offer the voters a choice about national policy and leadership. One would naturally expect to see both sides presented in the news. What is perhaps unexpected is the recent growth in the media's concern with the game. In the 1940s, Paul Lazarsfeld and Bernard Berelson found that about 35 percent of election news dealt with the fight to gain the presidency; a considerably larger amount, 50 percent, was concerned with subjects of policy and leadership.[8] In 1976 those proportions were reversed. As indicated by Table 3.1, most of the coverage during that election was of the race.

A number of factors appear to underlie this change. For one, strategy and maneuver play a larger and more visible role in today's campaign. Candidates now organize earlier and more thoroughly than in the past, place more emphasis on tactics, and depend more on paid consultants whose advice usually concerns technique rather than substance. More than before, many of the candidates' activities are strictly for show, staged in the hope that the press will cover that side of their campaigns. Nevertheless, the game emphasis primarily reflects the interests of the press. The messages that are tightly controlled by the candidates are dominated by substance. During the 1976 campaign the candidates devoted their televised advertising messages mainly to substance, mostly addressing issues and policies, traits and records. So too did the facts and imagery that filled their campaign speeches, their convention speeches, and their debates pertain primarily to the nation's policy and leadership needs.[9] Yet substance is now a smaller part of the news that the press presents to the public.

Changes in election journalism are one reason. Specifically, the press has come to make greater use of opinion polls and behind-the-scenes accounts of candidates' strategies and organizations. In the 1940s ten reports based on opinion polls would have been a medium's quota for an entire campaign. In 1976 the same number of poll reports appeared in the *Los Angeles Times* during the last week alone of the campaign, and almost all dealt with the election's likely outcome. Also affecting coverage has been Theodore White's innovation in the 1960s of behind-the-scenes reporting. [10] The use of inside accounts of the candidates' strategies, finances, and organizations are now regular features of election news.

The increase in the number of primaries is another reason that substance has been upstaged by the game. In the 1940s, the primaries accounted for about a third of the total election period. Now they cover nearly half of the campaign months, and it is during the primaries that the game is most heavily emphasized (see Table 3.3). Due primarily to predictions, reports, and analyses of primary election outcomes, the game receives 15 percent more coverage at this time than during the general election. It follows that the increased coverage of the game is partly a functioning of the lengthening of the primary period.

TABLE 3.3 News Coverage of Substance and Game during the Primary, Convention, and General Election Periods (percent)

Period	Network Evening Newscasts	*Erie Times/ News*	*L.A. Herald- Examiner*	*L.A. Times*	*Time/ Newsweek*
Primaries					
Game	64	64	62	59	62
Substance	24	26	24	28	24
Other	12	10	14	13	14
Total	100	100	100	100	100
Conventions					
Game	58	59	55	52	54
Substance	29	28	28	33	31
Other	13	13	17	15	15
Total	100	100	100	100	100
General Election					
Game	51	52	51	42	46
Substance	35	36	36	42	41
Other	14	12	13	16	13
Total	100	100	100	100	100

It is clear that the cause goes beyond the primaries alone. A comparison of 1976 and 1940 that includes only the convention and general election periods still indicates a substantially greater orientation toward the game in 1976. Again, the length of today's campaign is a reason, but the effect is an indirect one. Because the news is what is different about events of the past 24 hours, the newsworthiness of what a candidate says about public policies is limited.[11] To be specific, once a candidate makes known his position on an issue, further statements concerning that issue decline in news value. ABC News characterization of Carter's economic speech of October 14, 1976, as "old familiar lines," for example, was less a judgment that his positions were unimportant than an observation that they simply were no longer news. The fact is there are not enough major issues for the candidates to keep questions of policy at the top of the news for a full year. They can outline their priorities and positions on the key issues in two months. After that, all they can do is repeat their positions or take stands on lesser issues, neither of which is considered very newsworthy.

Thus the principle effect of a longer campaign is to spread a somewhat fixed amount of substance over a greater period of time. Since news outlets now give much more of their election year news space to the campaign, the substance of a presidential election probably gets more news coverage, in absolute terms, than in the past. Still, there are not enough fresh issues and leadership material to satisfy the media organizations' demands for election news for an entire election year. A presidential campaign is considered inherently newsworthy, deserving of coverage even on those days when nothing terribly new or important happens. On such days particularly, reporters have greater freedom in their choice of news material. Given their general view of election politics and of news, they tend to use this freedom for updates on the players' strategies and standings, rather than reruns of the candidates' policy statements, records, backgrounds, and qualifications.

4

REPORTING THE ISSUES

On the campaign trail candidates fill much of their public exposure time talking about national problems, policy goals, issues, and government performance, and they routinely put out press releases that state their policy leanings and priorities. Although much of this activity appears perfunctory, it has a definite purpose—the establishment of the candidate's agenda in the minds of the voters. Operating on evaluations of the policy desires of the electorate, the candidate aims to develop and communicate a combination of appeals that will attract a winning coalition of voters.

The candidate necessarily looks to the press to get his platform across to the voters. Other means of communication, such as paid advertising and public gatherings, are available to the candidate, but they lack either the audience reach or credibility to substitute for news coverage. If the candidate is to impress his ideas on the public, he must have the cooperation of the press. It already has been shown, however, that the news media place less emphasis on questions of public policy than on the game. Consequently, the candidate may have to be satisfied with less issue coverage than he might desire. But is the candidate at least able to present the blend of proposals that he wishes? Are the policies that he emphasizes also the ones that are stressed by reporters? Or do reporters' values lead them to prefer issues that are different from those stressed by candidates?

The press has a liking for what Colin Seymour-Ure has labeled clear-cut issues. These are issues that, above all, neatly divide the candidates. Preferably, they also produce disagreement and argument among the candidates; rest on principle rather than complex details or relationships; and can be stated in simple terms, usually by reference to a shorthand label such as busing or détente.[1]

The press's bias toward clear-cut issues stems from a number of influences. Such issues often provoke conflict and controversy among both candidates and voters, thus providing colorful copy as well as a ready audience. But the major reason for the press's interest probably owes to its patterned view of events, an outlook best described by James David Barber. "The first fact of journalistic life," he writes, is that reporters "tend to notice those aspects of the situation that lend themselves to storymaking." Stories begin with the intersection of contrasts. "The reporter's raw material is differences—between what was and what is, expectations and events, reputations and realities, normal and exotic—and his artful eye is set to see the moment when the flow of history knocks two differences together."[2] Thus the issues that tidily separate the candidates are preferred to those on which the candidates agree or on which the differences are imprecise. Consistent with this outlook, the press relies on metaphors of confrontation in reporting the issues, using words such as clashes, fights, and attacks to describe the candidates' claims.[3]

Such words conjure an image of the campaign, however, that is largely a construct of the press. Even though candidates sometimes use the same metaphors, only occasionally do they pointedly exchange views. Most charges made by the opposition are in fact ignored by the candidate, for to respond would be to let the other side set the agenda. Moreover, when a candidate does respond to the opposition, it is usually on his terms, redefining more than replying to the argument.[4]

Indeed, rather than the clear-cut issues that are favored by the press, the candidates prefer what can be called diffuse issues. These diffuse issues include broad policy proposals where the candidates' appeals differ mostly in style and emphasis, as in the common commitment to maintain a healthy economy. Addressing the problem, one candidate may stress it more than another or have a somewhat different set of proposed solutions, but both agree on the goal. Except in emphasis, the candidates' spoken statements on these issues are usually so general (such as, "It's time to get the economy moving again,") as not to distinguish one candidate from another. The candidates' detailed proposals for handling such issues are usually found in position papers or one-time-only speeches, but even these do not produce ready distinctions between the candidates, for their proposals often overlap substantially and frequently differ primarily on intricate points.

One reason why candidates emphasize broad issues is that they often are of major concern to the voters. The economy, peace, government efficiency, and other general problems usually rank higher in the public's mind than do the more specific problems that lend themselves to clear-cut solutions. Broad appeals also can be a unifying force for a candidate, as well as posing little risk. Few voters will find objectionable a candidate's claim that he is against government waste or for a strong economy; some voters will almost certainly be lost, however, regardless of which position a candidate takes on a clear-cut issue like abortion.

The candidates' emphasis on diffuse issues also lies in the nature of coalition building. Each candidate naturally gears his campaign toward those interests that already lean toward him and his party. Since the party coalitions differ, each party's candidate pursues a line that only occasionally brings him into direct conflict with his opponent. Many of these coalition appeals involve assurances of continued support or distributive benefits for a specific group, assurances that do not clash with those of the opposing candidate because he is appealing to other groups. Only in some instances, such as a commitment to labor that also is a direct threat to business, are the coalition appeals of the candidates likely to collide head-on. Indeed, Gerald Pomper's study of national party platforms during the period from 1944 to 1964 revealed that only a minority of platform pledges were similar or bipartisan, while the majority were distinctive pledges by one or the other party, and only one in ten pledges placed the candidates in conflicting positions.[5]

Of course, the candidates use clear-cut issues. Each candidate normally has a number of clear-cut issues on which he would like to engage the opposition, and opportunities sometimes arise. As well, candidates rarely bypass opportunities to attack the opposition's stands when it is advantageous. In general, however, candidates depend more heavily on diffuse issues than on clear-cut ones. Each side, in the words of one of the Nueffield studies, "tends to campaign on its self-chosen battlefield against straw men of its own devising,"[6] a view supported by Benjamin Page's exhaustive study of campaign issues. Each candidate he researched—from Roosevelt and Hoover in 1932 to Carter and Ford in 1976, and including ideologues Goldwater and McGovern—stressed general goals and coalition appeals more than he emphasized specific disputes.[7]

REPORTERS' ISSUES AND CANDIDATES' ISSUES

That reporters and candidates have different issue biases can be seen in part when issue news initiated by reporters is compared with that initiated by candidates. In daily news coverage, clear-cut issues accounted for only 40 percent of the issue references where a candidate was the initiator (such as, "Ford called a press conference today to discuss . . . "), while accounting for nearly 80 percent of those where a journalist was the initiator (such as, "Carter was asked by a reporter today about . . .").[8]

The clearest indicator of the difference, however, comes when the content of election news messages are compared with media messages controlled entirely by the candidates. Since all news stories are filtered through reporters and editors, their preferences are necessarily reflected in the total issue output. The candidates' preferences also will be reflected in the news output, since the press feels some responsibility for carrying their appeals. On the other hand, two major forms of election communication are controlled entirely by the candidates—their televised convention speeches and their televised political advertising. These forms are unfiltered by the press and, hence the difference between their issue content and that of the news provides a rough indication of the differing interests of reporters and candidates.

Comparing these forms of communication for 1976, there was markedly less emphasis on clear-cut issues in the candidates' advertisements and convention speeches than in election news (see Table 4.1). About 50 percent of regular news content pertained to issues that were obviously clear-cut; only about 25 percent of the issue news was devoted to what were plainly diffuse issues. In contrast, over 50 percent of candidate-controlled communication related to diffuse issues and less than 25 percent to clear-cut issues. It is apparent that the news does not contain the blend of issues advocated by the candidates. The press's issue agenda is markedly different than the candidate's agenda.

Diffuse issues lack the qualities prized in news stories. The candidates' general appeals are too imprecise to permit easy use; their position papers are too long and occasionally too intricate to be fitted easily into available news space; and their coalition appeals are too narrow to be of general interest.

Refraction of the candidates' appeals was typical of all news outlets in 1976, but none more clearly than television. Of the issue coverage on the ABC, CBS, and NBC nightly newscasts, 67 percent was devoted to clear-cut issues, compared, for example, to 48 percent of issue news in the *Los Angeles Herald-Examiner*. The networks' extraordinary emphasis on such issues owes mostly to television's preference for issues that do not require lengthy exposition and appeal to a diverse audience. The object is to broadcast a good deal of news of general interest in a short period of time, preferably using action film. As William Bicker notes, "the medium abhors the idea of a 'talking head' or the reading of a position paper."[9] Only news stories that are regarded as especially important are likely to run longer than a minute or two, and only rarely would a diffuse issue be considered to have compelling importance. In fact, it is uncommon for any policy issue to provide the entire content of a television news story. Most issue references on the evening newscasts occur in news segments of 20 seconds or less, usually embedded in other news of the campaign. Even newspapers are reluctant to make room for the hundreds of words sometimes required for explicating the candidates' positions on broad issues. With more severe space limitations and a desire to use action film, the networks almost never make room for such positions, thus centering their coverage on clear-cut issues that can be conveyed in a few words.

Some clear-cut issues that arise during a presidential campaign are more appropriately called campaign issues than policy issues. [Campaign issues are ones that develop from campaign incidents, usually errors in judgment by the candidates. Examples from the 1976 campaign would include Ford's remark during the second presidential debate that Eastern Europe was free from Soviet domination, and Carter's comment during the primaries about ethnic purity.]

TABLE 4.1 Amount of Emphasis on Clear-cut and Diffuse Issues in News Coverage and in Candidate-controlled Communication

Type of Issue Content	TV Ads	Convention Speeches	Network Evening Newscasts	Erie Times/ News	L.A. Herald- Examiner	L.A. Times	Time/ Newsweek
Clear-cut	26	22	67	44	48	54	46
Mixed	23	22	14	26	25	18	19
Diffuse	51	56	19	30	27	28	35
Total	100	100	100	100	100	100	100

Note: Definitions of clear-cut and diffuse issues are provided in the text. Mixed issues are those that combine elements from both of the other types.

[Campaign issues receive preferred treatment from the press.] At least when they first break, their customary positions are in the headlines, in lead paragraphs, on the front pages, and at the top of television newscasts.] For a week or more after they break, they remain major news items. In 1976 this was true for several such issues, among them Eastern Europe, ethnic purity, Carter's *Playboy* interview, and Reagan's remark about investing social security funds. The following headlines, for example, appeared over *Los Angeles Times's* news stories in the week immediately following Ford's statement about Eastern Europe:[10]

> Carter Aides Assail Ford for His Remark on Poland
> Carter, Ford Do Battle Over Eastern Europe
> Dole Says Ford's Remarks on Poles Poses Problem
> U.N. Envoys Find Remark Incredible
> Ford May Have Added To East Europe's Confusion
> But He Might Have Said—
> Carter Pressing Attack on Ford Relentlessly
> Carter Softens Rhetoric But Continues Attack
> Advisors Urge Ford to Hit Back at Carter
> Ford Admits He Made Error on Eastern Europe

Policy issues seldom receive this kind of attention during the campaign. Generally, they are neither placed in the headlines nor covered for more than a day or two. Indeed, there is a truly substantial difference in the press's attention to policy issues and campaign issues (see Table 4.2). Over 50 percent of the campaign issues were heavily reported during the 1976 campaign; only about 15 percent of policy issues can be said to have received heavy coverage. Here again, the television networks provided the extremes: their nightly newscasts gave heavy coverage to almost 70 percent of campaign issues, but to only about 10 percent of policy issues.

Campaign issues have a special appeal to the press in part because they conform with traditional news values—they are unexpected, colorful, and unique.[12] Who could possibly have predicted, for example, that given his political beliefs and experience, Ford would declare Eastern Europe free from Soviet domination? Most policy issues, on the other hand, are anything but sensational. The candidates are expected to address public policy problems such as unemployment and, usually consistent with the tradition of their party, their stands are familiar and predictable.

Campaign issues, furthermore, frequently build upon themselves, creating suspense and expectation as they unfold. They involve what Barber identifies as the most common type of developing news story, that of "action-reaction," and what Jules Witcover has described as the "I said-he said-I said" election issue.[13] A candidate's opponents are certain to try to capitalize on the opportunity provided by the precipitating incident, and the candidate is certain to try to minimize the episode. While the candidates fight over how the incident should

**TABLE 4.2 Amount of News Coverage of Policy
and Campaign Issues (percent)**

Type of Issue and Amount of Coverage	Network Evening Newscasts	*Erie Times/ News*	*L.A. Herald- Examiner*	*L.A. Times*	*Time/ Newsweek*
Campaign issues					
Heavy coverage	70	54	46	54	62
Moderate coverage	15	23	31	31	23
Light coverage	15	23	23	15	15
Total	100	100	100	100	100
Policy issues					
Heavy coverage	11	19	13	21	21
Moderate coverage	50	47	47	42	34
Light coverage	39	34	40	37	45.
Total	100	100	100	100	100

Note: Heavily covered issues are those receiving twice as much coverage in that medium as the average issue, and lightly covered issues are those receiving only half as much coverage as the average issue. Moderately covered issues are those whose coverage fell between these extremes.[11]

be interpreted, reporters can speculate on whether or not the errant candidate will publicly confess his mistake. For where there is error there is potential for dramatic resolution, as in 1976 when Ford admitted he had been mistaken on Eastern Europe and Carter apologized to black Americans for his choice of the words ethnic purity.

Christopher Arterton suggests that the appeal of campaign issues also lies in the opportunity they provide the press to reduce the candidates' control of the agenda. He conceives of press-candidate interactions as a power relationship in which each side has a major source of influence, the press through its control of the selection process and the candidates through their ability to decide what and how much they will say. Following an incident that creates a campaign issue, however, the candidate's influence is greatly diminished; he has little choice but to confront the problem that he has created for himself and that the press refuses to ignore. Behind the press's emphasis on the issue, Arterton proposes, is its frustration over the control that the candidates have during normal periods of the campaign. This can be seen in the fact that the press usually makes no pretense of finding the issue's significance in its face value. Ford's statement on Eastern Europe was seen immediately as a slip or blunder. The significance of such an issue is symbolic, resting on the contradiction it creates between the impression the candidate has been trying to establish and that suggested by the incident. Ford's Eastern Europe statement, for example, was in sharp relief to his cultivated image as a knowledgeable leader, and Carter's ethnic purity remark seemed to conflict with his claim to represent the new South. The incident provides the press with an opportunity to reveal the "real" candidate to the public.[14]

Nevertheless, reporters are disinclined, because of professional norms, to say directly that such an incident demonstrates a personal flaw or hidden policy preference of the candidate. These criticisms are voiced in the news through the words of the candidate's opponents. The connection that reporters themselves are likely to make is the electoral one. The exposure of a weakness of the candidate is seen by the press as a serious threat to his candidacy and is reported accordingly. Of the nearly 30 stories on the evening news about Carter's ethnic purity statement, all but six were built around themes of its endangerment to his chances for nomination and erosion of his support among black Americans. Implicitly, these evaluations suggested that Carter's position was weakened because of doubts raised about what he was really like, but explicitly the message concerned the health of his candidacy. Similarly, Ford's Eastern Europe gaffe was interpreted largely as a blunder that had caused him to lose the second debate, threatened his ethnic support, and halted the momentum his campaign had been gathering in the two weeks before the second debate.

THE ELECTORAL CONNECTION

As the 1976 campaign wore on, the press became increasingly critical of the candidates' use of issues. Ford was thought to be avoiding the issues by acting presidential—that is, campaigning from the White House, where press access to him was limited. During the campaign, roughly 65 percent of news references to Ford's accessibility were unfavorable ones. Carter was said to be fuzzy on the issues. According to reporter Carl Leubsdorf, the press felt that Carter "had a way of stating issues so that he drew support from those with opposing views . . . he often refused to state things in a precise way that would give reporters a sharp, easy quote.[15]

Underlying such criticisms are the contrasting beliefs of reporters about how the candidates *ought* to behave and how they *do* behave. The press's game perspective rests on assumptions about how candidates actually behave. What journalists see, says Weaver, is "an endemic tendency for players to exaggerate their good qualities and to minimize their bad ones, to be deceitful, to engage in hypocrisies, to manipulate appearances." [16] Yet against this, the press feels that the democratic bargain obligates candidates to be open with the voters. When the press perceives the candidates as dishonest or evasive, it feels responsible for placing the matter on the public agenda. The claim that Carter was avoiding the issues, for example, was voiced by a number of reporters very early in the primaries. It then was picked up by Carter's opponents and became the major criticism of him in election news coverage. Over 80 percent of news references to Carter's use of issues were unfavorable in nature.

Thus it was when the Ford-Carter televised debates were first announced, the press hailed them as an opportunity for the electorate to discover where the candidates stood on the issues. As the debates approached, however, reporters began to build the debates as pivotal to the election's outcome, and the news focus turned to questions of how the candidates would perform, who would win, and how the campaign might be affected. Would the debate help Ford to close the gap between Carter and himself or would it enable Carter to solidify the lead he then held in the polls? Said *Time* magazine in its preview of the first debate:

> A television audience of perhaps 100 million Americans will be watching. A large percentage of them might well decide which man to support on the basis of what they see that night. Even though there will be two more debates between Carter and Ford, first impressions are difficult to shake, as the 1960 opening debate between Jack Kennedy and Richard Nixon demonstrated. It may well be that the Philadelphia showdown is a more crucial test for Carter than it is for Ford.

> That had not seemed true when Ford issued his debate challenge at the Republican Convention in mid-August. Then Carter was far ahead in all the opinion polls and Ford seemed to be playing a desperate catch-up game. The President still trails, but much more narrowly. Yet for better or worse, depending on the voter, he is a known quantity. By contrast, despite Carter's all-out post-convention campaigning, he remains the man on whom millions of voters are still reserving judgment. If he reassures his shaky majority, he might breeze on toward certain victory. If he fails to do so, his support could erode badly.

By the time the first debate had taken place, the race theme clearly dominated news coverage and it was largely in this context that the presidential debates were reported (see Table 4.3). Over half of the postdebate coverage centered on the competitive aspects; about a fourth of that coverage dealt directly with the question of who had won, the rest with matters of performance and the debates' effect on the candidates' chances of election. Only about a third of all news space was given to the issues that the candidates addressed. These proportions were remarkably similar across news outlets: whether on television, newspapers, or newsmagazines, the race theme accounted for the large share of debate coverage.

To expect news about the debates to mirror the content of the debates themselves would be to misunderstand the nature of news. It is indicative of the press's orientation, however, that there was only minimal analysis of the issue content in debate news—most issue-pertinent coverage consisted of quotes or summaries of the candidates' remarks. The evaluative aspect of the coverage, for example, seldom studied the policy implications of the candidates' statements.

TABLE 4.3 News Coverage of the Televised Presidential Debates (percent)

Subject of Coverage	Network Evening Newscasts	*Erie Times/ News*	*L.A. Herald Examiner*	*L.A. Times*	*Time/ Newsweek*
Issues, policies	34	31	33	36	35
Winning, performance	50	54	51	53	46
Other	16	15	16	11	19
Total	100	100	100	100	100

Note: Table based on all news about presidential debates after the first debate had been held. The largest contributor to the other category was debate logistics, for example, timing, location, technical difficulties.

Nor did the many polls of the debates address questions concerning what voters considered the key issues, whether they had learned something important, and so on. Rather, these poll reports typically focused on one topic—"Who won?" It is the press's orientation to the election game rather than campaign substance that is the major explanation for this focus. After all, the emphasis on winning and losing was evident even before the first debate was held. As Donald Matthews notes, "the press corps mostly ignores campaign talk about policy issues unless it appears likely that this talk will affect electoral outcomes. The political consequences of issues are what matter to them."[17]

Journalists' reactions to the debates, however, also appeared to be a response to what the candidates said and failed to say. After the first debate, the *Erie News* reported, "There were no dramatic new proposals," and the *Los Angeles Herald-Examiner* said of the third debate, "the litanies were familiar." With the exception of the second presidential debate, in which Ford stumbled over a question about Eastern Europe, the consensus of the press generally was that the debates had failed to raise any new issues. Reporters heard basically the same things they had been hearing for months on the campaign trail—while it may have been new to some of the voters, it was old to the reporters and thus not highly newsworthy.

More importantly perhaps, the debates failed to meet the press's expectations for dialogue on the issues. The first debate was described in one news story as "side-by-side press conferences." The more strident tone of the second debate, though emphasized in press accounts, was modified by the observation that there appeared to be few differences between the candidates, evident in an *Erie Times* headline that read: "Tough Talk Hides Basic Agreement." The third debate was characterized in the *Los Angeles Times* as "subdued." In general, the press felt that neither Carter nor Ford had bothered to define sharply their positions or to respond to each other's charges. Instead, they were said to have framed replies in their own terms, to have aimed much of what they had to say at their separate constituencies, to have addressed general concerns in answers sprinkled with statistics ("like pocket calculators," said one news report). Journalists had seen the debates, rather than postdebate news coverage, as the opportunity finally to air "the real issues" of the campaign. In their eyes the candidates had largely evaded this responsibility.

OPPOSING CONCEPTIONS OF THE ISSUES

At the conclusion of recent presidential campaigns, the press has expressed its "weary distaste" for the candidates' handling of the issues. [18] Said James Reston of the *New York Times* after the 1976 campaign:

> If President Ford or Governor Carter had really raised a new issue, or defined an old one in new terms, the press would have been startled into reporting it. In the whole of the campaign, neither Mr. Ford nor Mr. Carter made a single memorable speech, so the press summarized their dreary cliches and the candidates were lucky that the press didn't print the full text of what they said.

Presidential candidates are almost always surprised by such attacks. Not only do speeches, position papers, and statements about policy take up much of their campaign time, it is the rare presidential candidate who has not served in high public office and therefore lacks a policy record that reporters could refer to. Reporters may see the candidates as evasive; at the same time, the candidates find it difficult to understand why reporters ignore so much of what they say and do.

That each group reacts so differently simply reflects their fundamentally different conceptions of election issues. Candidates tend to think in terms of broad policy questions and narrow coalition appeals. Reporters tend to see clear-cut issues as the real issues of election politics. The difference is almost irreconcilable. One type of issue usually does not provide the makings for good political messages, nor the other for good news messages.

Although the press is not positioned so as to force the candidates into a dialectic on clear-cut issues, there is no doubt that, because of its increased influence in the campaign, the agenda now has less of the balance of issues that the candidates themselves stress. Berelson, Lazarsfeld, and McPhee found in their study of the 1948 election that issue news was dominated by the candidates' official speeches and statements in which they talked " 'past each other,' almost as though they were participating in two different elections." [19] Today, however, the press is less willing to act as a common carrier and is intent on playing a more active part in setting the agenda. Ironically, the medium around which the candidate now organizes his campaign is the one that provides him the least control. It is television news that finds the least use for the candidate's diffuse policy appeals. Television's preference for action film, brief statements, and interpretive reporting produces an issue agenda that is the severest distortion of the one that the candidate is trying to establish.*

---

*The press's coverage of the issues also will be discussed in Chapter 13, where issue coverage will be related to voters' issue awareness.

5

PRESENTING THE
CANDIDATES

The journalistic model of election politics affects presidential campaign coverage in almost every respect, and reports on individual candidates are no exception. The effects may vary depending on the specific candidates and situation, but news values play a major role in how the candidates are presented. With the press's emphasis on the game, its concern with activity, and its preference for the indisputable fact and easy interest, certain aspects of presidential candidacy stand out against others in the news.

WINNERS AND LOSERS

In theory there is nothing total about a narrow victory or even a landslide in a state's presidential primary. First, a single primary is just one indicator of the candidates' popularity in a system of 50 state contests. The outcome in one state does not necessarily represent the thinking of voters throughout the nation. Second, a presidential primary lacks the finality of the general election. It has a relative rather than an absolute outcome. The difference in the popularity of one candidate who gets 51 percent of a state's primary vote and another who gets 49 percent is insignificant—both have about the same following. Recognizing this, the Democratic party has in recent years outlawed winner-take-all primaries; a state's delegates are not awarded in total to the first-place finisher, but distributed among the candidates in proportion to the votes they receive.

Press coverage of the 1976 Democratic primaries, however, operated on different principles. ⌊The press tended to project a single state's results to the nation as a whole, and something close to a winner-take-all rule applied. No matter how close the balloting, the state's leading vote getter was awarded the headlines and most of the coverage.⌋ To finish second, even a close second, was to receive little attention from the press. ⌐

These tendencies were evident as early as January 19, 1976, when Democratic precinct caucuses were held in the state of Iowa. Only some 50,000 Iowans participated in the caucuses, and they were greatly divided in their preferences—nearly 40 percent cast uncommitted votes, and the leading candidate received less than 30 percent of the votes cast. Nevertheless, Iowa's caucuses were the first chance for voters anywhere in the nation to judge the candidates and, in the words of the *Los Angeles Times*, "the first important test of the candidates' grass-roots strength."

Heavily covered, they foreshadowed the extraordinary emphasis that the press was to place on the candidates' order of finish throughout the primaries. Said CBS correspondent Roger Mudd in his report direct from Iowa:

> With 88 percent of Iowa's caucuses in, no amount of bad-mouthing by the others can lessen the importance of Jimmy Carter's finish. He was the clear winner in this psychologically crucial test. With thirteen projected national convention delegates, almost 28 percent of the total, he had opened ground between himself and the rest of the so-called pack.

With Mudd providing the lead, CBS then singled out Carter for extra coverage: "So the candidate with that highly prized political momentum tonight is Jimmy Carter, covered now by Ed Rable in New Hampshire."

After Iowa's caucuses, New Hampshire's primary was the next event to draw heavy press coverage. On the eve of the voting, ABC's Harry Reasoner said: "For some, New Hampshire will be fatal to their ambitions; for others it could be the lift needed to receive the party's nomination." Such a decisive position hardly owed to New Hampshire's delegate share, for the state contributed less than 1 percent of the Democratic national convention delegates, and by most standards the result of its 1976 primary were equivocal. In a state where only 80,000 Democratic votes were cast, Carter, the lone centrist candidate, received 28 percent to gain a 4,500 vote margin. The remaining four candidates, all liberal, who together received 60 percent of the vote, were led by Udall with 23 percent.

Yet these facts were at best only peripheral to the reporting of New Hampshire's primary. The salient point was that Carter had the lead, regardless of its frailty. Said NBC's Tom Pettit: "So Carter emerges from New Hampshire as the man to beat." *Newsweek* reported: "On the Democratic side, former Georgia Governor Jimmy Carter was the unqualified winner, with 30 percent of the vote in a crowded field." To the winner went the balance of news coverage until the next primary. *Time* and *Newsweek* put Carter's face on their covers and his story in 2,600 lines of their inside pages. The second-place finisher, Udall, received 96 lines; all of Carter's opponents together received only 300 lines. The television and newspaper coverage given Carter that week was about four times the average amount given each of his major rivals.

A more systematic look at the relationship of the amount of coverage a candidate receives to his rank in the order of finish is provided in Table 5.1. In

TABLE 5.1 Weekly News Coverage of the Democratic Candidates, Depending on Their Order of Finish in That Week's Primary (percent)

Position Candidate Finished In	Network Evening Newscasts	*Erie Times/ News*	*L.A. Herald- Examiner*	*L.A. Times*	*Time/ Newsweek*
First place	59	58	52	60	62
Second place	17	18	29	19	14
Third place	16	16	17	15	13
Fourth place	8	8	2	6	11
Total	100	100	100	100	100

Note: Based on average for the 13 primary weeks of 1976.[1]

the typical week following each primary, the first-place finisher received nearly 60 percent of the news coverage given the primary's participants; the second-place finisher received about 20 percent, the third-place finisher about 15 percent, and the fourth-place finisher about 5 percent. In the 13 primary weeks of 1976, the one substantial gap in coverage allotment occurred between the first and second places, making the difference between a first-place finish and anything less a crucial one for the candidates.

This imbalance reflected no obvious bias by the press toward a particular candidate. In the weeks that Carter finished first, he received more coverage than he did other weeks. In the weeks that Jackson, Brown, and Church won primaries, their coverage was heavier. By the time other candidates started winning more often, Carter had accumulated enough delegates to be marked as the probable nominee and therefore to receive more coverage even during winless weeks than did the others. He received by far the largest share of 1976 coverage of the Democratic race (see Table 5.2).[2] But there is nothing to suggest that the press would have covered another candidate differently had he been in the same position.

During the 1968 and 1972 elections the press was criticized for reporting the Democratic primaries in terms of expectations it had helped to create. In 1968 Lyndon Johnson received more votes than Eugene McCarthy in New

TABLE 5.2 News Coverage Received by Each of the Democratic Candidates during the Primaries (percent)

Candidate	Network Evening Newscasts	Erie Times/ News	L.A. Herald- Examiner	L.A. Times	Time/ Newsweek
Brown	10	9	20	22	10
Carter	48	44	41	46	54
Church	8	7	8	7	5
Jackson	12	13	14	11	11
Udall	13	11	12	10	13
Wallace	5	12	2	3	5
Bayh, Harris, and Shriver	4	4	3	1	2
Total	100	100	100	100	100

Hampshire's primary, but because McCarthy fared better than predicted, that primary was widely reported as a defeat for Johnson. The pattern was repeated in 1972 when Edmund Muskie had more votes than George McGovern in New Hampshire's primary, but was called the loser because he failed to win by the predicted margin. In 1976 the press consciously avoided basing its judgments on such expectations. Although it made predictions, winning and losing were treated strictly as a matter of how many votes the candidates received.

Whether coverage is based on expectations or vote counts, however, the critical fact is that the press treats primary elections much as it does the general election: there must be a winner. Each primary is only incidentally treated as part of a larger nominating system, particularly in the early stage when no candidate has accumulated enough delegates to bring the nomination close within his reach.*

In the signal tradition of which Lippmann wrote, the naming of a winner in each primary meets almost every criteria for good news. The results are the real story and reporters are careful not to submerge them in the intricacies of

---

*The 1976 primaries in New York and Wisconsin illustrate this point clearly. In Wisconsin Udall finished second to Carter by less than 1 percent of the popular vote, gaining 25 delegates to Carter's 29. On the same day, Udall easily bested Carter in New York's primary, receiving 70 delegates to Carter's 35. Thus Udall collected 95 delegates while Carter received 61, yet Carter got more news coverage and bigger headlines. Why? Because Udall failed to win either primary, finishing second to Jackson in New York. Wrote *Time* about Udall: "To stay in the race as a serious contender, he needed to win in Wisconsin. The narrow loss there was only partially offset by his unexpectedly strong showing in New York."

the presidential nominating system, for to do so would be to ignore the limited news space available, the gravitation toward the most salient fact about an event, and the need to capture what Lippmann called "the easy interest." The exaggerated emphasis on the outcome of single contests also results from a belief that the dynamics of the nominating system are more important than its abstract form. In the eyes of most reporters, the nominating system is not a network of 50 state contests weighted according to the number of delegates that each contributes. It is instead, from the very beginning, a test of the candidates' abilities to demonstrate immediate support. "The fact is that the reality in the early going of a presidential campaign is *not* the delegate count at all," Jules Witcover states. "The reality at the beginning stage is the psychological impact of the results—the perception by press, public, and contending politicians of what has happened."[3]

Press buildup of the early contests certainly contributes to the psychological impact of their results, particularly in New Hampshire's primary. Michael Robinson and Karen McPherson report that the preprimary election coverage, presumably higher in 1972 than in 1968, was a third again higher in 1976. Their study of election coverage in a three-month period also indicated that the New Hampshire primary received over half of all network evening news stories and over a third of the newspaper stories in the 1976 preprimary period; the next most heavily emphasized contest received less than 10 percent of the coverage.[4]

The extraordinary emphasis on New Hampshire is somewhat justified by the press's game perspective on the campaign. The voters of New Hampshire are not representative of the nation's, but the candidate's task there is not much different from his task in other states: he must raise money, mold an organization, gain press coverage, and make personal appearances. Since the press regards his ability to do these things as more important to his success than his politics or the nature of his audience, it sees a state like New Hampshire as a valid test of his ability to attract a national following.

Moreover, the press has a bias toward hard events. Until New Hampshire happens and the first votes are taken, the press must rely on soft indicators such as the candidates' poll standings and finances, that have only a potential relationship to the candidates' success.* Given its traditional emphasis on activity, the press would prefer to focus on actual outcomes, even if they involve few voters, narrow margins, and a questionable relationship to the thinking of the national electorate. "The early caucuses and primaries are seen as the first 'hard news' stories of the presidential race, a perception which almost guarantees an inflated

---

*For comparison, a Gallup poll taken at the time of the Iowa caucuses that first provided Carter with the front-runner label showed that less than 5 percent of the country's Democrats preferred Carter as their nominee. Kennedy, Humphrey, Wallace, Jackson, McGovern, and Muskie all rated higher while Bayh, Udall, Harris, and Shriver had about the same level of support.

value placed on the results of these events," writes Christopher Arterton. "The unrepresentative nature of the early contests is neglected because *finally* the contest has begun."[5]

The importance of early results was exaggerated in coverage of Republican as well as Democratic primaries. New Hampshire's contest between Ford and Reagan was built up enormously, and when the results were in, great significance was attached to Ford's 51 percent to 49 percent victory there. Because of his loss, it was said that Reagan had to win the upcoming Florida primary.

Although alike in this way, the Democratic and Republican races were nevertheless dissimilar in the application of the winner-take-all principle of news exposure. Both Reagan and Ford received heavier coverage when they won, but the imbalance was nowhere near as large as among the Democrats.[6] The number and nature of the candidates involved in the two races account for this difference. Excepting Wallace, the Democratic race involved a group of men whose presidential credentials owed not to any claim of a national following or major accomplishments, but to their personal ambitions and the fact that they were or had been governors or members of Congress. None of these candidates had the standing of a Ford or Reagan and, as such, none was expected by the press to last more than a few primaries without an early win. It was in terms of this expectation that initial Democratic primaries were reported. The candidacies of Bayh and Harris were pronounced dead after New Hampshire, as were those of Shriver and Udall after Massachusetts, that of Wallace after Florida, and even that of Jackson, who had a large number of delegates at the time, after Pennsylvania. Without standing in the eyes of the press, these candidates were no longer very newsworthy.

On the other hand, because the Democratic candidates were unknowns, the candidate to break out of the pack first was virtually assured intense coverage. While victory in New Hampshire produced only a slight publicity edge for Ford, it gave Carter a considerable edge. Carter was a new face and a fresh personality and, because of his newly gained prominence, eminently newsworthy. From New Hampshire to Pennsylvania, during the first nine of 30 primaries, Carter received about half of all the coverage awarded the seven Democratic candidates who began the primaries together.

Carter's performance also provided him with news coverage that was more favorable than that received by his opponents. Evaluations of the candidates were keyed primarily to their success. A winning candidate was said to be an effective campaigner and organizer while a loser was normally presented as lacking in these talents. Moreover, since popular support is considered a *sine qua non* of success, a winning candidate usually was described by such adjectives as likable and appealing. Although a losing candidate normally was not described in opposing terms, it was often stated or implied that voters were not particularly attracted by his personality and style. During the primaries Carter received more than two favorable news mentions about his performance and personality for each unfavorable one. No other candidate received even a favorable balance of coverage.

ELECTIONEERS AND REPRESENTATIVES

A second case illustrating how the journalistic model of election politics affects candidate coverage is the 1976 Republican race. It was a contest in which the press's predictions frequently missed their mark. In March Gerald Ford was named by the *Los Angeles Times* as "a solid favorite" in North Carolina one week before Ronald Reagan easily won that state's primary. *Time* magazine wrote in the same month that Reagan had been "practically eliminated . . . from the running" by Ford's Florida win, and that his candidacy "had died" after his fifth straight loss in Illinois; several weeks later Reagan surpassed Ford in total delegates won. In April NBC News asserted that Ford was the heavy favorite to win the Republican nomination. Shortly thereafter, however, Reagan ran off a string of five primary victories in 11 days and took the delegate lead from Ford. Perhaps this prompted *Newsweek* to write in early May that Ford faced a stiff test in Michigan and that "a defeat there would leave his candidacy tapped out and might even force his withdrawal from the race." Yet Ford won 65 percent of the Michigan vote and led Reagan within a week by more than 100 delegates.

When their predictions went awry, journalists responded with surprise, speaking in their postprimary analyses about "shocking wins," "stunning turn-abouts," and "eleventh-hour reprieves." The day after Reagan's North Carolina win, ABC's Herb Kaplow said,

> Aside from foreign policy and inflation maybe turning the voters towards Reagan, there's talk that maybe local politics helped him to win, and maybe better organization, and maybe Bo Calloway's problems, and maybe sympathy for the underdog, particularly when the President's men tried to pressure Reagan to quit, but so far it's just maybes, just speculation. And so nobody knows just what happened here yesterday. . . .

Reviewing the Republican primaries, *Time* magazine concluded that the voters had upset "many an expert forecast." A leading newspaper columnist echoed that sentiment when he wrote: "A weary reporter, unpacking his suitcase and sorting through his jumbled impressions of the last five months, is struck by the paradoxes of the primary season. Almost any generalization that springs to mind is immediately contradicted . . . there were so many surprises."

Nevertheless, there was actually a remarkably consistent pattern to the 1976 Republican race. For some time there has been an enduring ideological split between moderate and conservative rank-and-file Republicans. Evident for the past quarter century, it has occurred in each primary election involving strong contenders identified clearly with the right and the center. It appeared in 1952 when Republican voters had to choose between conservative Robert Taft and moderate Dwight D. Eisenhower, in the 1964 contest among conservative Barry Goldwater and moderates Nelson Rockefeller and William Scranton, and once again in 1976 when the conservative Reagan and the moderate Ford vied for the Republican nomination.

The persistence of this split is clearly illustrated by a comparison of the 1964 and 1976 races. In 1964 Goldwater received his most solid support from Republicans in these 25 states: Alabama, Arizona, California, Georgia, Idaho, Illinois, Indiana, Kansas, Louisiana, Mississippi, Missouri, Montana, Nebraska, Nevada, New Mexico, North Carolina, Oklahoma, South Carolina, South Dakota, Tennessee, Texas, Utah, Virginia, Washington, and Wyoming. All but three of these states also produced wins for Reagan in 1976. Only in Kansas, Mississippi, and Illinois did Reagan win fewer delegates than Ford. Together, Reagan acquired from these states 833 delegates, while Ford received only 276. Moreover, the 25 states providing Goldwater his least solid support in 1964 were: Alaska, Arkansas, Colorado, Connecticut, Delaware, Florida, Hawaii, Iowa, Kentucky, Maine, Maryland, Massachusetts, Michigan, Minnesota, New Hampshire, New Jersey, New York, North Dakota, Ohio, Oregon, Pennsylvania, Rhode Island, Vermont, West Virginia, and Wisconsin. These states meant poor showings for Reagan as well. With the exceptions of Arkansas and Colorado, each state supported Ford, providing him a total of 881 delegates to Reagan's 237.

Although the conservative Reagan's victories in North Carolina, Indiana, Idaho, and Nebraska were labeled surprising by the press, these states also were dominated by Goldwater in 1964 and by Taft in 1952. Ford's surprising wins were in New Hampshire, Florida, Kentucky, and West Virginia, but these states had been neither Goldwater's nor Taft's best.[7] Primary results presented by the press as voter upsets, then, were actually parts of a recurring pattern.

If there was any real surprise in 1976, it occurred because of the timing of the primaries. What resulted when the state legislatures of the 30 primary states made their schedules was a calendar with built-in drama. By scheduling primaries in the conservative southern and western states for early May and the last three weeks of the campaign, they clustered together those primaries where Reagan's prospects were best. Similarly, primaries in the moderate northern and eastern states, where Ford's chances were good, were clustered in early spring and in mid-May. The Republican primaries were thus positioned so that each candidate was able to respond to a series of his opponent's first-place finishes with a winning streak of his own.

The press was not entirely unmindful of either the split within Republican ranks or the regional concentration of the split. In late May, for example, *Time* magazine said of a Ford victory, "The President needed that lift because the fight now moves to Reagan's friendly southern and western turf." In April an AP report in the *Erie News* noted: "Ronald Reagan, meanwhile, began a tour of Texas as part of his Sun Belt strategy to wrest the Republican nomination from President Ford." Early in the election year the *Los Angeles Times* had analyzed the regional and ideological aspects of the Ford-Reagan race.

But these aspects were only used occasionally by the press to explain primary results. Instead, the press usually cited campaign promises, events, strategies, styles, and organizational activities as the reasons behind the developments in the Ford-Reagan race (see Table 5.3).

TABLE 5.3 The News Media's Explanations for the Outcomes of the Republican Primaries (percent)

Explanation	Network Evening Newscasts	*Erie News/ Times*	*L.A. Herald-Examiner*	*L.A. Times*	*Time/ Newsweek*
Organization/ Financing	18	21	22	25	19
Strategy/ Momentum	22	17	17	15	20
Issues/ Episodes	19	21	20	21	21
Style/ Vigor	25	21	22	17	23
Subtotal	84	80	81	78	83
Ideology/ Region	16	20	19	22	17
Total	100	100	100	100	100

After Reagan's poor showing in New Hampshire, for example, *Time* magazine suggested that he might have won had he not declined an appearance on NBC's "Today" show on the morning of the primary. When Ford won in Florida, the *Erie Times* carried a report giving much of the credit to a switch in his state campaign manager just before the election. Then Reagan won in North Carolina and the media accepted it as a result of the voters' negative response to the recent airing of Ford's attempts at détente with the Soviet Union. On NBC News the size of one of Ford's wins was attributed to his presidential demeanor, the size of another to his momentum. Reagan's win in one primary was associated with "his Hollywood glamour—still a factor in the rural Midwest." A UPI story in the *Erie Times* indicated that Ford's victory margin in Michigan owed to his "whistle-stopping across the state by train in the style of his political hero, Harry Truman." In mid-May the *Los Angeles Times* said that "Ford had the strongest organization in Maryland, with telephone banks and mass mailings, and it showed in the election results."

There are a number of reasons for the press's emphasis on explanations such as these. It results in large part from the reporters' particular vantage on the campaign. Their attention is focused so tightly on the candidates that their first consideration is likely to be differences in candidates' strategies, organizations, promises, and the like. It also results from the press's concern with the marginal vote. In elections that are close or whose margins differ substantially from what had been predicted, the press looks past the larger group of voters whose allegiance depends mainly on enduring influences, such as ideology, to the smaller group that is more easily persuaded by campaign activity and may have provided the difference. Thus reporters sometimes point to things such as Reagan's failure to appear on the "Today" show or Ford's decision to change campaign managers as critical, in spite of their patented insignificance to the thinking of the vast majority of primary voters.

Such explanations also conform with the press's gamelike conception of the campaign. In this model, as Wicker notes, the press sees the electorate as a people influenced mostly by tactics and strategy, and thus exaggerates dynamic influences such as momentum, discounting such factors as the differences in the political views of the voters in separate states.[8]   Such reasoning prompted reporters to predict that Ford would easily win the primary in North Carolina because he had won the five preceding primaries. After Reagan won in North Carolina, one columnist wrote that "the Reagan campaign revived only when he stopped shaking hands and headed for a Hollywood television studio to film his half-hour speech."

There are few constraints on such conclusions for elections are complex activities. Once it is assumed that campaigning is decisive in election outcomes, it always is possible to find something that the winner did better than, or at least differently from, the loser. This in turn may affect the press's views of the candidate: the better campaigner will win and the winner will be the better candidate. In the average week of the 1976 Republican primaries, 75 percent of the press's evaluations of the winning candidate's strategy, organization, and so on were positive in nature, while only 30 percent of such evaluations of the loser's effort were positive. This type of circular reasoning occurred regardless of the winner's identity. In the weeks that Reagan won his effort was interpreted as superior to Ford's; the opposite was true in the weeks that Ford placed first.

A LIMITED PERSPECTIVE

The press's handling of the two situations just described obviously resulted in part from factors unique to each situation. The specific amounts and types of news coverage the candidates receive in future elections will, consequently, vary with the situation. It is possible that circumstances similar to those in 1976 will exist in some future election. Indeed, the Democratic race in 1976 race was a close replay of the 1972 race in which a relative unknown, McGovern, emerged from a large field of Democratic contenders and received a much larger share of the news than he did of the votes or the delegates.

But the central point here is that, regardless of the situation, what is reported to the public depends as heavily on journalistic values as on political considerations. This was only somewhat less true during the 1976 general election than it was during the primaries. In the general election the news agenda was dominated by the game; major events like the debates were reported mainly in terms of their impact on the race; and the candidates' standing with the voters was pictured as resulting more from their skills as electioneers than from the political alternatives they represented.

The power of the press rests largely on its ability to select what will be covered and to decide the context in which these events will be placed. Through this influence and because the press is guided substantially by its values, conventions, and organizational imperatives, certain aspects of an election are magnified and others muted in news of the campaign. The press's version of election politics elevates competition over substance, outcomes over process, and the immediate over the enduring. While these favored aspects are not an insignificant part of the election, focus on them represents an unquestionably limited perspective.* *Some prime examples of the mistakes or interferences the press makes in covering a campaign.*

---

*The press's coverage of the candidates also will be discussed in Chapter 12, where the themes of the candidates' coverage will be related to their images.

PART III
THE ELECTION AUDIENCE

6

THE AUDIENCE FOR
NATIONAL NEWS

Because most adult Americans read a newspaper or watch television daily, it is tempting to assume that the national news carried by these media is an everyday part of their lives. National opinion polls seem to confirm this impression. Asked about the current issues facing the nation, most people offer an opinion, giving the appearance, says Barber, that they have been keeping up with the news.[1]

The image of an intrusive national politics results particularly from the emergence of network television as a major news source. Unlike the newspapers that are locally based and divide their coverage between local and national affairs, the networks are national organizations whose coverage is almost completely limited to national politics. While about 70 percent of U.S. homes receive a daily newspaper, nearly 98 percent have a television set. In many homes the television is left on for several hours each day, often regardless of what programs happen to be on at the time. Facts like these have convinced many observers that the networks are the preeminent source of public information. "The three New York-based networks, via their news and documentary programs, have become the principal arbiters of American opinion," declares Kevin Phillips. "Survey after survey spotlights television as the most influential medium in the United States."[2]

Indeed, there are many observers who feel that television has in effect revolutionized the political audience. The newspaper's audience, so their argument goes, is necessarily limited because its use requires motivation and effort. But watching television is effortless. Besides presenting a more appealing version of the news, it almost seeks out an audience. Many television viewers are said to watch the news regularly, not because they are especially interested in politics, but because they spend so much time watching television. "One unique characteristic," writes Michael Robinson

> is that its audience is an *inadvertent* one—which, in large proportion, does not come purposely to television for news, but arrives almost accidentally, watching the news because it is "on" or because it leads into or out of something else . . . the people who "watch" the news—more often than not—have almost literally fallen into the audience.[3]

As a result, television's audience is said to be much larger than and different from the newspaper's. It is said that whereas the newspaper appeals primarily to the relatively small group of politically interested people, television news appeals to the masses. "So large is the viewing audience," writes Dan Nimmo

> that exposure cuts across such sections of the population as age groups, educational levels, economic strata and races. . . . The printed media—newspapers and magazines—are "high effort" media compared to television and radio. The contrast is so sharp that only a small proportion of heavy readers of newspapers and magazines are part of regular television news audiences.[4]

Robinson even claims that the two audiences are reverse images of one another:

> The people who watch television news the most, in absolute and proportional terms, are among the least well educated and least "connected" individuals in our mass society. This is unprecedented for a news audience and completely reverses the general pattern of correlation between news consumption and socioeconomic status.[5]

The evidence for these claims comes from a number of different polls, chiefly the Roper Poll on Television and Other Media conducted almost yearly since 1959. These polls have asked people where they get most of their news.* Responding to this question in the 1976 Roper poll, about 40 percent mentioned television, 25 percent said the newspaper, and 25 percent indicated both sources. The more frequent references to television support the conclusion that its

---

*These questions are of the following form: "Now, I'd like to ask where you usually get most of your news about what's going on in the world today—is it from the newspapers or radio or television or magazines or talking with others?" Questions like this have appeared in the Roper, Gallup, SRC, and other surveys. Perhaps the major reason why people's media exposure has been measured this way is the economy of using a single question.

audience is larger. The rather consistent mention of only one source prompts the judgment that the two news audiences are basically different. The lower education and income levels of those who mention only television seem to indicate that its greatest following is among those of lower status.

THE REAL AUDIENCES OF TELEVISION
AND THE NEWSPAPER

The judgment that television's audience is much larger than and different from the newspaper's, however, is a faulty one. The problem stems from the evidence on which the judgment is based. To ask people where they get most of their news is to fail to regard distinctions in the *amounts* of news they receive. For instance, as long as they have less exposure to other news sources, individuals can say that they get most of their news from television even if they seldom watch its newscasts.

A more precise assessment of the political audience is obtained by asking people how often they see the news on television or in the newspaper. When this is done a much different picture emerges. It is actually the newspaper, not television, which has the larger regular news audience (see Table 6.1). In Erie 48 percent of those polled said they regularly read a daily paper's news sections, while 34 percent said they regularly watched the evening newscasts of ABC, CBS, and NBC. In Los Angeles 33 percent claimed to be regular readers and 24

TABLE 6.1 Exposure to Network Evening Newscasts and the Daily Paper's Political News Sections (percent)

Level of News Exposure	Erie		Los Angeles	
	Newspaper	Network News	Newspaper	Network News
Regularly	48	34	33	24
Somewhat often	21	30	15	27
Once in a while	11	23	10	30
Infrequently	7	12	15	16
Never	13	1	27	3
Total	100	100	100	100

Note: Table percentages are average of respondents' replies for the five interviews. That respondents were questioned as many as five times provides a control on measurement error. To be classified as a regular user, a respondent had consistently to indicate frequent exposure. Typical of the questions asked was the following: "Most people don't have the time or interest to read the entire newspaper. They normally read only certain parts such as the sports, the comics, the news, the business pages, the women's pages, and so on. How often do you read the *news pages* of your daily newspaper? Do you read the news pages regularly, somewhat often, only once in a while, or almost never (infrequently)?" People who did not receive a newspaper or did not have a television set were placed in the never category.

percent were regular viewers. Moreover, the frequency of use is higher among newspaper regulars. On the average, regular newspaper readers said they read their paper's news pages six days a week, while regular viewers said they watched the evening news three or four times a week.[6]

Only among nonregular news users are there more people who depend on television than the newspaper. There were one and a half times as many television viewers as there were newspaper readers among respondents who reported being exposed to the news somewhat often (once or twice a week). Over twice as many saw the nightly newscasts once in a while (approximately once every two or three weeks) as read the newspaper this often. Among those receiving infrequent exposure (once a month or less), a somewhat larger number watched the evening news than read a daily paper's news pages.

Further, it is not the case that "only a small proportion of heavy readers" are part of the regular television news audience, as Nimmo suggests. In fact, respondents who read the newspaper regularly also were more likely to watch the newscasts on a regular basis ($r=+.38$). Roughly half of all regular readers watched the evening news consistently; only a fifth of nonregular readers did so. As a result of this overlap in the two audiences, television viewing alone does not greatly expand the proportion of the population that follows at least one news medium regularly. Television enlarges the attentive public by roughly one fourth of what it is when newspaper readership alone is considered.

It is further instructive to look at where people at each level of news exposure got most of their news (see Table 6.2). The newspaper was more likely to be the preferred source among people who used at least one news source regularly. Only among less avid news consumers was television the source used most often. In fact, the less closely people followed the news, the greater the chance that television provided most of their news. For example, among those whose maximum exposure to either television or the newspaper

TABLE 6.2 News Source Used Most Often, Depending on Frequency of News Exposure (percent)

Highest Level of Exposure to Either News Source	Network News	Newspaper	TV and Paper Equally
Regularly	11	22	18
Somewhat often	12	9	6
Once in a while	10	2	3
Infrequently	4	0.4	2
Never	0	0	1
Total	37	33	30

Note: The table combines Erie and Los Angeles respondents. The pattern was similar in both locations.

was infrequent (once a month or less), ten times as many received most of their news from television. The reason: these people had television sets and, though they rarely watched the evening news, they did not subscribe to and thus never read a newspaper.

This also unmasks television's supposed appeal to those of low status. This relationship exists only when the television news audience is defined by where people get most of their news; then it includes those people of low educations and incomes who generally ignore the news, but get most of what little they receive through television. When the amount of people's television exposure is considered, a different conclusion is demanded:

	Regular Viewers	Not Regular Viewers	Significance of Difference
Average income			
Erie	$13,724	$14,521	.28
Los Angeles	14,976	13,384	.09
Average education			
Erie	12.2 yrs.	12.2 yrs.	.81
Los Angeles	13.0 yrs.	13.1 yrs.	.77

There actually are no significant differences in the incomes and educations of those who watch television news regularly and those who do not.

Television news, then, does not find its audience primarily among people of low status; nor does it typically attract people with little political interest. In both Erie and Los Angeles, regular viewers of the evening newscasts, as well as regular readers of the newspaper, had significantly more interest in politics (at the .01 level) than those who seldom followed the news.

None of this is to say that the network evening newscasts are an unimportant source of news. On the contrary, television has enlarged and changed the regular political audience somewhat. For while the differences are small among regular and nonregular viewers, education and income levels are higher among a disproportionate number of regular newspaper readers. Moreover, television has provided most regular newspaper readers with additional frequent news exposure and has increased the casual political exposure of most Americans. But this is much different from saying that television has fundamentally altered the public's attention to politics. To accept the argument that television's regular audience is much larger than and different from the newspaper's is to believe that the news fully penetrates U.S. society when, in fact, the attentive public neither includes the large majority of citizens nor fully represents the whole public.

ATTENTION TO THE NEWS

Even when people read or watch the news, there remains a question of how much attention they give it. Often people's intake of the news is shared simultaneously with another activity, such as holding a conversation. Often the news is communicated against a background of noise, perhaps engulfed by the clamor of the dinner hour. Even when external disturbances are minimal, consumers of the news may have other things on their minds.

Some indication of the attention given to the news is provided by the interviews. When respondents reported news exposure within the past 24 hours, they were asked to describe whatever they remembered best. The choice was theirs, so this test of memory was not particularly demanding. Yet the ability of respondents to recount what they had seen was not particularly high. About half the time they were able to provide the basic facts of a news report:

> It was about what Ford said on Eastern Europe. That it was not dominated by the Soviet Union. What he said hurt his position in the polls.

> It was about the problems with the present primary system of selecting presidential candidates. The suggestion was made that there should be regional primaries.

> The President wanted to revamp the CIA and FBI and the rest of the intelligence agencies. He wants to bring them under better control.

About 30 percent of their descriptions were only partly complete:

> Ford was talking about working people.

> Can't pinpoint it exactly. Carter is coming up so fast was the main point though.

> Governor Brown trying to get uncommitted delegates. I don't remember any of the details.

About 20 percent of the time they were unable to recall much at all of what they had seen:

> It was something about the election. That's all I remember.

> Ford was campaigning someplace. I don't recall what it was or what he was saying.

> About the man that is challenging the Republican candidate. I can't remember his name.

Such evidence suggests that people often are not closely attentive to the news they see.

One factor emerged as important to people's ability to recall what they had seen: the medium used (see Table 6.3). Newspaper coverage left a more lasting impression than did television news. While over 55 percent of the newspaper readers could accurately recall a news story seen within 24 hours, only about 45 percent of network news viewers could do so. This difference held regardless of people's backgrounds. Within each category of education, income, sex, and age, the recall level was higher for newspaper readers than it was for television viewers.

The difference inheres in the media and their uses. Newspaper readers have more control over the content of their source. Its news can be read and digested as quickly or as slowly as the individual's reading ability and inclination permit. Television viewers, on the other hand, watch their news stories flow one after another, never able to spend more time on each than is determined by the speed with which they are communicated. Viewers also take in less information, for television stories are shorter, typically equivalent in length to the first two paragraphs of newspaper stories.[7] Longer and more detailed, newspaper stories and their content undoubtedly leave a greater impression on those readers who do more than simply glance at the headlines.

The impact of television news also is limited by the nature of its communication. Although a highly visual medium, television transmits its most important political information through sound, for politics is an activity dominated by words. Yet, as Thomas Patterson and Robert McClure found in their 1972 election study, people actually are more attentive to the pictures than to the words of television news.[8] As a consequence, television viewers sometimes fail to get the message. Regardless of what viewers focus on, moreover, the ear is not as adept a receiver as the eye—what is read is more apt to be retained than what is heard.[9] The newspaper, as well as being read, has little nonverbal

TABLE 6.3 Ability to Recall News Stories Seen within the Past 24 Hours (percent)

Level of Recall	Network News Stories	Newspaper Stories
Mostly complete	45	57
Partly incomplete	37	30
Fully incomplete	18	13
Total	100	100
	(n=1,298)	(n=1,665)

Note: Examples of each recall level are included in the text. Table based only on respondents who claimed to have seen a news report in the medium within the past 24 hours. Los Angeles and Erie respondents are combined for the table; the pattern was similar in each location. The n's are for stories recalled. Since questions were asked in each of the five personal interviews, the n's total more than the number of respondents.

communication to distract the reader from the essence of its message.

Finally, television news receives comparatively less attention from its users than does the newspaper. Early television was correctly labeled by Marshall McLuhan as a high-involvement medium, but this description is less accurate today. [10] As television's novelty has passed, notes Barber, so has the image of viewers riveted to their seats, staring intently at the pictures on the screen. [11] Television no longer draws the complete attention of its users. It has not gone as far as the radio, which is now almost solely a background medium, for its pictures help to hold its audience in place. But while television often accompanies dinner, knitting, or homework, newspaper reading is necessarily a primary activity. Readers often are distracted in their pursuit, but they must involve themselves more deeply than television viewers, thus increasing their chances of retaining what they see.

OCCASIONAL SOURCES OF NATIONAL NEWS

The conclusions drawn from the evidence on daily newspapers and the network evening news are not altered substantially by an account of other sources of national news.

Concerning the weekly newsmagazines such as *Time* and *Newsweek*, for instance, only 8 percent of the respondents read the political sections regularly. The use of such a magazine was reported by a small minority, and by only one out of every 100 respondents as the only news source followed regularly. Newsmagazines, then, tend to reach those already reached by the newspaper or television.

Local television news, in contrast, does have a large audience. But people's local and network news exposure overlapped substantially (r = + .70). Furthermore, national news reports shown on local television often were taken from the network newscasts, suggesting that local television primarily complements national political information communicated by the networks. Viewers of local news, moreover, were least attentive of all news audiences to politics, especially to national affairs. Asked whether they had seen anything about politics through their medium in the past 24 hours, frequent local viewers were 30 percent less likely than frequent network viewers or newspaper readers to say they had. Presumably, this reflects the local newscasts' emphasis on and viewers' interest in weather, sports, local crime, accidents, cultural events, and the like. When local viewers were able to recall something about politics, they were as likely to mention a report on local or state politics as one about national politics.* What-

---

*Of relevance here, though the newspaper also covers these levels of politics, 85 percent of newspaper readers described a report on national affairs.

ever contribution local television makes to public awareness of national politics, it apparently is a modest one.

Personal discussion also does little to extend the political audience. In their studies of presidential elections in the 1940s, Lazarsfeld and Berelson claimed that there was a penetrating two-step flow of communication: "Ideas often flow *from* radio and print *to* the opinion leaders and *from* them to the less active sections of the population." [12] Reflecting on the enormous implications of this conclusion, Key wrote in 1961: "By this means the audience of the media may be enlarged; their messages reach indirectly many people who pay no direct attention to the media." [13]

The interviews, however, provide no evidence for a pervasive two-step flow of information. Only 11 percent of the respondents claimed to discuss politics regularly. More to the point, those individuals who for the most part ignored the news media largely refrained from talking politics. Less than 5 percent of these said they talked politics regularly; the large majority said they seldom or never discussed politics with others. This was as true in the smaller, more neighborly city of Erie as it was in the Los Angeles metropolis. In both locations personal communication was a weak source of day-to-day news for those who did not depend on the media.

Discussions with others, however, were more useful than the formal channels of mass communication in serving occasional and special needs. Although the total electorate's exposure to television and the newspaper varied only slightly from time to time in the election year, political conversations changed markedly at one point. Discussion rose about 50 percent during the last three weeks of the campaign. In October, although a majority still was not talking politics regularly, a fairly sizable minority was doing so. As Chapter 9 will indicate, their conversations had several purposes, one being the transmission of information received from the media. But many of these discussions provided the people with something not available through mass communication, namely, feedback on their views and intentions toward the candidates. People were looking to others for help in making and crystallizing their opinions about the election.*

TIME, INTEREST, AND POLITICAL EXPOSURE

That the electorate responds to the media as it does is a reflection primarily of people's time for and interest in politics. Every breakthrough in commun-

---

*It was, however, the case that most conversations, even in October, were taking place among people who followed the media closely. This study produced little evidence of the two-step flow of which Lazarsfeld and Berelson spoke. The note to their work above contains a brief criticism of their methodology, suggesting that their evidence was insufficient to justify their claim.

ication, from the printing press to the telegraph to television, has extended the political audience. Each breakthrough, however, inevitably confronts the basic barrier to universal attention: many citizens have neither the political concern nor the time requisite to following the news on a daily basis.

From one perspective, television news places unusually heavy demands on its users, a fact often ignored in evaluations of television's impact. To see the news people must be near their television sets at the proper time and with 30 minutes to spare. A delay in coming home from work, a neighbor stopping by, an errand that needs to be run, losing track of time—any of a dozen such things can keep the intended viewer away from the news. In comparison, the newspaper is a readily available medium. It can be carried inside the home or out and read most any time there is a moment to spare. This is one reason why, as shown earlier, regular newspaper readers usually read the news each day, while regular viewers of the evening news usually missed a newscast or two each week. Newspaper reading also was more consistent on a week-by-week basis. In each of the five interviews during 1976, respondents were asked how many times in the last seven days they had read their daily paper's political news or watched the evening newscasts, and their answers indicate that the correlation between any two weeks of newspaper exposure was higher than the correlation between the same two weeks of television viewing. The newspaper is simply more conducive than television to consistent use.

From another perspective, however, television news has a unique answer to the obstacle of time: people are willing to surrender so many of their spare hours to television that the news it offers gains some followers. Those people for whom television was the only regular source were characterized by their heavy use of the medium for entertainment. Compared with people who read the newspaper regularly, they watched 30 percent more prime-time television programming each week.

Habitual television viewing is not, however, a sufficient cause of heavy news exposure. For the fact is unless heavy viewers also are interested in politics, they do not pay much attention to the newscasts. Two in every three people who were chronic viewers and had high interest in politics watched the evening news regularly. But only one in six people who were chronic viewers and had low interest in politics watched the nightly news consistently. These television addicts obviously organized their viewing hours so as to miss the evening newscasts.

Jay Blumler and Denis McQuail quite accurately say that television has resulted in "in the availability of a large group in the electorate who are prepared to tolerate political messages without being keen to receive them." [14] The difficulty comes when this observation is extended, as it has been, to the claim that television has made politics an everyday experience for those who traditionally have ignored politics. Tolerance is not the mainspring of ongoing attention to the news. Only an interest in politics, and the availability of time to pursue it, can create that result.

INTEREST IN THE CAMPAIGN

A presidential election campaign is an intense news event. Where most events are in the news for a few days or weeks, the campaign is an everyday topic for nearly a full year and often is the subject of special news coverage. Truly, the campaign stands as an extraordinary effort to involve U.S. citizens in the nation's politics.

How do people react to this massive effort to arouse and keep their attention? Do they take a strong interest early in the campaign? Or do they, as is often claimed, wait until the last few weeks of the campaign before taking note? There is not much evidence available that would answer these questions. Since 1952 the Survey Research Centers' presidential election studies have questioned Americans about their election interest, but these studies are based on single interviews and thus do not reveal the changes that occur during the campaign. Lazarsfeld and Berelson measured people's interest at different periods of the 1940 and 1948 elections, but their studies were conducted three decades ago, and what was true in the 1940s may not characterize the significantly different campaigns of today.

INTEREST AT EACH STAGE OF THE CAMPAIGN

Before the 1976 campaign got under way, most people gave the election little thought (see Table 7.1). In the February interviews completed just before New Hampshire's opening primary, only 20 percent of the respondents reported

TABLE 7.1   Election Interest at Various Times during the Campaign (percent)[1]

Level of Interest and Location	February	April	June	August	October
Erie					
Strong interest	22	28	26	33	32
Some interest	28	30	34	33	34
No interest	50	42	40	34	34
Total	100	100	100	100	100
Los Angeles					
Strong interest	19	27	32	37	29
Some interest	26	28	33	32	33
No interest	55	45	35	31	38
Total	100	100	100	100	100

strong interest in the election. Half of those questioned indicated a total lack of interest. Some claimed to have a general distaste for politics; others simply felt that it was too early in the campaign to be concerned:

> I just won't be interested until the campaign gets going.

> It's ridiculous how much they're trying to make of the campaign already . . . there's nothing to be interested in yet.

> At this point, my opinion is that things don't matter very much. I'll be interested later on.

With the primaries, however, there came a surge in voters' interest. By the April interviews, halfway through the primaries, 27 percent were strongly interested in the campaign and less than 45 percent expressed no interest. In both absolute and proportional terms, this was the most significant rise in interest for any period in the campaign. The general rise in interest that occurred during the early primaries was not, however, matched during the late primaries. Only in Los Angeles did interest grow between the April and June interviews, due mostly to the success of Californians Jerry Brown and Ronald Reagan in the later primaries. In fact, interest at this time was particularly high among supporters of Brown and Reagan.

The period of the Republican and Democratic national conventions produced a second general growth in public interest. In the August interviews, completed after the last convention, 37 percent of the respondents in Los Angeles expressed strong interest and 31 percent said they were not interested, while 33 percent of the respondents in Erie were strongly interested while 34 percent were not. For the first time in the campaign, highly interested voters equaled in number those with no interest.

Interest did not continue to rise during the general election, however. In fact, in Los Angeles the interest level was substantially lower at the end of the general election than it had been in August. The October interviews indicated high interest among only 29 percent of its respondents, a decline of 8 percent. This decline can be attributed to the failure of the Brown and Reagan candidacies to survive beyond the convention period, for diminished interest was concentrated among prenomination backers of Brown and Reagan. For other Los Angeles voters, there was no substantial loss of interest between August and October; at the same time, however, there was no increase in the interest of this group. Nor was there an increase among Erie voters; 33 percent of them had been highly interested in August and 32 percent were strongly interested in October. Thus the common assumption that interest rises sharply in the campaign's final weeks is certainly questionable.

Indeed, the ability of today's campaign to induce and expand interest is somewhat limited. From February to October, after nine months of intensive campaigning, strong interest among the electorate increased from about 20 percent to slightly more than 30 percent. In this respect, today's campaign is not much different from those studied by Lazarsfeld and Berelson in the 1940s. Then, as now, the peak of public involvement was reached when about a third of the electorate expressed strong interest.[2] Thus the lengthening and increased activity of the current campaign has not significantly changed the overall level of voter interest.

There is another respect in which the public's response to today's campaign is remarkably similar to that of the 1940s. Beneath the stability apparent in the interest of the public as a collective group of voters lie constant upward and downward fluctuations in the interest of individuals. Election interest can be fragile. A particular event or period in the campaign may spark a voter's interest, but this interest often subsides as quickly as it materializes. Over 40 percent of the respondents either gained or lost interest from one interview to the next. Interestingly, Lazarsfeld and Berelson also found roughly a 40 percent turnover in election interest between interviews.[3]

NEWS EXPOSURE AFFECTS INTEREST

Today's election appears to have resulted in one notable change: public interest now peaks more quickly. Whereas interest in the 1976 campaign rose sharply in the early primaries, interest in the 1940 campaign did not increase significantly until the general election.[4] Higher interest during the early stage of the campaign and particularly during the primaries is surely due in part to the larger role the public now plays in the nominating process. But it also is surely a function of changes in election coverage and its impact on news audiences. Election coverage today is more intense and less easily avoided than it was three decades ago. In the 1940s, the campaign received only 40 percent of the front-page newspaper coverage given it during the 1976 primary period.[5] Also, there was practically no television coverage of presidential elections in the 1940s.[6]

The onslaught of election news that accompanies the start of today's primaries promotes early interest. Repeated interviews with the same respondents indicate a significant relationship between people's media use and changes in their interest. Even when their interest in the earlier interview was controlled for, the more closely people followed the news, the more likely their interest was to have increased by the next interview (see Table 7.2).* This was true at every stage of the campaign—the primaries, the conventions, and the general election—but the impact of news exposure in 1976 was particularly strong during the primaries. It was at the start of the primaries that the most abrupt change in the flow of election news occurred. Once the primaries were underway, television and newspaper coverage of the election was nearly three times as heavy as it was in the weeks preceding the primaries, surely making more difficult a passive avoidance of the campaign.

Television coverage contributed most to the early upturn in election interest. Television viewing and newspaper reading were about equally responsible for rising interest during the latter part of the 1976 campaign, but in the primaries the evening newscasts had the greater impact. This is perhaps because its pictorial presentation of news gives television an immediacy not to be found in newsprint, an immediacy, it might be argued, that hastens interest. Television during the early part of the campaign also is a more invasive medium than the newspaper. Readers who are not yet interested in the campaign can simply bypass election news. Those who look to be informed by television news, however, are a somewhat captive audience to whatever election news stories the networks decide to include in their newscasts. Moreover, viewers are more likely than readers to encounter a high proportion of election stories early in the campaign. During the 1976 primaries the campaign was the subject of one in five national political news stories on evening newscasts, but only one in eight of such stories in the newspaper. Not surprisingly, when recalling news stories they had seen, viewers were nearly 15 percent more likely than readers to describe one about the primary campaign.

----

*A panel survey uniquely provides the basis for a finding of this type. Only because the same individuals were interviewed each time is it known whether an individual's interest increased, decreased, or stayed the same from one interview to the next. Such changes can then be related to people's news exposure. The reader might note that there is a positive association between news exposure and interest during the general election, despite the fact that the overall interest level did not increase during this period. The reason is that a positive relationship between one variable and another can result either because increases in the change variable are associated with higher values of the other variable or because decreases in the change variable are associated with lower values of the other variable. The statistical values found in many of the tables in this and subsequent chapters reflect both of these types of associated change. For a discussion of the use of beta coefficients in panel analysis, see note to Table 7.2.

TABLE 7.2 Relationship of News Exposure to Changes in Election Interest

Time of Interest Change	Erie		Los Angeles	
	Newscast Exposure	Newspaper Exposure	Newscast Exposure	Newspaper Exposure
Primaries (Feb. to June)	+.26 (.01)	+.17 (.01)	+.19 (.01)	+.12 (.01)
Conventions (June to Aug.)	+.05 (.25)	+.10 (.01)	+.15 (.01)	+.11 (.05)
General election (Aug. to Oct.)	+.09 (.05)	+.08 (.05)	+.10 (.05)	+.05 (.25)

Note: Top figures are beta coefficients from regression equations in which people's interest at the time of the later interview was the dependent variable. Their newscast exposure, their newspaper exposure, and their interest at the time of the earlier interview were the independent variables. That the betas are positive indicates that higher news exposure was related to increased or consistently high interest from one interview to the next. The figures in parentheses are the statistical significance levels of the respective betas. These levels indicate the statistical probability that the observed relationships are due to chance alone, for example, the level .01 indicates that the odds are less than one in 100 that the relationship of higher interest was due simply to chance.[7]

In addition to regular evening newscasts, special coverage also contributes to the impact of television during the primaries. Programs such as the Tuesday night telecasts of primary returns and frequent appearances of the candidates on "Meet the Press" and "Face the Nation" reached about 20 percent of the voters during the typical primary week in 1976. Heavier exposure to these telecasts was significantly related to increases in people's interest during the primaries (see Table 7.3). As the data indicate, however, these telecasts were not as important to television's early impact on election interest as were the evening newscasts.

Once the primaries were over, the national conventions and presidential debates came to the forefront, and television's coverage of those events replaced the nightly newscasts as the major inducer of public interest. Almost 60 percent of the respondents watched at least one debate and an additional 25 percent said they saw at least some of one debate. While smaller, the audience for the televised conventions also was substantial. Nearly 30 percent claimed to have watched most of one or both televised conventions, and another 35 percent said they saw some of at least one convention. Generally, such exposure led to increased interest. Respondents who saw more of the conventions were likely to have higher interest in August than they did in June; those who saw more of the debates were likely to have more interest in October than in August (see Table 7.3).

In fact, during the last stages of the campaign the effect of television on

TABLE 7.3 Relationship of Exposure to Televised Coverage of the Primaries, Conventions, and Debates to Changes in Election Interest during the Primary, Convention, and General Election Periods, Respectively.

Time of Interest Change	Special Telecast Exposure	Evening Newscast Exposure	Daily Newspaper Exposure
Primaries (Feb. to June)	+.13 (.01)	+.27 (.01)	+.16 (.01)
Conventions (June to Aug.)	+.25 (.01)	+.03 (.25)	+.11 (.01)
General election (Aug. to Oct.)	+.14 (.01)	+.07 (.05)	+.09 (.05)

Note: Top figures are beta coefficients from a regression equation in which people's interest at the time of the later interview was the dependent variable while their special telecast exposure (such as, viewing of primary returns, the conventions, and the debates, respectively), their evening newscast exposure, their daily newspaper exposure, and their interest at the time of the earlier interview were the independent variables. The figures in parentheses are the statistical significance levels of the respective beta coefficients.

voter interest derived almost totally from coverage of the debates and conventions. It was found by controlling the impact of these special telecasts that only a weak association existed at this time between interest and viewing of the evening newscasts (see Table 7.3).

The type of television viewing most strongly related to rising interest in the latter part of the campaign was that of the conventions.[8] The impact of convention coverage was stronger than that of debate coverage, perhaps because the conventions came at a time when interest was at a lower level and the potential for media impact was greater. But the conventions also are the campaign's turning point, when competition within the parties is replaced by competition between them and the complexion of the attentive electorate changes. Interested voters in the primary period of 1976 tended to be strong party identifiers.* Indeed, partisanship has been the traditional explanation for high interest. A strong party preference, it is argued, leads one to perceive a greater stake in the election's outcome and, in turn, to higher interest.[9] During the convention period, however, the interested electorate came to include a greater proportion

---

*Partisanship, however, was less closely associated than was news exposure to rising interest at every point in the campaign. On average, the beta coefficients for partisanship were only slightly more than half the size of those for news exposure.

of weak partisans. Interest was particularly likely to increase among weak identifiers who happened to see parts or all of the conventions. Apparently convention coverage helps to arouse latent partisanship, in the process enlisting people's interest in the campaign.

The impact of television coverage was not matched by the newspaper at any point in the 1976 campaign. The newspaper, however, had a steady and independent influence on voters' interest. When people's exposure to television's newscasts and special broadcasts was controlled, their newspaper exposure remained significantly related to changes in their interest. [10] The newspaper's dependable though undramatic effect on interest may be characteristic of the medium; while its presentation limits its capacity for dramatic impact, its depth of content assures a cumulative and lasting effect. [11] This would help explain why, when the newspaper was the unrivaled campaign medium a few decades ago, interest developed more slowly than at present.

INTEREST AFFECTS ELECTION EXPOSURE

The public's interest in the campaign clearly is affected by election coverage, but surely the relationship must be a reciprocal one. It seems natural, after all, that one's level of interest would help to determine the frequency and intensity of one's news exposure. Survey responses do indeed indicate that high interest at the time of one interview was related to increased or consistently high daily news exposure at the time of the next interview (see Table 7.4). Just

TABLE 7.4 Relationship to Election Interest to Changes in News Exposure

Change in News Exposure	Primaries (Feb. to June)	Conventions (June to Aug.)	General (Aug. to Oct.)
Erie			
Network news exposure	+.01	+.19	+.03
	(.75)	(.01)	(.50)
Newspaper exposure	+.07	+.06	+.03
	(.05)	(.05)	(.50)
Los Angeles			
Network news exposure	+.11	+.11	+.13
	(.01)	(.01)	(.01)
Newspaper exposure	+.02	+.03	+.06
	(.50)	(.50)	(.10)

Note: Top figures are beta coefficients from a regression equation in which people's news exposure at the time of the second interview was the dependent variable. Their election interest and news exposure at the first interview were the independent variables. The figures in parentheses are the statistical significance levels of the respective betas.

as news exposure in 1976 affected interest, interest levels influenced amounts of news exposure.

Still there were significant and distinguishing differences in the two-way relationship. First, changes in levels of news exposure were much less extensive than changes in interest levels, for while interest is a direct response to the campaign, daily news consumption is determined mostly by habit and only marginally by the presence of the campaign. Second, the strength of each influence developed at different rates. During the primaries the impact of news exposure on interest was at its peak (see Table 7.2), but the impact of interest on news exposure was insignificant (see Table 7.4). Higher interest voters were not spurred during the primaries to seek more daily news than they normally did, suggesting that interest was not a powerful motivating influence at this point in the campaign.

Rather, the influence of voter interest was at its strongest in the last stages of the campaign, particularly during the convention period. Those who expressed higher interest in June were more likely by August to have increased their daily news use or, more commonly, to have maintained a high level of news exposure. The impact of interest was mainly on viewing of the evening newscasts, which is not surprising since newspaper readers tend to read their paper's news pages almost daily anyway. Television viewing is more variable; regular exposure requires that the individual make an effort to be in front of a television set at the proper time each day. High interest in a presidential campaign apparently encourages viewers to continue to make that effort or even to tune into an additional newscast now and then, creating a net change in the television audience that is marginal but nonetheless evident.

Where interest in the election matters most is not in daily news exposure, but in the viewing of television's special broadcasts—its coverage of primary election returns, the conventions, and the debates. Those respondents who expressed high interest in the interviews immediately preceding these broadcasts comprised a disproportionate share of the audience. In a typical primary week, 31 percent of high interest voters compared with 15 percent of low interest voters saw a special telecast about the election. Nearly 45 percent of those voters with high interest claimed to have watched most of one or both televised conventions; only 15 percent of low interest voters did so. Similarly, the constant audience of each presidential debate included 67 percent of the high interest voters but only 27 percent of the low interest voters.

THE LIMITS ON ELECTION INTEREST

Interest and exposure are part of a cyclical process: heavier news exposure encourages higher interest, which leads to heavier exposure, which promotes higher interest. Of these two effects, that of news exposure on interest is the more powerful. In terms of the total electorate, however, the campaign does not result in a continuously upward spiral of interest: the process eventually encounters resistance from people's marginal concern for politics. Not all voters have the potential to join the ranks of the strongly interested. Those citizens who developed high interest in 1976 were, by and large, citizens who were at least somewhat committed to politics in the first place. Few citizens who were political neutrals took a strong interest in the campaign. That peak interest was defined by the involvement of only a third of the electorate is evidence less of the scope of the modern campaign than of the secondary importance of politics to most people. However ambitious the campaign and however invasive the news, politics can reap interest only where its seeds have been sown.

That the news cannot reverse people's fundamental dispositions does not indicate that it is ineffectual. For while the campaign and its news have never been able to create interest, they can activate interest. The significant fact about today's election coverage is that it can activate interest at a point very early in the campaign, helping to mobilize interest months before the voters make their final decision at the polls. The news media, and television particularly, welcome the primaries with such extensive regular and special coverage that a large part of the potentially interested develop an early interest. This is an effect of considerable importance, for the level of voters' interest helps determine what they will learn and think about the campaign. Even within the same level of news exposure, as subsequent chapters will show, people who are more interested in the campaign benefit more from news of the election. Moreover, the ability to accelerate people's interest carries with it the ability to affect their subsequent exposure to the campaign. In the summer of 1976, for example, it was those voters who expressed high interest in June, not those who acquired it as the campaign was ending, who were the ones most likely to watch the televised conventions.

good

8

THE VOTERS' CONTROL OF INFORMATION

The image of voters emerging from early election studies was that of individuals firmly in control of the information they received. If they encountered information that was inconsistent with what they already believed, they would reject or distort it to conform with their beliefs. They would even limit their intake of dissonant news by selectively ignoring such messages. Describing the voter, Lazarsfeld, Berelson, and Gaudet wrote:

> As interest increases and the voter begins to be aware of what it is all about, his predispositions come into play. Out of the wide array of available propaganda, he begins to select. He is more likely to tune in some programs than others . . . to understand one point in a speech than another. His selective attention thus reinforces the predispositions with which he comes to the campaign. At this stage the initiative is almost wholly with the prospective voter rather than with the propagandists. Whatever the publicity that is put out, it is the selective attention of the citizen which determines what is responded to.[1]

THE LIMITS OF SELECTIVE EXPOSURE

At first look, today's voters also would appear to exercise firm control over their information. When respondents were asked during the 1976 presidential primaries what news stories they had seen on television or in the newspaper

TABLE 8.1 Relationship of Candidate Preference of Respondent to Recall of News Stories about the Candidates during the Primaries (percent)

Candidate Who Was Subject of Story	News Stories Recalled by Supporters of:								
	Republicans	Democrats	Ford	Reagan	Brown	Carter	Humphrey	Udall	Others
Television stories									
Gerald Ford	29	19	30	28	10	20	18	13	29
Ronald Reagan	35	20	32	41	19	19	22	19	25
Jerry Brown	3	7	5	0	24	3	8	0	4
Jimmy Carter	17	34	21	10	33	41	31	38	13
Hubert Humphrey	8	7	7	10	0	8	10	6	4
Morris Udall	0	4	0	0	0	5	2	13	4
Other Dems.	7	9	5	10	14	5	8	13	21
Total	99	100	100	99	100	101	99	102	100
	(n=86)	(n=196)	(n=57)	(n=29)	(n=21)	(n=86)	(n=49)	(n=16)	(n=24)

Newspaper stories

Gerald Ford	29	15	34	18	9	13	16	13	29
Ronald Reagan	27	17	21	41	6	19	18	19	19
Jerry Brown	5	7	6	3	25	3	5	6	0
Jimmy Carter	24	46	26	21	53	52	36	31	43
Hubert Humphrey	6	7	4	10	3	6	9	19	0
Morris Udall	1	1	0	3	0	0	5	0	0
Other Dems.	8	7	9	5	3	6	9	13	10
Total	100	100	100	101	99	99	98	101	101
	(n=128)	(n=222)	(n=89)	(n=39)	(n=32)	(n=98)	(n=55)	(n=16)	(n=21)

Note: Based only on news reports about one of the candidates listed. The Other Democrats category includes Harris, Bayh, Shriver, and Wallace. For this table and subsequent ones in this chapter, the n's refer to news stories recalled rather than respondents. This table, for example, is based on interviews conducted in February, April, and June; thus the same respondent conceivably could account for as many as three of the television or newspaper responses. A respondent's candidate preference is what the respondent indicated it to be in the interview during which the news story was recalled.

within the previous 24 hours,* a candidate's supporters recalled a higher proportion of newspaper and television stories about him than did other voters (see
Table 8.1). Moreover, Democrats more frequently mentioned news about the
Democratic race while Republicans more often recalled stories about the Republican race. Consider the following examples:

Of television's candidate stories recalled by Republican voters, 64 percent
were about a Republican candidate. Only 39 percent of the stories recalled by
Democratic voters were about a Republican candidate.

Of the newspaper stories recalled by Republicans, 56 percent were about a
Republican candidate. Only 32 percent of the newspaper stories recalled by
Democrats were about a Republican candidate.

About 40 percent of the evening news stories recalled by backers of
Ronald Reagan were about Reagan. Only about 30 percent of those recalled by
Gerald Ford's backers were about Reagan.

Of the newspaper stories recalled by Jimmy Carter's supporters, 52
percent pertained to Carter. Of those recalled by backers of Hubert Humphrey,
36 percent were about Carter.

Clearly, the differences in what people remembered seeing were often quite
substantial.

There is less to the evidence than first appears, however. To conclude that
voters are strongly inclined to select and ignore news stories based on the extent
to which the stories conform with their biases is to fail to explain the tendency
of television viewers to describe stories about their preferred party and candidate.
Although readers conceivably can scan the newspaper's smorgasbord of news
stories and select only those that appear to conform with their beliefs, viewers
of television news would find that difficult since they must sit passively while
news stories are served one at a time. Viewers certainly do not close their ears
and eyes when the opposition appears on the screen. As an explanation of the
findings, the notion of conscious avoidance of opposing stories is suspect for
television news, and consequently must be questioned as an explanation for
tendencies among newspaper readers, since the findings are almost identical
for viewers and readers.

An alternative explanation to selective exposure is selective attention, or
an inconstant level of attention. That is, on television people may watch less
intently when an opposing candidate is on the screen; in the newspaper they
may read stories about the opposition less closely. As a result, coverage of the

---

*The Lazarsfeld-Berelson studies of the 1940s also used people's recall of political
messages as the basis for assessing selective exposure. For this chapter the Erie and Los
Angeles respondents have been combined in all tables; no significant differences existed
between respondents in the two locations for any of the relationships shown.

opposition would leave a weaker impression.

During the primaries this does appear to be the case when partisanship is considered. Not only were people less likely to mention stories about the opposing party's candidates but, when they did, these descriptions lacked essential detail, being more often incomplete than those about candidates within their own party (figures are percents):

	News Stories about:	
Completeness of Recall of Television Stories	Candidates within Party	Candidates of Other Party
Mostly complete	59	56
Incomplete	41	44
Total	100	100
Completeness of Recall of Newspaper Stories		
Mostly complete	67	62
Incomplete	33	38
Total	100	100

This may indicate a need, conscious or otherwise, to avoid conflicting information. More likely it indicates that voters are simply more interested in news about their party's race. The nominating contest that voters follow more closely is the one that determines their own party's nominee.

A curious result occurs, however, when people's descriptions of news stories about candidates within their party are examined. If it were true that voters concentrate on news about their favorite candidate, their descriptions of these stories should be more complete than their descriptions of news about other candidates within their own party. Yet, for both newspaper and television reports, the opposite occurred (figures are percents):

	News Stories about:	
Completeness of Recall of Television Stories	One's Favorite Candidate	Other Candidates within Party
Mostly complete	56	63
Incomplete	44	37
Total	100	100
Completeness of Recall of Newspaper Stories		
Mostly complete	62	74
Incomplete	38	26
Total	100	100

Given traditional theories of political exposure, this is certainly an unexpected finding.

It is not inexplicable, however, for it is consistent with certain patterns of memory. Research has shown that within minutes after exposure to the media, people often are unable to recall readily what they have seen.[2] Occasionally a news story will linger and come to mind quickly when prompted by questioning. Frequently people must search their minds for something they have seen. In this process people are more likely to remember something about a central object, such as their favorite candidate. Assume, for example, that a Jimmy Carter supporter had read about both Carter and Udall in his daily newspaper, and that neither story had made a lasting impression on him. When interviewed several hours later, he tries to recall what he had seen, nothing comes immediately to mind. He then tries to think back on the day's stories, but still nothing occurs to him. He asks himself: "Did I read anything about the election?" But that general question fails to jog his memory. "How about Carter then?" With that, the Carter story comes to mind and he proceeds to describe it to the interviewer as well as he can. For this hypothetical Carter supporter, the name Udall in all probability would not enter his mind as quickly as the name Carter. Most likely, only if the Udall story had been particularly distinctive would it be remembered first and in relative completeness. Thus, consistent with the evidence, those news stories about less central candidates would be recalled less frequently, but reported more completely.

Further, when news exposure is brief or attention marginal, one is more likely to retain memory of exposure to salient objects, such as one's favorite candidate. When scanning the headlines people do not dwell on each one, but pass quickly from one to the next so that headlines about a candidate central to their thinking are likely to leave the stronger impression. "Udall Visits State," for example, probably would register with Udall supporters more so than with other voters. Similarly, a distracted viewer is more likely to remember the sight of a familiar figure on the television screen than to recall a brief glance at an unfamiliar one. Thus voters would be more likely to mention stories about their favorite candidate but less able to describe these stories fully.

The importance of salience to news recall is otherwise evident. People seldom mentioned news stories about a candidate of passing familiarity. Virtually all reports recalled about lesser known candidates like Udall and Harris, for example, were mentioned by respondents who were fully aware of these candidacies before having seen news about them. Certainly other people were seeing news about Udall and Harris now and then, but this news either failed to register or was quickly lost to memory.

On the other hand, people easily recalled news about the campaign's most prominent candidates, regardless of whether they supported one of these candidates or not. Carter, Ford, and Reagan were the candidates who received by far the heaviest news coverage during the 1976 primaries, and these three candidates together accounted for over 70 percent of the candidate news reports mentioned.

Without exception, supporters of other Democratic candidates referred more frequently to news reports about Carter than they did to news reports about their preferred candidate (see Table 8.1). For example, among respondents supporting Jerry Brown, although 25 percent of the newspaper and television stories were about Brown, an even greater number were about Carter. Thus voters are not able, even if so inclined, to avoid hearing or reading about candidates who are constantly in the news. Nor can they surround themselves with information about a favorite candidate who receives comparatively little coverage. Although backers of Udall, for example, mentioned more stories about him than did other voters, only 10 percent of the stories mentioned by his backers were about him.

It seems that selective remembrance and salience account for much of the tendency found in Table 8.1. If it does, then large differences in people's recall of news stories should not exist during the general election when there are only two candidates, both of whom are central to people's thoughts when the subject turns to election politics. In the general election of 1976, there was indeed no tendency to recall news about one's preferred candidate (see Table 8.2). In fact, Gerald Ford's backers recalled more newspaper and television stories about Carter than Carter's backers did. Moreover, substantially more of the stories recalled by both groups were about Carter, largely because Ford spent much of the general election period in the White House and thus received less election exposure than Carter. Further, during the general election people's descriptions

TABLE 8.2 Relationship of Candidate Preference to Recall of News Stories about the Candidates during the General Election (percent)

Candidate Who Was Subject of Story	News Stories Recalled by:		
	Carter Voters	Undecided Voters	Ford Voters
Television stories			
Jimmy Carter	61	66	66
Gerald Ford	39	34	34
Total	100	100	100
	(n=94)	(n=58)	(n=54)
Newspaper stories			
Jimmy Carter	57	60	58
Gerald Ford	43	40	42
Total	100	100	100
	(n=82)	(n=58)	(n=67)

Note: Based on interviews conducted in August and October. Table omits news stories recalled that were about both Ford and Carter. A respondent's candidate preference is what the respondent indicated it to be in the interview during which story was recalled.

of news stories about their candidate and his opponent were equally complete. Finally, there was no significant difference in the content of the stories recalled. Supporters of a candidate were nearly as likely as opposing voters to describe news stories critical of the candidate.

In short, the notion that people are strongly motivated to build a wall of supportive information around themselves is not supported by the evidence. Voters obviously do exercise some control over their exposure: they are more attentive in the primaries to news of their own party, more concerned with news of major candidates than with coverage of lesser ones, and undoubtedly marginally more interested in news about a preferred candidate. But the findings interpreted by some to indicate widespread selective news consumption are better explained by the influence of interest and memory. Certainly, what news people receive is influenced most by the content of that news—it is the heavily covered candidates to whom people are most frequently exposed.

Whether these findings indicate that today's voters are greatly different than those of the 1940s is another matter, however. Lazarsfeld and Berelson did not explore alternative explanations for their finding that people tended to recall more news stories about their preferred party or candidate. As David Sears and others have suggested, Lazarsfeld and Berelson may have overstated the extent to which voters of the 1940s resisted the intake of dissonant material.[3]

INTEREST, COMMITMENT, AND PREFERRED MESSAGES

A recent approach to the study of the media's impact, following upon work done on British elections by Jay Blumler and Denis McQuail, has been to assume that news exposure and response are affected in large part by people's needs.[4] Some people, for example, may attend to election news primarily for guidance in choosing among the candidates, while others may follow the election mainly for the enjoyment it provides.

If this is so, it might be thought that substance news would have special appeal for undecided voters who seek assistance in choosing a candidate. These people would focus on stories about the candidates' issue stands, the types of leadership they promise, the groups they represent, and similar subjects that indicate the nature of the candidates' politics. It also might be conjectured that certain voters would be particularly attentive to news coverage of the game, concerning themselves with the candidates' strategies, appearances, and standings much like the baseball fan who follows the pennant races. Presumably these voters would be concentrated among those with considerable interest in politics, people who already had made their choice of a candidate but who had an innate interest in presidential campaigns.

Although high interest voters showed no unusual interest in news about the game, undecided voters were, as Blumler and McQuail's theory predicts, unusually attentive to reports about the election's substance (see Table 8.3). At every level of interest, those people who had not yet made a choice were more

TABLE 8.3 Relationship of Election Interest and Decisional Certainty to Recall of Game and Substance Election News Stories (percent)

| | News Stories Recalled by: | | | | | |
| | Committed Voters | | | Undecided Voters | | |
Subject of News Story	Low Int.	Mod. Int.	High Int.	Low Int.	Mod. Int.	High Int.
Television stories						
Game	77	71	75	75	67	72
Substance	23	29	25	25	33	28
Total	100	100	100	100	100	100
	(n=98)	(n=155)	(n=219)	(n=61)	(n=57)	(n=44)
Newspaper stories						
Game	78	79	72	69	69	66
Substance	22	21	28	31	31	34
Total	100	100	100	100	100	100
	(n=113)	(n=204)	(n=256)	(n=52)	(n=66)	(n=67)

Note: Based on interviews conducted in February, April, June, August, and October; interest and commitment are for the same interview during which the news story was recalled.

85

likely to have described news stories about the issues, the candidates' abilities, and the like. On the average, undecided voters were 9 percent more likely to recall newspaper stories and 2 percent more likely to recall television stories about substance than were decided voters. That the relationship was stronger for newspaper reading where people have greater control over content further indicates a true preference among undecided voters for substance news.

Overall, however, there can be no doubt that the dominant influence on what people recalled seeing was the thrust of the news media's communication. The game was the major subject of the press's coverage of the campaign, easily dominating substance in emphasis. In every group of voters the game accounted for at least 66 percent of the news reports that were recalled; for one group, it accounted for 79 percent of the recalled stories. Furthermore, variations in voters' recall of the news about the game correlated with variations in its emphasis in the news. During the primaries, when the game received its greatest coverage, 80 percent of the news stories recalled were about candidate appearances, winning and losing, strategy and tactics, and other game-related subjects. In the general election, when the press's emphasis on the game declined, only 60 percent of the recalled stories pertained to the game.*

Thus, although the special needs and interests of voters can have a slight influence on their news story exposure, the major influence is the content of news coverage. No matter what type of story an individual would prefer to see, it is the prevailing type that will be seen most often.

NEWS CONTENT AFFECTS SELECTIVE PERCEPTION

The news media clearly influence what voters receive, but do they influence significantly how voters perceive this information? It is well documented that voters' preferences can affect what they see when exposed to political information.[5] Two voters of opposite persuasion, for example, can be watching the same candidate on television yet receive highly different impressions of him.

---

*The reader will note that the frequency with which voters recalled news about the game exceeded even the frequency with which the game was covered by the press. This might be taken to indicate that voters take more interest in this facet of election coverage. Such a conclusion seems unwarranted, however, in view of the fact that people's descriptions of game stories were incomplete more often than were their descriptions of substance stories. For television stories that were recalled, 55 percent of those about the game and 67 percent of those about substance were mostly complete. For newspaper stories, 63 percent of those about the game and 71 percent of those about substance were mostly complete. An alternative explanation for excessive recall of game news, and one consistent with the earlier argument about salience, is the prominence of game news in terms both of its dominance of election news in general and of lead election news stories in particular. The game is so pervasive that people's thoughts are drawn to it, even though they make less note of its particulars.

The one who supports the candidate might detect sincerity in his face and voice; the one who supports the candidate's opponent might think he looks insincere and conniving. That such divergent impressions can result from the same exposure is an example of selective perception, the tendency for people's biases to influence their perceptions of what they see.

Noting selective perception in their 1940s studies, Lazarsfeld and Berelson concluded that it was a major reason for the campaign's "minimal effects."[6] The importance of selective perception in the communication of election news, however, depends on how fully it dominates the voter's response. Do voters selectively perceive nearly all of the election messages they receive through the media? Or do most messages reach voters largely unfiltered by their preference for one candidate over another? To examine this, respondents were asked, upon describing a candidate news story they had seen, to indicate their reactions to it.

Whenever reactions about the candidates' postures or abilities were provoked by news stories, they reflected the voters' preferences (see Table 8.4). Typically, those favoring a candidate found his actions agreeable and his ability apparent:

> He [Carter] was very concerned. You could tell he cared about those people.
>
> —Carter supporter

> I have to agree with what he [Reagan] said on this. He knows what he is talking about.
>
> —Reagan supporter

> It showed what a quick thinker he [Udall] is.
>
> —Udall supporter

> He [Brown] is doing the right thing with this. It will help him.
>
> —Brown supporter

Those favoring an opposing candidate typically found his actions disagreeable and his ability questionable:

> It was just another of his [Reagan's] wrong ideas. He's off-the-wall about half the time.
>
> —Ford supporter

> I don't know why he [Ford] would do that, except that he's not very aware of things.
>
> —Carter supporter

> He [Wallace] was not being completely honest. I don't think Wallace has changed that much on the race issue.
>
> —Udall supporter

> I thought he [Carter] was being vague. He's like that.
>
> —Ford supporter

TABLE 8.4 Relationship of Candidate Preference to Reaction to Election News Stories (percent)

Reaction to		Reaction to a Candidate's Television Stories by:			Reaction to a Candidate's Newspaper Stories by:		
		His Voters	Undecided Voters	Other Voters	His Voters	Undecided Voters	Other Voters
Ability/ Character	Pro	13	4	2	6	1	2
	Con	8	10	11	2	6	11
Postures/ Actions	Agree	11	7	5	11	9	4
	Disagree	6	5	16	4	15	14
Chances of winning		24	16	22	30	20	29
Noncandidate		17	27	16	22	23	23
No reaction		21	31	28	25	26	17
Total		100	100	100	100	100	100
		(n=106)	(n=102)	(n=208)	(n=121)	(n=109)	(n=261)

Note: Based only on election news stories recalled by respondents in which a candidate was mentioned. Includes recalled stories from both the primary and general election periods; there were no significant differences in people's reactions during these two periods.

88

This tendency was quite pronounced. Three in every four reactions toward the postures and abilities of one's favorite candidate were favorable; four in every five reactions of this type toward opposing candidates were unfavorable. This was true even during the primaries, for once voters had committed themselves to a candidate, their reactions even to an opposing candidate within their own party were largely unfavorable. It also was true regardless of the news medium. Though television stories provoked more reactions to candidates' personalities and newspaper stories to their actions, people tended in each case to see their candidate positively and his opponents negatively.

This may lead one to think that selective perception renders the content of information received from the media inconsequential to the judgments voters make. Such a tendency is not, however, representative of the total picture, for most election news does not provoke a response to the candidates' abilities or actions. More commonly, people reported having no reaction to what they had seen or a reaction that included no evaluation of the candidates (such as, "It was interesting," "I didn't learn anything new"), or they indicated having reacted to what it suggested about the candidates' chances of winning.*

In fact, the respondents abstracted from the news aspects of the candidates' chances for victory about as often as they responded to the candidates' personalities or political postures, surely a consequence of the emphasis the press places on the race for the presidency. But does the subject of an election news story affect people's response? Do they react differently to stories about the game than they do to stories about the election's substance?

Reactions to news about the game are much different than those to news about substance (see Table 8.5). Only 20 percent of the game stories elicited reactions about the candidates' abilities or postures; over 40 percent of substance stories did so. Responses about the candidates' prospects for victory were provoked by 25 percent of the game stories, but only 10 percent of the substance stories. Finally, news about the game more frequently elicited no reaction from the people seeing it. About a third of the game stories drew no reaction; only about a fifth of all substance stories were not reacted to.

It is with relative passivity, then, that people respond to news about the game—stories about winning and losing, strategy and tactics, and the like. Voters behave more like spectators than election participants when they encounter such information, usually responding not to what the candidates represent but to the status of the contest, if they respond at all. On the other hand, substance news—

---

*Although the method used here to study selective perception is a common one, the author is convinced that it greatly overestimates the level of selectivity. Most people are not highly involved when reading the newspaper or watching television news. When asked in an interview, however, about their reaction to a news story they have just described, they usually supply a reaction, one that the author feels is often only a response to the interview situation.

TABLE 8.5 Reaction to Game and Substance Election News Stories (percent)

Reaction to		Reactions to Television Stories about the:		Reactions to Newspaper Stories about the:	
		Game	Substance	Game	Substance
Ability/	Pro	2	6	2	3
Character	Con	9	12	5	11
Actions/	Agree	2	13	2	12
Stances	Disagree	8	13	7	15
Chances of winning		20	9	30	12
Noncandidate		26	26	24	27
No reaction		33	21	30	20
Total		100	100	100	100
		(n=376)	(n=136)	(n=423)	(n=191)

stories about the issues, the candidates' qualifications, and the like—brings out the politics in voters, eliciting evaluations of the candidates' leadership and personal traits and of their actions and policy postures. It also cultivates more involvement, evident in voters' greater reaction to and more complete recall of such stories.

A MOSTLY PASSIVE AUDIENCE

The conclusions of the classic Lazarsfeld and Berelson studies always seemed stretched a little beyond their useful applicability. To ignore one side of the news, to read one's biases into all types of political news—these behaviors seem to defeat the reason why most people follow the news, which is to keep abreast of events. Furthermore, the classic view seems at odds with the relaxed way in which people use news sources; to screen out one side of the news surely demands more vigilance than most people give the news.

The interpretation of selectivity presented in this chapter conforms better with other facts about news use. In other words, voters have a slight preference for some types of news, but it is based as much on their interests as a psychological need for reinforcing information. While voters do engage in selective perception, it is inconstant and depends considerably on whether people encounter the type of information that is most likely to activate their defenses. In general, voters who differ in their political commitments and interest are considerably more alike than different in the types of news messages they consume and in their immediate response to most messages.

Indeed, the news media have considerable power to direct the public's attention and political response. Those candidates, activities, and ideas that dominate election coverage cannot be ignored, even when the voters' sentiments lie elsewhere. From this it is apparent that the major control people exercise over their information environments occurs before, not during, their news exposure. The critical choice that people make, one that becomes habit, is whether or not to follow the news regularly. There is more variation in the amounts of news citizens receive than in the types of news they receive, and much more news passes to them straight than is distorted by their political biases.

It would be misleading to infer from this that the news audience is powerless before the messages of the media. Such a view is as inadequate a conception of the political audience as the one that claims citizens have almost total control of their information environments. To hold to the opinion that the electorate is easily manipulated is to ignore their selective response to certain types of information and to discount the other influences operating on them. The ultimate uses of information also are not necessarily reflected in people's immediate response. Nevertheless, whatever the situation in the 1940s, it is simply inappropriate today to say that "the initiative is almost wholly with the prospective voter" in any election-year encounters with the news media.[7]

PART IV

THE IMPACT OF THE MEDIA CAMPAIGN ON VOTERS

9

THE VOTERS' AGENDA

Early election researchers studied the mass media's impact on the voter's basic attitudes. Having found that attitudes generally were unaffected by the campaign, they concluded that mass communication was not a significant influence on the voters' behavior.[1]

If attitude change were the criterion for media influence, the same conclusion would apply today. Consider, for example, party attitudes; between February and October of 1976, only 8 percent of the respondents switched their allegiances from one party to the other.[2] Indeed, the effect of the modern campaign on attitudes is limited by the campaign's intensity. As propaganda theorist Jacques Ellul has noted:

> The individual can clearly discern any propaganda when it suddenly appears in a social environment normally not subject to this type of influence. The contrast is so strong that the individual can recognize it clearly as propaganda and begin to be wary.[3]

Wary as many are, however, citizens still expect the campaign to inform them, thereby putting the media in a position to influence their perceptions. What voters see in the newspaper and on television will affect what they perceive to be the important events, critical issues, and serious contenders; it will affect what they learn about the candidates' personalities and issue positions. As V. O. Key, Benjamin Page, and others have noted, voters' decisions may depend on what they perceive to be at stake when they make their choice.[4] If they become convinced, for example, that unemployment and not inflation is the nation's most pressing concern, they may revise their preference, overlooking the candidate with the know-how to handle inflation in favor of the one they think could resolve the unemployment problem. As a potential influence on vote choice, the media's effect on perceptions is worthy of analysis.

Moreover, the study of perceptual effects as opposed to attitudinal effects is more consistent with the purpose of most election communication. The messages originating with the press are intended primarily to inform and alert the public to the campaign's developments. Even the candidates seldom try to overturn basic attitudes, but work instead to create perceptions that they feel will elicit those attitudes beneficial to their candidacies. Thus their messages are directed at the voters' perceptions.

A study of perceptual effects, furthermore, is important beyond what it reveals about voters' decisions. For every minute people spend actively deliberating their decisions, they spend hours simply following the campaign. What do they learn from this exposure? Do they develop an understanding of the candidates' qualifications? Do they acquire an awareness of the major issues? Answers to such questions are central to any judgment about the quality of today's campaign. A democratic election is meaningfully measured not by the number of votes that it changes, but by its ability to enable voters to perceive more accurately their stake in its outcome.

To test for media impact, two approaches were used. One is panel analysis, in which people's media exposure is related to changes in their thinking from one interview to the next. Evidence suggesting that people who follow the news closely become better informed about election issues, for example, would be taken to indicate media influence. Usually, however, this type of analysis will underestimate the media's impact, because almost every citizen is reached to a degree by the media. It certainly is not the case that a proportion of citizens are totally isolated from election news while the remaining people are totally exposed to it. In a laboratory experiment on communication, messages can be transmitted to one group and withheld entirely from another. In real life this neat division does not exist. For every specific effect of the media, some people with less media exposure will be reached and influenced, and some of those with more exposure will remain unaffected. Thus, when comparing the two groups, the differences between them will not reveal the full impact of the media.*

---

*In the analysis of panel data, there also is a statistical reason why the media's impact is underestimated. It is a technical point, but an example may provide some understanding of it. Assume that the researcher wants to see how people's media exposure in the time period between two interviews relates to their information about the election. The hypothesis is that the more exposure people have, the better informed they will become. It cannot be assumed, however, that everything people know about the election was learned during the period between the interviews. Consequently, it is necessary to control for what

Sometimes the impact of the media touches the public so fully that the voters' perceptions, regardless of their level of news exposure, are much the same. An example would be public recognition of the two presidential nominees. The nominees' identities are known eventually to nearly all Americans who obtain their knowledge directly or indirectly from the news media. The slight differences in recognition associated with different amounts of news use would vastly underestimate the media's impact. In situations of this type, time-series analyses were done: that is, comparisons were made between patterns of news coverage and patterns of public perceptions over periods of time.* The congruence of these patterns was taken to indicate the extent of the media's influence.

The media's effect on the voters' perceptions are the topic of this chapter and the four that follow. The analysis begins with a brief look at the voters' agendas—what they thought was important in the campaign and what they talked about during it.

WHAT VOTERS SEE AS IMPORTANT

By emphasizing certain campaign events, simply by placing them repeatedly and prominently in the news, the press signals their importance to the public. By neglecting and underemphasizing other aspects, the press relegates them to the background, hidden from all but a few directly involved people. The distinction is a vital one. Without firsthand contact, citizens are highly dependent on the news for their images of the campaign. Events placed high on the agenda catch and hold the public's attention; events that are given little emphasis are unlikely to attract much concern. "The power of the press is a primordial one," Theodore White has written. "It determines what people will think and talk about."[5]

---

they knew when the period began. The odds are, however, that people who are better informed at the time of the first interview also will be better informed at the time of the second. This is particularly true when the media are having their predicted effect. Then the media would have contributed to the initial differences in people's information and would have worked to maintain these differences in the period between the interviews. This creates a statistical problem that is referred to as high autocorrelation. When people's initial information level is controlled statistically, much of the variation in their later information level is eliminated, leaving little variation to be explained by their media exposure. The result is a correlation that underestimates the true relationship between exposure and acquired information.

*Panel analysis would be useful in these situations if the time period between interviews coincided exactly with the time of the media's impact. Then the analysis would reveal how the speed of response was related to people's news habits. As things are, however, the times do not coincide, and this works to depress lagged correlations rather severely. Consequently, when the association between people's perceptions and news coverage is obvious and extremely high, it makes sense to use time-series analysis.

This power was evident during the 1976 campaign. What the press emphasized in its coverage was precisely what the public said was important about the campaign. As shown in Chapter 3, election news emphasized the game rather than matters of policy and leadership, and it was the game that dominated people's thoughts. The correlation between journalistic emphasis and public preoccupation was in fact very high, more than +.85 at every point once the campaign was under way (see Table 9.1).

In April and June over 80 percent of the respondents mentioned some aspect of the game as the election's most important feature, usually citing either Carter's success in the primaries or the closeness of the Ford-Reagan contest. The game was at the top of the voters' lists at every stage of the campaign but one: it fell behind the debates during the general election. In contrast, substantive matters were named the campaign's most significant feature by about 30 percent of the respondents in February, and by only 12 percent in April. To the public the election's substance declined in importance as soon as the primaries began, and remained low until the general election when 26 percent of the respondents again felt substance was the campaign's most significant aspect. Much of this rise, however, was attributable to people's perceptions of the importance of campaign issues—Ford's Eastern Europe statement, Carter's

TABLE 9.1 Perceptions of Election's Most Important Aspect at Different Times during the Campaign (percent)

Type of Aspect Mentioned	February	April	June	August	October
Game	56	85	81	72	22
Substance					
Policy issues	24	7	9	6	10
Campaign issues	2	3	1	1	13
Candidate traits	3	2	2	2	3
Subtotal	29	12	12	9	26
Events (e.g., debates)	8	1	1	16	44
Other	7	2	6	3	8
Total	100	100	100	100	100
	(n=212)	(n=520)	(n=585)	(n=610)	(n=550)

Note: The table is based on replies to the following question: "So far during the presidential campaign, what do you think is the most important thing that has happened?" Only those respondents who indicated they were paying at least some attention to the campaign at the time of the interview were asked the question. Their replies are grouped by general type; for example, a reference to a candidate's performance in the primaries was placed in the game category. Erie and Los Angeles respondents are combined for this table as the responses were similar in the two locations.

Playboy interview, and the like.

These tendencies were common to all kinds of voters. Interest levels, for example, made no substantial differences. Individuals with little interest were about as likely as the more interested to mention a feature of the game as the campaign's most significant aspect during the early periods and to cite the debates in the general election. In their agendas, voters were distinguished clearly by only one characteristic. During the primaries, Democrats and Republicans were more likely, by about a three-to-two margin, to find significance in some aspect of their own party's race. Voters not only take a little more interest in the nominating process of their party, but also find it to be somewhat more significant as well. Even this, however, did not affect the tendency to see the game as more important than substance.

News coverage was not the sole reason why voters overlooked substantive matters to concentrate on the outcomes of the primaries and the debates. Indeed, citizens tend naturally to think of the election in terms of a contest. It is true that the public believes the election is a time for it collectively to determine the directions of national policy and leadership, but their mental images of the campaign are not those of abstract leadership needs and policy matters. They think of the campaign concretely, in terms of its events and participants. Additionally, events within the campaign, particularly the large number of primaries, draw voters' attention to the race. Even if the election's contestual aspects did not receive such thorough press coverage, they would still rate very highly in people's minds.

Nevertheless, the nature of election news exaggerates this natural concern. As Chapter 8 indicated, voters' attention is drawn to the personalities and subjects that dominate news coverage. Lightly reported aspects often pass unnoticed and certainly are infrequently regarded as significant. The public's collective perceptions are not representative of total news content, reflecting instead its most salient aspects. In the October interviews, for example, the closeness of the Ford-Carter race ranked second out of all the specific things people designated as important about the election, clearly a response to the emphasis that the press, through its polls and commentary, placed on the candidates' standings.* Many of those who cited the debates as important, furthermore, did so in relation to the debates' impact on the race.

The press's capacity to focus public attention is further evident in the prominence of campaign issues on the public's agenda in October. The most intensely reported substance topics during the general election were Ford's

---

*In each interview about 30 separate aspects were mentioned by more than one respondent as being significant about the election. The ranking of the closeness of the Ford-Carter race is its position among these specific mentions.

Eastern Europe gaffe, Carter's *Playboy* interview, and Butz's racial joke and resignation. Having developed into issues only during the campaign's final stage, each was a major news story for a week or two. They ranked third, fifth, and eighth out of all of the specific things that people mentioned as important in the October interviews.

During the entire campaign only one policy issue ranked high on the lists of people's concerns. When Reagan won in North Carolina to reestablish his candidacy, reporters attributed his success to his criticisms of Ford's foreign policies. Once this electoral connection was made, foreign policy was thereafter a more prominent subject in news of the Republican race. Though its coverage was not as heavy as that given the status of their race, Ford and Reagan's clashes over policies like détente, Rhodesia, and military spending were covered regularly, and voters ranked the candidates' foreign policy dispute as the seventh and fifth most significant aspect of the campaign in the April and June interviews respectively. During the general election, no policy issue received extensive coverage. Similarly at this time, no policy issue commanded significant public concern: about 5 percent of the respondents mentioned one policy or another of the Ford administration as important, but these references were distributed among several policy areas.

The press's view of election politics, along with the distribution of its coverage, contributes to the public's response. Besides being reported less heavily than the game, substance often is presented in the context of the game, frequently appearing as an object of strategy and manuever that is significant for its impact on the race as much as for its policy and leadership implications. This interpretation of election politics, moreover, enables campaign issues to be presented as more compelling than policy issues. The public does not accept this perspective completely, but it is vulnerable because the large majority of voters never consider the relationship of the news to events. The campaign is what the daily newspaper and the evening newscasts show it to be. Aspects of the campaign that are not highly visible on the news agenda go unmissed. Although active in the inferences they draw from news received, the voters are largely passive recipients of the news—the content of the campaign is defined for the most part by the content of election news.

NEWS EXPOSURE AND OBTRUDING ASPECTS

The public's acceptance of the press's version of the campaign is facilitated by the consistency of coverage by the various news outlets. Although the press is not monolithic in how events are reported, it is in which events are covered. Print and television journalists alike are mostly concerned with campaign activity and the game, and their shared news values make the same events and subjects the focus of each medium's coverage. Consequently, there were not large differences in the judgments of television and newspaper audiences concerning the election's significant aspects.

Nevertheless, there was some association between changes in people's perceptions of the election's important features and the levels and types of their news exposure (see Table 9.2). Exposure particularly to the newspaper inclined voters to accept as significant the prevailing topics of election news. In April, June, and August, when the game was at the top of the agenda, heavier newspaper readers were most likely to develop concern with the game from one interview to the next. Then in October, when the debates and election substance moved higher on the agenda, heavier newspaper readers again contributed disproportionately to these increases. Television viewing, in contrast, had no added impact. Although heavy viewers were likely to cite some aspect of the game as important during the campaign's early periods and to mention the debates as important during the general election, they did not differ significantly in these tendencies from people who paid infrequent attention to the evening newscasts.*

This finding supports other research on agenda setting—newspaper reading has consistently been found to be more important than television viewing in creating audience agreement with general themes of news coverage.[7] The newspaper simply is more able to impress these themes on its users. With more news space it can cover topics in greater depth, thus reinforcing people's awareness of them. Some writers also have suggested that the newspaper's headlines are important to its agenda-setting power.[8] The messages that repeatedly appear in the headlines have been found to be those imprinted most clearly in readers' thoughts. This certainly was the case during the 1976 campaign. Nearly half of all front-page headlines during the primaries referred to the status of the race, and the word "Debates" was one of the five most frequently mentioned subjects in headlines of the general election.

Although it might be thought that television's pictures would give it an edge as an agenda setter, they appear generally to weaken its effect. To be sure, there are times when dramatic pictures can fix events in viewers' minds, as illustrated by the filmed sequences of the Iranian student takeover of the U.S. embassy in Tehran in late 1979. But not all political activity lends itself fully to television's pictures. Most political information must be communicated with the spoken and written word. Often significant developments occur outside the range of the camera; are produced by a talking head, as in a press conference or speech; or involve processes, patterns, or trends. In such instances, which account for the large majority of political news stories, there are no dramatic

---

*It is important to recognize exactly what is being said here since panel analysis can easily be misinterpreted. Television did contribute to the making of the election agenda. Its dominant themes were the dominant dimensions of that agenda. Unlike the newspaper, however, television does not give added salience to the dominant dimensions. Heavier viewers' perceptions increased at the same rate as those of lighter viewers. For a discussion of the use of dummy variables in regression analysis, see the note to Table 9.2.

TABLE 9.2 Relationship of Network Newscast Exposure, Newspaper Exposure, and Televised Convention and Debate Exposure to Changes in Perceptions of Election's Most Important Aspect

Time of Perceptual Change	Erie			Los Angeles		
	Network Exposure	Newspaper Exposure		Network Exposure	Newspaper Exposure	
February to April						
Game	+.02	+.14[a]		+.04	+.11[b]	
Substance	+.05	+.08		-.03	+.10[b]	
April to June						
Game	+.01	+.13[a]		-.06	+.10[b]	
Substance	+.04	.00		+.09	+.02	
June to August			Convention Exposure			Convention Exposure
Game	-.13[a]	+.08	+.09[b]	-.02	.00	+.16[a]
Substance	-.02	+.03	+.11[a]	-.06	-.03	+.10[b]
Events	+.06	-.01	+.05	-.03	+.03	+.06
August to October			Debate Exposure			Debate Exposure
Game	-.07	+.05	-.06	+.05	-.03	+.05
Substance	-.04	+.06	+.07	+.02	+.09[b]	+.04
Events	+.03	.00	+.14[a]	-.04	+.07	+.06

[a]Relationship significant at the .01 level.
[b]Relationship significant at the .05 level.

Note: From the answers people gave to the question about the campaign's most important aspect, three dummy variables were created for each interview. One was the game variable: if respondents mentioned an aspect of the game, they were given a score of 1 for the game variable, and if they mentioned something else they were given a score of 0 for the game variable. Similarly, people were assigned scores of 1 and 0 for the substance and events variables depending on whether or not they mentioned this aspect when asked the question. The figures in the table are beta coefficients from regression equations in which the respective dummy variable for the second interview was the dependent variable, and media exposure and the same dummy variable from the first interview were the independent variables. The coefficients from the event variable are not presented for the first two time periods because too few respondents mentioned events at this time to provide meaningful estimates.[6]

pictures with which to convey the story and television must rely on the talking heads of newsmakers and its reporters. Or, as happens frequently on the evening newscasts, the essential message conveyed by the reporter's narrative is accompanied by pictures tangential to the message. In its election coverage, for example, a candidate is often pictured getting off an airplane or greeting a crowd while the reporter discusses the day's events in a voiceover. Yet television's pictures dominate the viewers' attention, sometimes even distracting from television's verbal communication. Thus the evening news is less likely than the newspaper to impress upon its audience the messages it communicates.

Television's influence, however, is not always reduced by the medium of pictures. Television communication is powerful when the subject is a live event. In 1976, exposure to the televised debates and conventions had a clear impact on the public's agenda (see Table 9.2). One effect of this exposure was to increase the salience of the events themselves. People who watched the debates were more inclined in the October interviews to note the debates as significant events. Similarly, those who saw the televised conventions were more likely (in August) to identify the conventions as important.

Several important differences exist between television's live coverage and its daily news coverage. While viewers of an evening newscast catch a 90-second glimpse of the campaign, viewers of a convention or debate are exposed at length to the event, resulting in a strengthened impression that what they see is significant. Moreover, television's images of a debate or convention are direct—the pictures and the words flow together. Indeed, a debate is nothing but talking heads and a televised convention consists mainly of speeches and interviews. Finally, televised convention and debate coverage takes viewers directly to the scene; what they receive is not a stylized rendition of earlier developments, but a largely unfiltered and immediate view of the actual event.

Televised convention and debate exposure also had one other noteworthy effect—it increased the salience of the election's substance. People who watched the conventions were more likely, by August, to have formed the judgment that some aspect of policy or leadership was the campaign's most significant feature. Similarly, debate exposure was related to increases in October of people's assessments of the importance of election substance. Indeed, debate and convention viewing was more closely related than either newspaper or evening newscast exposure to a heightened belief in the significance of policy and leadership matters (see Table 9.2). These telecasts provided the candidates with an opportunity to present their views in some detail. The convention and debate telecasts contained considerable substance, while daily news coverage in these periods centered mainly on the game.

WHAT VOTERS TALK ABOUT

The capacity of the media's news coverage to constrict and focus voters' attention on the race is enhanced by the structure of the present nominating system. For nearly four months the weekly parade of some 30 primaries over-shadows everything else in people's minds. The scheduling and reporting of the primaries channel voters' attention so completely that they seldom even talk about anything but the race.

Election conversations can be placed roughly in two categories. Some revolve around news events that gain people's attention. The topic of these conversations depends on the nature of the news stories, whether about substance or the game, that attract people's attention and provoke discussion. Other conversations that voters have are less specific in origin, consisting mainly of people's general thoughts about the campaign and the candidates. The topic of these conversations also varies, although in 1976 these centered on substance, since they usually were exchanges of opinion about the candidates' good and bad points. Typically short discussions between individuals with similar opinions, these conversations were seldom elaborate or contentious, but the usual subjects were the candidates' abilities and political views.

These two types of conversation occurred with unequal frequency during the primary and general election periods. Respondents were much more likely during the primaries to discuss news developments. The major reason was that the primaries provided the hard events that create news stories that are more likely to provoke discussion. Most often people conversed not in response to news of amorphous events, such as a routine day on the campaign trail, but in response to hard events, those of apparent proportion and importance—the type that attracted the heaviest news coverage. Further, a kind of Gresham's law governed political discussion; when a hard news event occurred, it dominated conversation. Presented with an event at the top of the news, people usually talked about it rather than other aspects of the campaign.

Since the primary period is essentially a series of hard events (for example, the primaries), scheduled at almost the precise intervals necessary to hold the public's attention, it is a time when people's conversations are inclined to focus on the news. As the campaign moves into the general election period, however, the number of hard events drops considerably, precipitating a change in political discussion. During the primaries in 1976, the race was the overwhelming topic of conversation (see Table 9.3). In August and October the election's substance was talked about more often than was the race. The change was actually quite remarkable. Conversations based on the candidates' abilities and political views more than doubled when the campaign entered its general election phase, while those centering on the race occurred only half as often.

The scheduling and reporting of the primaries were not the only factors involved in these changes. In October when election day was only a week or two away, people were more concerned about their voting decisions than they had been earlier, a concern resulting in more frequent discussion of the candidates' views and qualifications. Significantly, the election's substance was proportionately a more prevalent subject in August than it was in October. The election was then more than two months away and voters were not overly concerned at

TABLE 9.3 Topics of Election Conversation at Different Times during the Campaign (percent)

General Topic of Conversation	February	April	June	August	October
Game	45	64	69	32	37
Substance					
Policy issues	5	12	11	31	19
Campaign issues	3	1	1	4	8
Candidate traits	15	8	6	16	16
Subtotal	23	21	18	51	43
Events (e.g., debates)	12	3	5	10	15
Other	20	12	8	7	5
Total	100	100	100	100	100
	(n=40)	(n=128)	(n=81)	(n=108)	(n=161)

Note: Table based on the reported conversations of those who indicated they had talked with another person about the election in the 24 hours prior to their interview. Erie and Los Angeles respondents have been combined for this table.

the time with their choice of a candidate. What, then distinguished this time period? The interviewing was conducted in late August and early September, when the campaign was in its traditional postconvention lull. At this time there was nearly a complete absence of hard events—the conventions were past and the debates had not yet begun—and a sharp reduction in news about the race—the delegate contests were over and poll results had not yet become an almost daily news subject. In this period people talked mostly about the candidates' abilities and views when discussing the election.

In general, however, the substantive side of the election seems to be losing ground in the bid for people's expressed interest. In their study of the 1948 election, Berelson, Lazarsfeld, and McPhee found that 67 percent of the voters' conversations were concerned with the candidates' positions and qualifications.[9] Only about a fourth of voters' discussions focused on the question of which candidate was likely to win. In 1976, however, only 34 percent of people's conversations were concerned with substance. Even in October 1976, only 43 percent of the voters' conversations dealt with the candidates' abilities and views. The game was the major topic of conversation in 1976. The obvious reasons for this dramatic change in what people talk about during a presidential campaign are the changes since 1948 in the structure of the campaign and in election news. The spectatorlike response to the primary period particularly is a perfectly natural reaction to the flow of information and events in this stage of today's campaign. Faced with contest after contest and exposed to news centered on the competition, election conversation is certain to concentrate on the game.

10

AWARENESS OF THE CANDIDATES

Today's presidential campaign encourages self-starters, candidates who enter the race not so much in response to public demand for their presence, but more because of a personal desire to be the next president. Self-starting candidates whose backgrounds include state or national office and periodical appearances in the national news usually are taken seriously by fellow politicians and the press. But if they have been just ordinary figures in the news in the years leading up to the election, they enter the primaries as politicians unknown to large numbers of voters.

An example from the 1976 campaign is Fred Harris. He first won national news attention in 1964 when he upset footballer Bud Wilkinson in Oklahoma's race for the Senate. Touted as a comer within the Democratic party, Harris continued to appear in national news—cochairing Hubert Humphrey's 1968 presidential campaign, receiving the Democratic national chairman appointment, and making a belated bid for the 1972 presidential nomination. When he sought the presidency for the second time in 1976, he hit the campaign trail a full year before the first primary in New Hampshire, crisscrossing the nation in a motor home, stopping wherever he could attract a crowd or the press. Like most Democratic presidential aspirants that year, Harris seldom made front-page news, but he was nevertheless among the candidates regularly mentioned in news reports on the upcoming election.

Even so, the public remained largely unaware of Fred Harris. Only 47 percent of the respondents questioned just before the New Hampshire primary recognized even his name. More importantly, only 12 percent felt they knew something about him.* Eleven months of vigorous campaigning and nearly 12 years of occasional national exposure had produced for Harris very little public recognition.

Several of the other candidates' attempts to penetrate the public's awareness were just as quixotic. A majority of the people knew the names of Morris Udall, Birch Bayh, Jimmy Carter, and Frank Church, but only 20 percent indicated knowledge of any one of these candidates beyond his name. When asked about Sargent Shriver, most of the 44 percent who felt they knew him were unable to cite anything more than his Kennedy connection or his 1972 nomination for vice-president. A full 37 percent of the Erie respondents did not even recognize by name the most publicized of the nation's governors, Jerry Brown. Even Henry Jackson, one of the more visible Democratic candidates prior to the campaign, was not very well known. After his long tenure in the Senate, years of speculation about his presidential ambitions, and his prominence in congressional hearings over détente, national defense, and oil prices, 37 percent of the people said they had never heard of him, and another 36 percent said they knew him only by name.

A comparison of these candidates with three familiar public figures provides a clear indication of just how unknown they were. No less than 99 percent of the respondents knew Gerald Ford, Ronald Reagan, and George Wallace by name; and most felt they knew each candidate better. Over 90 percent felt they knew something about Ford, the nation's president since August 1974. Reagan, whose film and television career and two terms as California's governor had made him a national figure, was known to 85 percent. In his fourth presidential race, Wallace was familiar to 76 percent of the respondents.

CHANGES IN CANDIDATE AWARENESS DURING PRIMARIES

When the presidential primaries begin, the focus of political news swings toward and stays on the candidates. They are no longer merely the occasional subjects of news reports, for hardly a day passes without mention somewhere in the news of every active campaigner. Of course, the amounts of coverage that the various candidates receive may be quite unequal. Among self-starting Democrats running in 1976, Carter clearly dominated the headlines and news space; Jackson, Brown, and Udall got moderate coverage; Church had some

---

*Recognition of a candidate's name is the standard measure of public recognition of that candidate. As will be demonstrated later in the chapter, however, simple name recognition is relatively unimportant to vote casting. What matters is whether people feel they know something about a candidate; only when their familiarity with him reaches this stage are they likely to consider him when making their voting decision.

exposure; Harris, Bayh, and Shriver received very sparse coverage (see Chapter 5).

How did unequally weighted coverage affect these candidates' recognition levels? What happened, in other words, to the public's awareness of each one? Only Carter, who received most of the coverage, became dramatically more visible to the voters (see Table 10.1). The proportion of citizens who felt they knew something about him rose from 20 percent in February to 81 percent by June, a jump of over 60 percentage points during the primaries. Their recognition of his Democratic opponents, however, increased only modestly. Recognition levels rose by about 14 percent for Udall, Brown, and Jackson, and by only 9 percent for Church. They remained fairly constant for Harris, and even declined

TABLE 10.1 Awareness of the Candidates at Different Times during the Primaries (percent)

Candidate	Percent saying they knew something about him in:			Change from Feb. to June
	Feb.	April	June	
Birch Bayh	21	27	—	- 4
Jerry Brown (Erie)	—	25	43	+18
Jerry Brown (L.A.)	—	87	91	+4
Jimmy Carter	20	77	81	+61
Frank Church	20	21	29	+9
Gerald Ford	93	93	94	+1
Fred Harris	12	12	16	+4
Henry Jackson	27	42	34	+7
Ronald Reagan	85	89	88	+3
Sargent Shriver	44	36	—	-8
Morris Udall	23	37	37	+14
George Wallace	76	74	74	-2

Note: Respondents were read a list of candidate names and asked to indicate which of the following categories best described their recognition of each candidate:

1. I've never heard his name before.
2. I've heard his name, but I really don't know anything about him.
3. I know something about him.

The proportions in the table are those giving the third response which, as later analysis will show, is the recognition level that is critical to vote choice. Except in their recognition of Brown, Erie and Los Angeles respondents have been grouped for this table. Los Angeles respondents, however, had somewhat higher recognition levels of the candidates throughout the period. No entry in the table indicates that respondents were not asked about the respective candidate in that interview. This method of measuring candidate recognition was validated with open-ended questions. Unless a respondent was in the third category, there was a 90 percent probability that the respondent would not be able to say anything about a candidate when asked an open-ended question about him.

for Bayh and Shriver.

The amount of coverage a candidate received was strongly related to the public recognition he gained—the correlation exceeded +.90.[1] Importantly, though, the relationship was not strictly linear. Small amounts of coverage resulted in stable or even declining recognition, a moderate amount contributed modestly to the public's awareness of the candidate receiving it, and intense coverage led to a dramatic increase in the public's familiarity with a candidate. In other words, within the relationship were thresholds at which the impact of news coverage on public awareness changed significantly. Below a certain level of news coverage, the effect was muted; above that level the effect was magnified.

At the base of this threshold effect lies the voter's approach to political news. The names, facts, and events in the news are simply too numerous for anyone to comprehend or remember. Voters trying to gain awareness of all public personalities and problems, big and small, would simply bury themselves in a mound of data for which they have neither the time nor the interest. The only practical way for most citizens to proceed is simply to follow the news, paying attention only to its obtruding features, and thus being certain of acquiring only that information placed at the top of the news again and again. The news signals what and who are important and gets across the message with repetition and placement.

When a presidential candidate is fortunate enough to find himself constantly in the headlines, the effect can be as sudden as it is dramatic. Carter had become a well-known figure by April. He was known to four of every five adults only two months into a campaign he had entered as a virtual stranger. Other factors were involved in public recognition of Carter during the early primaries. He did, after all, best his rivals in seven of the first nine Democratic primaries, making him the favorite to win nomination. Surely, even if he had received only slightly more coverage than his closest rivals, he would have gained wider recognition.

Yet if the Brown candidacy is indicative, the amount of coverage a candidate receives matters greatly to his recognition. Brown was a late starter in the race; all of the primaries he entered were held during the final stage. In each state where he was on the ballot, Brown beat Carter but shared the headlines with winners of other contests, for all of his wins came on Tuesdays when two or more primaries were held. He received only about a fourth of the news space awarded the Democratic candidates during the late primaries, about as much coverage as Jackson had received earlier, when the calendar consisted of a single primary each Tuesday. The amount of recognition Brown gained as a result of his victories was very close to what Jackson had gained during the initial two months. Despite a primary performance that rivaled Carter's early showing, Brown's recognition level did not even double.

So complete was Carter's domination of the news in the early primaries that he became familiar even to a large portion of the citizens who were outside the regular news audience. The more closely people follow the news, the more likely they are to feel they know the candidates. But regular news exposure does not result in familiarity with each candidate, and infrequent news exposure may result in awareness of some candidates. As the following figures show, the proportion of nonregular news users who felt they knew Carter in April 1976 exceeded the proportion of regular news followers who thought they knew the two men who were his principal opponents at the time (figures are percents):

	Not Regular Reader or Viewer	Regular Reader or Viewer
Carter	64	85
Jackson	24	55
Udall	23	48

Most people, regardless of how closely they follow the news, will become familiar with an intensely reported candidate, while only a few outside of a moderate amount of news regulars will learn to recognize a candidate who receives infrequent coverage.

NEWS EXPOSURE AND CANDIDATE AWARENESS

It is widely believed that recognition of any candidate is more likely to result from television viewing than from newspaper reading. Familiarity is thought to be gained more easily and more rapidly from watching and listening to a candidate than from reading about him. In the words of Robert Agranoff, television "can thrust unknown candidates into prominence."[2] Yet the evidence points to the newspaper as the most effective means of building public awareness. For each of the 1976 presidential candidates, recognition was higher at the end of the primaries among people who followed the newspaper regularly than among those who watched the evening news regularly.

Further, increases in recognition levels from one interview to the next were more closely associated with newspaper reading than with television viewing (see Table 10.2). People who read a daily newspaper frequently became more familiar than infrequent readers with every candidate; only about 60 percent of the candidates became more familiar to frequent television viewers than to infrequent viewers. This is not to say that television viewing was without impact. For 36 percent of the candidates among Erie respondents and 18 percent among Los Angeles respondents, there was a significant relationship between heavier viewing and increased awareness. But heavier newspaper reading had a much more substantial impact on people's awareness—73 percent of the Erie relationships and 91 percent of the Los Angeles ones were significant.

TABLE 10.2 Relationship of Television and Newspaper Exposure to Increases in Candidate Awareness during the Primaries

Candidate and Level of His News Coverage	Erie		Los Angeles	
	Network Exposure	Newspaper Exposure	Network Exposure	Newspaper Exposure
Heavily reported				
Carter	.00	+.08[b]	+.01	+.21[a]
Ford	-.02	+.11[b]	+.18[a]	+.13[b]
Reagan	-.01	+.11[b]	+.10[b]	+.08[b]
Moderately reported				
Brown	+.03	+.07[b]	+.02	+.03
Jackson	+.10[b]	+.06	+.01	+.22[a]
Udall	+.19[a]	+.07	.00	+.25[a]
Wallace	-.02	+.10[b]	-.02	+.09[b]
Lightly reported				
Bayh	+.03	+.09[b]	.00	+.12[a]
Church	+.13[a]	+.09[b]	-.04	+.30[a]
Harris	+.12[a]	+.05	+.03	+.18[a]
Shriver	+.01	+.10[a]	-.06	+.19[a]
Median Coefficient	+.03	+.09	+.01	+.18
Significant (.05)	36	73	18	91

[a]Relationship significant at the .01 level.
[b]Relationship significant at the .05 level.

Note: Figures are beta coefficients from regression equations in which awareness of the candidate at the end of the primaries was the dependent variable and evening newscast exposure, daily newspaper exposure, and awareness of the candidate at the beginning of the primaries were the independent variables. Figure's insignificant row are percents.

The newspaper is in this dominant position for the simple but easily overlooked reason that voters' awareness results largely from the frequency and depth of their exposure. Seeing a candidate on television may help viewers to recognize him when he appears again, certainly a step toward a sense of familiarity, but meaningful recognition results from repeated exposure to a candidate and the reception of information about him. It is when the candidate becomes more than just a face or name that voters come to think they know who the candidate is. With greater news space, the newspaper is more able than the evening newscasts to communicate large amounts of information about the candidates.

Of course, most of this news material goes unheeded; if readers saw and remembered even half of it, every candidate would be readily recognized by most citizens. The odds are, however, that the more information a news source makes available about the candidates the more likely it is that its users will come to recognize the candidates. This can be seen even in the greater impact of newspaper exposure on candidate recognition in Los Angeles than in Erie. Most newspaper readers in Los Angeles subscribed to the *Times*, a paper whose candidate coverage is as extensive as that in any of the nation's dailies. By chance alone, readers of the *Times* would encounter more news of the candidates than would readers of the less comprehensive Erie dailies.[3]

The Erie dailies, in turn, provide several times the amount of national news presented in the evening newscasts. The words spoken on a newscast will fit with room to spare on the front page of the *Erie Times* or *News*. In Erie, newspaper exposure was more highly related to increased recognition than was television exposure. The network newscasts, however, made a greater difference to recognition in Erie than in Los Angeles, indicating that when the depth of newspaper coverage is not considerable, television news makes a more substantial contribution to public awareness of the candidates. Indeed, the nature of the media environment appears to affect overall awareness levels. In media-rich Los Angeles, about 5 percent more voters, on average, felt they knew each candidate than was the case in Erie, where the available media are limited.

People's newspaper habits are particularly important to their recognition of less-publicized candidates. When a candidate dominates the news, the extent of his familiarity to television viewers and to newspaper readers differs only marginally. At the end of the 1976 primaries, Carter's recognition was only a tenth higher among newspaper-only regulars than among television-only regulars. But for candidates who were not heavily covered by the press during the primaries, recognition was a fourth higher among people depending on the newspaper. Again, this seems to result from differences in the media's news space. Although the proportions of coverage given all candidates may be roughly the same for both television and the newspaper, the absolute volume of coverage given the lightly covered candidates is considerably greater in the newspaper. This is particularly true of a newspaper like the *Los Angeles Times*; in 1976, voters exposed to this newspaper were better informed about the less-publicized candidates than were readers of other newspapers.

The importance of the information people receive from the news to their awareness of the candidates is further revealed by differences in the media's impact on voters of high, moderate, and low interest (see Table 10.3). Low interest voters benefited the least from newspaper exposure; those who looked at the news pages more frequently became only slightly more familiar with the candidates than those who largely ignored the newspaper. The reason is that most low interest readers seldom put much effort into their reading of the political sections of the newspaper. They infrequently read more than the lead paragraphs of political news stories, and usually move on after a glance at the headlines, thus bypassing nearly all of the information that the newspaper provides. Indeed, low interest voters derive about as much benefit from exposure to television.

Among moderate and high interest voters, however, the newspaper's

TABLE 10.3 Relationship of Television and Newspaper Exposure
to Increases in Candidate Awareness amoug High,
Moderate, and Low Interest Voters during the Primaries

Level of Voter Interest	Erie		Los Angeles	
	Network Exposure	Newspaper Exposure	Network Exposure	Newspaper Exposure
High interest voters				
Median coefficient	-.02	+.08	+.01	+.19
Significant (.10)	0	36	18	73
Moderate interest voters				
Median coefficient	+.02	+.10	-.11	+.09
Significant (.10)	9	46	9	27
Low interest voters				
Median coefficient	+.11	+.03	+.01	+.11
Significant (.10)	36	18	18	27

Note: Based on changes in people's awareness of the 11 candidates listed in Table 10.1 The median coefficient is the median beta coefficient from 11 regression equations where awareness of each candidate at the end of the primaries was the dependent variable and evening newscast exposure, daily newspaper exposure, and awareness of the candidate at the beginning of the primaries were the independent variables. Figures in significant rows are percents.

impact was significantly greater than television's. For citizens in these categories of interest, those who followed the newspaper frequently became substantially more aware of the candidates than those who paid infrequent attention to the newspaper. On the other hand, the frequency of television viewing was relatively unimportant to the candidate recognition of moderate and high interest voters. Whether they watched the evening newscasts frequently or rarely, they were nearly as likely to gain awareness. Those who were not heavy viewers had alternative and just as effective ways of learning about the candidates. The newspaper, however, contains enough information to have an independent effect. High and moderate interest voters include nearly all of the citizens who take the time to read the newspaper somewhat carefully. Those who read the newspaper frequently therefore gain significantly higher awareness of the candidates than their high and moderate interest counterparts who read the newspaper only occasionally.*

---

*The relationship between recognition levels and party affiliation also was examined. It might be thought that a party's candidate would be more familiar to voters within that party. However, there was little difference across party lines; Republicans were actually slightly more likely to be familiar with the candidates of both parties, presumably the result of their slightly greater attention to politics.

AWARENESS AND VOTE CHOICE

Austin Ranney and others have shown that primary election voters are more interested in politics than other citizens.[4] As could be expected, they also are more familiar with the candidates. It is not the case, however, that primary voters think they knew each of the candidates on their ballots. Democratic voters in Pennsylvania, for example, faced the choice of voting for Carter, Jackson, or Udall.[5] Of those respondents who voted, almost 90 percent felt they knew Carter, but only slightly more than 50 percent were familiar with Jackson or Udall.

These differences in candidate recognition were important to the voting decisions that Erie's primary voters made, for few people selected a candidate known to them only by name (see Table 10.4). Nearly all picked a candidate they knew something about, which provided Carter with a decided edge on

TABLE 10.4 Relationship of Candidate Awareness to Vote Choice during the Primaries (percent)

Candidates Whom They Felt They Knew	Candidate for Whom They Voted		
	Pennsylvania Primary		
Erie voters	Carter	Jackson	Udall
Only Carter	20	2	0
Only Jackson	0	1	0
Only Udall	4	0	0
Only Carter and Jackson	12	8	0
Only Carter and Udall	4	0	4
Carter, Jackson, and Udall	20	11	8
None of the candidates	4	2	0
Percent of total vote	64	24	12

Candidates Whom They Felt They Knew	California Primary			
Los Angeles voters	Brown	Carter	Church	Udall
Only Brown	3	1	0	0
Only Carter	0	1	0	0
Only Brown and Carter	18	8	0	2
Only Brown and Church	1	0	0	0
Only Brown, Carter, and Church	5	4	2	0
Only Brown, Carter, and Udall	8	3	0	2
Brown, Carter, Church, and Udall	23	9	4	5
None of the candidates	1	0	0	0
Percent of total vote	59	26	6	9

Note: Table omits categories that include no respondents. For example, there was not a single respondent in California who knew Udall and Church, but not Carter or Brown.

Jackson and Udall:

About 25 percent of the voters knew only one of the three candidates. This candidate usually was Carter. He received 90 percent of the votes cast by this group.

About 30 percent knew two candidates, usually Carter and Jackson or Udall. Carter received 60 percent of the votes of this group.

There were 45 percent who knew all three candidates. Carter received half of the votes cast by this group.

Carter received about 12 percent more votes than he would have received if each candidate had been equally familiar to the voters. In many presidential primaries, this advantage would have exceeded the margin of victory.

California's primary presented a different situation, since two of its candidates, Carter and Brown, were highly familiar to the voters. Both were known to 95 percent of the respondents who voted. Church and Udall were the unfamiliar candidates on the ballots, known to only half of those who voted. As in Pennsylvania, almost all of the voting respondents cast their ballots for a candidate they knew. Church and Udall received virtually no consideration from the voters who knew them only as names, gathering from them only 10 percent of their votes; 90 percent of the votes they received came from the half who knew them.

Voter support obviously is not based on familiarity alone. Voters may regard one known candidate more highly than another, or they may not care for a candidate they know, a position that Wallace held for many voters in 1976. But a candidate has little chance of gaining support from those to whom he is not familiar, for the voters' awareness defines the range of alternatives they consider. In the right circumstances, this can result in votes that are won and lost almost by default. When a candidate is known and not widely disliked, as was Carter, and when each of his opponents suffers from a lack of recognition, as did Jackson and Udall in Pennsylvania, his advantage is enormous.

Thus the way in which the press distributes its coverage among the candidates can make a difference: its reporting helps to define voters' alternatives. The press's coverage does not necessarily determine how people will react to their known alternatives—a candidate who gains their recognition must still gain their confidence. Nevertheless, without party labels to guide their choice and often with limited information about what each potential nominee represents, some voters are primed for uncritical acceptance of a candidate. Few voters, moreover, will change their news habits to try to discover which of the presidential hopefuls is best for them. There may be another candidate out there who offers more of what they want in their party's nominee, but they are unlikely to plunge into the news looking for him. Most people simply take the news as it comes, skimming the top and even doing that in a casual way. Indeed, it is precisely the voters with fewer known alternatives who are less critical in their choices and less likely to gain awareness of additional alternatives. Under the appropriate conditions, such voters have a high probability of choosing the candidate emphasized by the press.

11

VIEWS OF WINNERS
AND LOSERS

The dominant theme of presidential election news coverage is one of winning and losing. The returns, projections, and delegate counts of the primaries and the frequent polling and game context of the general election make the candidates' prospects for victory a persistent subject of news coverage throughout the campaign. The outcomes of the races are of considerable interest to the voters as well; in 1976 this was the most frequently discussed political subject during the primaries and continued to be a large part of political conversation during the general election.

The voters' opinions about the candidates' chances are heavily dependent on information received from the news media. To decide where a candidate stands on the issues, voters might rely on what they know of the candidate's partisanship, but for knowledge of the candidates' competitive positions, they must depend for the most part on news about primary outcomes, poll results, and so on. Indeed, in 1976 people's perceptions of the candidates' chances for nomination and election followed closely what the news coverage indicated those chances to be. When press accounts indicated uncertainty about likely winners and losers, the judgments of the electorate mirrored that uncertainty. When the news spoke of an almost certain winner, the voters expressed the same optimism for that candidate.

PERCEPTIONS OF THE CANDIDATES' CHANCES

Just before the first primary in late February, news reports generally expressed uncertainty about the outcome of the Democratic race; respondents also were uncertain, though they granted Humphrey, Carter, and Jackson a somewhat better chance than candidates such as Bayh and Udall (see Table 11.1). Halfway through the primaries, however, people's doubts about the Democratic contest had largely disappeared. Interviews conducted in late April and early May showed that people were now quite sure that Carter would win nomination, that only Brown and Humphrey had an outside chance of stopping him, and that candidates such as Jackson and Harris were simply out of the running. Voters had changed their assessments dramatically, but so had the press, for Carter had won seven of the first nine primaries and reporters were projecting him to win nomination. At the end of the primaries in June, news reports virtually conceded the Democratic nomination to Carter. Again, voters followed suit—most respondents felt the race was over.

On the Republican side, people were convinced that either Ford or Reagan would be nominated, but were uncertain throughout the race as to which man

TABLE 11.1 Perception of Candidates' Chances of Winning Nomination at Different Times during the Primaries

Candidate	February		April		June	
	Mean	S. Dev.	Mean	S. Dev.	Mean	S. Dev.
Ford	+1.81	1.57	+1.99	1.41	+1.88	1.41
Reagan	+1.16	1.60	+0.89	1.66	+1.16	1.63
Bayh	-0.37	1.61	-2.20	1.16	–	–
Brown	–	–	-0.05	1.74	-0.11	1.85
Carter	+0.36	1.69	+2.20	1.11	+2.54	1.03
Church	-0.35	1.55	-1.13	1.54	-1.58	1.61
Harris	-0.52	1.56	-2.01	1.34	-2.39	1.17
Humphrey	+0.78	1.71	+0.46	1.81	-0.76	1.85
Jackson	+0.21	1.53	-1.13	1.56	-2.11	1.27
Shriver	-0.86	1.58	-2.21	1.17	–	–
Udall	-0.47	1.45	-1.31	1.48	-2.08	1.36
Wallace	-0.72	1.87	-2.01	1.25	-2.30	1.25

Note: Respondents were asked to rank each candidate's chance of nomination on a seven-point scale that ranged from extremely likely (+3) to extremely unlikely (-3). The left entry for each candidate is his average score for all respondents. Thus the closer to +3.00 a candidate's average score, the higher his chances, and the closer to -3.00 his score, the lower his chances as seen by the voters. A score of about 0.00 indicates that the respondents were unsure of his chances. The right entry is the standard deviation of people's estimates. A large standard deviation indicates that different people had quite different estimates of the candidate's chances. A small standard deviation indicates that most people were in agreement of his chances. Erie and Los Angeles respondents had roughly the same estimates of the candidates and have been grouped together for this table. No entry in the table indicates that respondents were not asked about the respective candidate in that interview.

would prevail. The February interviews indicated that, like the press, the voters saw Ford as the favorite to win nomination, but regarded Reagan as an unusually strong challenger. Halfway through the primaries, after Ford had won more primaries and was being portrayed in the news as the man with the edge, the voters felt that prospects had improved for Ford and weakened for Reagan. At the end of the primaries, however, the electorate believed that Reagan had gained slightly on Ford, a reflection of Reagan's strong second-half showing.

Voters' perceptions continued to parallel news coverage in the general election. Immediately after the party conventions, news analyses based on polls gave Carter a substantial but insecure lead deriving from soft support. Interviews conducted at this time indicated that voters also considered Carter comfortably ahead of Ford, yet far from securing election. By late October, as election day approached and Carter's lead in the polls narrowed, journalists spoke of a close election. The voters also were less certain of which candidate would win.*

Throughout the campaign voters' perceptions of the candidates' chances were related in a general way to news coverage. People who followed the news more closely, however, were more likely to have accurate perceptions. From one interview to the next, heavier readers and viewers were more likely to be correct in their reassessments of their candidates' chances (see Table 11.2). In the primary period, in fact, television viewing had nearly as large an impact on these assessments as newspaper reading, making winning and losing an area in which newspaper reading was not overly dominant. Certainly the fact that television primary coverage is dominated by the race helps to account for its influence.

The greater accuracy of judgment that came with heavier news exposure was a marginal one. Most citizens had reasonably accurate perceptions. Messages about the candidates' chances were communicated so often and were so highly placed in news reports that they were almost certain to get through to most voters. The ease with which people learned about the race also reflected the simplicity of the information involved, for indications of a candidate's prospects are fairly straightforward, particularly during the primaries. A candidate's competitive position in the nominating race is rather succinctly revealed by election returns and delegate counts. It is not even necessary that the citizen receive news messages about all of the candidates or know them all; if one candidate is strongly favored to win his party's nomination, others cannot be expected to do well.

In its ability to transmit information about winning and losing, the news media are surely aided by interpersonal communication. The previous evidence on personal discussion probably underestimates rather severely the frequency

---

*The means and standard deviations respectively in August were: Ford (+ 0.32, 1.78), Carter (+1.30, 1.51). In October they were: Ford (+0.46, 1.56), Carter (+0.98, 1.37).

TABLE 11.2 Relationship of Network Newscast Exposure and Newspaper Exposure to Changes in Accuracy of Perception of Candidates' Chances of Winning Nomination

Time Period	Eire		Los Angeles	
	Network Exposure	Newspaper Exposure	Network Exposure	Newspaper Exposure
Early primaries (Feb.-Apr.)				
Median coefficient	+.07	+.08	+.05	+.10
Significant (.05)	40	50	20	50
Late primaries (Apr.-June)				
Median coefficient	+.08	+.09	+.06	+.14
Significant (.05)	55	67	22	, 67
Postprimaries (June-Aug.-Oct.)				
Median coefficient	+.01	+.05	+.01	+.06
Significant (.05)	0	50	25	50

Note: Figures based on chances from one interview to the next in people's estimates of the candidates' chances. The median coefficient is the median beta coefficient from regression equations (one for each candidate) where the voters' estimates of the candidate's chances at the time of the second interview was the dependent variable and their newscast exposure, newspaper exposure, and estimate of the candidate's chances at the time of the first interview were the independent variables. A positive coefficient indicates change in the correct direction. The text indicates what these directions are, for example, for Udall, accurate change was a belief that his chances were decreasing. All candidates are included in the early and late primaries estimates; only Ford and Carter are included in the postprimaries estimates. The significant row indicates the percentage of betas that were significant at the .05 level.

with which the race comes up in conversation. "Who do you think will win?" may not rival "What do you think of the weather?" as a passing comment during an election year, but it is a common enough remark. Although this casual question and its answer may not be thought of as a political conversation by most voters, and hence not mentioned when they are asked whether they have talked politics recently, it is a way by which the media's race messages are extended beyond their direct audience.

WINNING AND LOSING: TWO EXAMPLES

Further insight into the diffusion of information about winning and losing is gained by looking at voters' responses to two situations: a critical juncture in the Ford-Reagan race and the second presidential debate.

When the Ford-Reagan race changed direction midway through the primaries, voters revised their perceptions greatly. On April 27 Ford wrapped up his eighth first-place finish in Pennsylvania, the state of the ninth primary. Only

Reagan's win in North Carolina on March 23 prevented Ford's sweep of the early primaries. But Reagan then retaliated with a winning streak of his own, winning in Texas on May 1 and in both Indiana and Georgia on May 4, then winning in Nebraska but losing in West Virginia on May 11.

The interviews conducted between April 28 and May 18 indicate that people's estimates of the two candidates' chances were highly sensitive to these developments (see Table 11.3). People interviewed in the three days immediately following Pennsylvania's primary regarded Ford as an almost certain nominee and saw Reagan's chances as slim. As the days passed and Reagan's victories accumulated, however, there was a significant change in these estimates. Reagan's prospects were thought to have improved somewhat following his win in Texas, to have improved dramatically after his double victory in Indiana and Georgia, and then to have leveled off after he split Nebraska and West Virginia with Ford. Meanwhile people's estimates of Ford's chances slipped gradually before stabilizing near the end. Over the interviewing period, voters felt that Ford's advantage over Reagan had declined by about 60 percent. In their minds Reagan still trailed Ford, but by a much narrower margin than before.

Close attention to the news during this period sharpened people's reactions and judgments. First, those with heavier news exposure reacted more quickly to the changing situation. In early May, for example, nearly every voter thought that Reagan was gaining ground on Ford, but those who followed television or the newspaper regularly came to this conclusion two to three days sooner than most nonregulars. Also, the reactions of close followers of the news were stronger. Collectively, those having attended carefully believed that Reagan had closed Ford's lead by 65 percent; nonregulars felt the gap between the candidates had shrunk by 55 percent.

The impact of new information on public judgment is even more evident in a competitive situation of another kind—the presidential debates. After each debate, the news focused on analysis of its outcome. The journalistic consensus after the second debate was that Ford had lost because he had mishandled the question of Eastern Europe. Although a number of hours passed before this message reached the voters, its effect was dramatic, for while respondents who were interviewed within 12 hours of the second debate felt that Ford had won, most of those interviewed later felt Carter had won. The passing of time required for the news to reach the public brought with it a virtual reversal of opinion (figures are percents):

Which Candidate They Felt Won the Debate	Time Elapsed Between Interview and Second Debate:	
	12 Hours or Less	12 to 48 Hours
Ford	53	29
Undecided	12	13
Carter	35	58
Total	100	100

TABLE 11.3 Perception of Republican Candidates' Chances of Winning Nomination, Depending on Time of Interview

	April 28-30	May 1-3	May 4-6	May 7-9	May 10-12	May 13-15	May 16-18
Ford's chances	+2.10	+2.15	+2.13	+1.79	+1.73	+1.94	+1.77
Reagan's chances	+0.20	+0.40	+1.09	+1.35	+1.21	+1.13	+1.30

The change was clearly due to news exposure, for in their evaluation of the debate only 10 percent of the people interviewed early mentioned Ford's statement on Eastern Europe. On their own, voters failed to see in his remark the significance that the press would later attach to it. Yet over 60 percent of those interviewed late discussed his Eastern Europe statement, most indicating that they, like the press, saw it as a major error causing him to lose the second debate.

In this situation close attention to the news again intensified people's reactions. About 50 percent of nonregular news users interviewed late believed that Carter had won the debate, but nearly 65 percent of news regulars interviewed late felt he had won. News regulars also were a third more likely to cite Ford's statement on Eastern Europe as the reason for his defeat.

THE MAKING OF A BANDWAGON

Information about the candidates' chances can result in a bandwagon—the situation where large numbers of voters choose to back the candidate who is ahead. For a bandwagon to occur, however, two conditions must be met: first, voters must be a largely unfettered by other influences; second, they must be convinced that the leading candidate is almost certain to win.

A case in point is the 1976 Democratic nominating contest. When the Democratic primaries began, most rank-and-file Democrats had few constraints on their thinking. They were concerned about the nation's unemployment level and still troubled by Watergate, but this discontent was directed at the Republican party. Unlike Vietnam in 1968 and 1972, no issue dominated their thoughts about the party's primaries. Excepting Wallace, most Democrats had no strong feelings one way or the other about their party's active candidates. Only one in five of the Democratic respondents clearly preferred one of these candidates before the primaries started. Another one in five preferred either Humphrey or Kennedy, who were not actively seeking nomination. Nearly three in five Democrats said they had no preference.*

Lacking any firm notion of what or whom they wanted, many Democrats were influenced by the news coverage and outcomes of the early primaries. When a voter is firmly committed to a particular candidate or viewpoint, this

---

*In the Gallup poll, as well as most other polls, respondents are provided a list of the primary candidates and asked to indicate their favorite. This procedure, however, tends to force respondents to make a choice and can result in a considerable underestimation of the voters' uncertainty. In the survey for this book, respondents were not provided a list of the candidates, but were asked simply which candidate they favored for nomination. In February 1976, 60 percent of the Democratic respondents replied by saying they did not have a preferred candidate.

attitude provides a defense against change. The commitment leads voters to see events and personalities selectively, in the way they want to see them, thus resulting in the reinforcement of existing attitudes. When voters' attitudes are weak, their perceptual defenses also are weak. When this occurs, as Herbert Krugman, Muzafer Sherif, and others have noted, voters are likely to accept incoming information in a rather direct way, thus developing a conception of the situation consistent with this information. Their perspective becomes that of the communicator, a change that directs their attention toward certain ways of acting and away from other modes of behavior. Their perception of the situation may even point toward a single option, one that they find entirely satisfactory because they had no strong initial preference. They then act upon this choice and, in doing so, form attitudes consistent with their choice. Voters, in short, have been persuaded through perceptual change rather than attitude change. Their perceptions were altered first, and then appropriate attitudes were developed.[1]

This was the process of decision for many Democratic voters during the 1976 primaries. They had no strong commitments before the campaign began, but developed perceptions of the race that led them to accept Carter and reject his opponents. In their minds the central concern became the candidates' electoral success and, once the race was seen in this way, they embraced the winner and rejected the losers. Except for Udall, the candidates who were labeled as losers by the press lost favor with the voters (see Table 11.4). Jackson, Bayh, Wallace, Shriver, and Harris were regarded much less favorably after they failed to run strongly in the early primaries. This cannot be explained by the fact that Democrats had come to know and dislike these candidates' politics, for they acquired very little information of this kind during the primaries.* The only impression that most voters gained of any of these candidates was that they were not doing well in the primaries.

The response of Democrats to Carter was only somewhat less dependent on his performance during the early primaries. The first impression that most Democrats had of Carter was that he was doing extremely well in places like Iowa and New Hampshire, an accomplishment that evoked some surprise and a certain amount of admiration. As they heard more about him, most of them also regarded him as an acceptable nominee. This reaction was not based on the feeling that in Carter they had discovered their ideal candidate, for they knew very little about his politics or abilities. But he seemed like a sensible and personable individual and, since he had won the acceptance of voters elsewhere, he must have his good points. These were persuasive perceptions. The rush to Carter's side was not because large numbers of Democratic voters wanted to be

---

*Chapters 12 and 13 detail what voters learned about the candidates during the primaries.

TABLE 11.4 Changes in Favorability of Democrats, Independents, and Republicans' Feelings about Candidates during Primaries

Candidate	All Voters	Erie			L.A.		
		Dems.	Inds.	Reps.	Dems.	Inds.	Reps.
Republicans							
Ford	+.10	+.06	-.23	+.46	+.32	-.29	-.41
Reagan	-.04	-.05	-.22	-.33	+.04	+.01	+.14
Democrats							
Bayh	-.54	-.39	-.32	-.95	-.54	-.67	-.71
Brown	+.32	+.06	.00	-.25	+.26	+.02	+.24
Carter	+.40	+.78	+.67	+.11	+.03	.00	+.58
Church	+.01	-.25	+.68	.00	-.14	-.78	+.36
Harris	-.12	-.49	-.04	+.41	+.14	-.54	-.57
Jackson	-.42	-.05	-.95	-.39	-.35	-.71	-.82
Shriver	-.49	-.38	-.82	-.71	-.30	-.81	-.45
Udall	+.03	+.38	-.69	-.48	+.20	-.35	-.07
Wallace	-.27	-.04	-.60	-.44	-.34	-.04	-.62

Note: Respondents were asked to indicate how they felt about each candidate on a seven-point scale that ranged from extremely favorable (+3) to extremely unfavorable (-3). The scores in the table are the change in each candidate's average score from one interview to a second one. For Bayh, Harris, Jackson, Shriver, and Wallace the first interview was the February one and the second was the April one. For Brown the first was the April interview and the second was the June interview. For all other candidates the score indicates the change in people's evaluations between the February and June interviews.

in the winner's camp; that type of bandwagon effect was not operating during the early Democratic primaries. Rather, Carter's approval by other voters, his apparent command of the nominating race, and his lack of liabilities made him the natural choice of an electorate attuned to the race and devoid of strong preferences. The following responses, obtained during the April interviews when people were asked why they favored Carter, are typical of those given by about 75 percent of his backers at the time. Their thoughts reveal the importance of their perceptions of the race and of Carter, and indicate clearly that their attitudes toward him were still in the process of formation:

> He is the person the majority of the public is backing. He seems to be a nice man.

> He seems to be forthright, a good man. The voters like him and he is way ahead.

> I respect him. He doesn't have a machine behind him and yet is going to be nominated.

> I guess we haven't heard as many bad things about him as the others. He's popular, too.

> I know that he's doing good. He seems down to earth. He seems honest and sincere. He has a nice smile.

> He appeals to many people.

> I guess I like him best because I hear more about him.

> He seems to be honest. I don't necessarily really favor him, but I think he's going to be the one.

> I don't see anyone else with a chance. He's a fresh and engaging personality. Not committed to Washington, either.

> He must be doing the right thing. He's in popular demand.

A more systematic view of Democrats' reactions to their party's candidates is gained by looking at how their feelings changed from one interview to the next (see Table 11.5). Democrats' opinions about a candidate tended to align with their perceptions of his chances. If they regarded a candidate as having a good chance, they usually had acquired more favorable feelings toward him by the time of the next interview. On the other hand, less favorable thoughts usually followed the perception that a candidate did not have much of a chance. Moreover, this evidence probably underestimates the impact of viability considerations on voters' thinking. The February interviews were conducted before the first primary, but it was not until the start of the primaries that Democrats began to see the direction in which their party's race was going. By the time of the April interviews, however, Democrats also had substantially changed their feelings about the candidates. The statistical technique used for Table 11.5 does not measure dual change of this type.

TABLE 11.5 Relationship of Network Newscast Exposure, Newspaper Exposure, and Estimate of a Democratic Candidate's Chances of Winning Nomination to Changes in Favorability of Democrats' Feeling about Democratic Candidates during Primaries

Location	Network News Exposure	Daily Newspaper Exposure	Estimate of Candidate's Chances
Erie			
Median coefficient	+.04	+.05	+.11
Significant (.05)	20	20	40
Los Angeles			
Median coefficient	+.04	+.06	+.10
Significant (.05)	10	20	40

Note: Median coefficient is median beta coefficient from regression equations (one for each candidate) in which the dependent variable was the favorability of the voters' feeling toward the candidate at the time of the second interview, and the independent variables were favorability toward and success estimate of the candidate at the time of the first interview as well as newspaper and television exposure. The significant entry indicates the percentage of betas that were significant at the .05 level.

It is possible, however, to examine the nature of this change since respondents were asked in each interview how they felt about each candidate and his chances. The pattern of change that occurred was usually consistent—that is, Democrats tended either to regard both the candidate and his chances more highly by April or to regard both less highly. Moreover, from the evidence available it is certain that most Democrats reached a conclusion about a candidate's prospects before developing a firm opinion about him. Considering the uncertainty that the Democratic respondents expressed in the interviews completed just before the first primary, and the fact that the large majority did not even know Carter at this time, it is inconceivable that great numbers of them selected Carter before hearing about his success in the opening primaries. Thus this dual change reflects mostly the pull of their judgments about the candidates' chances on their feelings toward the candidates.

Interestingly, frequent followers of the news were slightly more likely than infrequent users to judge the candidates on the basis of performance (see Table 11.5). The opposite might have been predicted, since more attentive citizens generally have stronger political convictions, ones that might retard bandwagon effects. Nevertheless, heavier exposure to the newspaper and television was related to the tendency to respond favorably to winners and unfavorably to losers. Perhaps frequent users' heavier exposure to the news media's conception of the Democratic race impressed it more thoroughly on them.

An alternative explanation for why heavy media users were more responsive to winners and losers relates to the uncertainties surrounding the Democratic race—uncertainties about the identity of the candidates, about their prospects, and about their politics. Jacques Ellul posits that conditions of uncertainty make attentive citizens particularly vulnerable to mass persuasion. According to Ellul, attentive citizens feel a greater need to understand situations, and thus feel a greater compulsion to resolve uncertainty when it exists. Because the events they wish to understand are beyond their direct observation, however, they are susceptible to the media's interpretations of reality. The assessment that prevails in the press becomes their perception. Informed citizens, in fact, are often seen to be those who are able, early in the course of an uncertain event, to articulate the media's conception of it. To be sure, there are people who are deviationists, individuals who ignore the common response because of their superior understanding or strong personalities. He suggests, however, that only a very small percentage of citizens can receive information about an event and then draw unique and perceptive inferences about it. The ordinary response of the attentive citizen is to accept the communicator's definition of the situation. The inattentive citizen, in contrast, may not care or know enough to try to understand the situation, thus being somewhat less likely to adopt the media's interpretation.[2]

OBSTACLES TO BANDWAGONS

Unlike Democrats, Republicans were largely unaffected by the outcomes of their party's primaries. About 75 percent of the Republican respondents had chosen between Ford and Reagan before the campaign began, some selecting their candidate because they liked or disliked Ford's handling of the presidency, others choosing one of the two men because of a conservative or moderate preference. Moreover, the large majority of these Republicans stayed with their candidate; in June 80 percent preferred the same candidate they had preferred in February. Reasonably sure about which candidate they wanted and why, their commitments shielded them from bandwagon effects. Indeed, persuaded Republicans tended to react selectively to exposure to the candidates. Their candidate gained stature while his opponent lost it, shown clearly by a comparison of the Erie and Los Angeles respondents. Before New Hampshire's opening primary in February, Erie Republicans were generally pro-Ford and Los Angeles Republicans were primarily pro-Reagan. As the primaries progressed, as indicated in Table 11.2, Republican opinion of Ford became more favorable in Los Angeles and more critical in Erie. Meanwhile Reagan drew opposite reactions: he was viewed more favorably by Los Angeles Republicans, less favorably by those in Erie. Within each location, moreover, pro-Reagan and pro-Ford voters responded selectively to the two candidates.

Among rank-and-file Republicans, then, the candidates' successes were generally unimportant to public response. Indeed, another pattern was evident—

Republicans tended to think highly of their preferred candidate's chances. There is in fact a general tendency for voters to be optimistic about the prospects for the candidate they favor. People like to think that others will develop equally high opinions of their favorite contender; consequently, they overrate his prospects. Throughout the 1976 race, each candidate's supporters rated his chances more highly than did other voters, but the degree of exaggeration varied. People were especially positive when the indicators were soft or conflicting, as they were before the first primaries, when without a solid basis for assessing how the contests would go, voters were reasonably hopeful about their candidates' chances. It is true that Ford's backers were more confident than Reagan's and Democrats backing Jackson, Carter, and Humphrey were more optimistic than those behind other candidates, but each side held on to the possibility of victory.

Carter's success in the primaries, however, quickly dampened the hopes of opposing Democrats. Halfway through the primaries, regardless of whom they favored, Democratic voters saw Carter as the likely winner. Only Brown's supporters felt their candidate still had a reasonable chance.* Carter's showing had simply overwhelmed the ability of opposing voters to rationalize.

Republicans were less strongly affected by developments. After Ford's victory in Pennsylvania extended his domination of the early primaries, most of Reagan's supporters believed that Ford had the advantage. They were not convinced, however, that the race was virtually over, but felt that Reagan still had time to turn things around, an optimism apparently justified by the winning streak Reagan began in early May. His wins did more than simply persuade his supporters that his chances had improved; many felt that he had edged ahead of Ford. They were less optimistic than Ford's supporters that their candidate would prevail, but they felt he could prevail. Each side continued to feel confident through the remaining primaries—an outlook made possible by the reality of a close race. Almost certainly this impeded any bandwagon effect—most Republicans already believed their side had a good chance.

All of this helps to explain why the Republican and Democratic races, despite similar appearances at the outset, took such different routes. Ford and Carter each began the primaries with a series of victories, but only Carter's success produced a bandwagon. Once he had control of the headlines, there was little to stem the flow of Democrats to his side. To be sure, some people voted against Carter because he was winning. Jackson in Pennsylvania and Brown in

---

*The large proportion of Brown supporters among the Los Angeles respondents was what kept Carter from gaining as favorable a rating there as he did in Erie (see Table 11.2). Brown's voters saw Carter selectively, as do all committed voters. The Erie reaction is undoubtedly more representative of the nation's voters. Unlike California Democrats, many of whom had a standing loyalty to their state's governor, most of the nation's Democrats were uncommitted before the primaries began. Thus, like the Democrats in Erie, they were in a position to be influenced by the results of the primaries.

California gained some votes because people saw them not as their first choice, but as capable of stopping Carter, thus enabling another candidate, such as Humphrey, to gain nomination. Voters of this type, however, were easily outnumbered by those attracted to Carter because of his success.

The Republican vote was decidedly more stable. Despite the appearance from early losses that his voters were deserting him, Reagan actually retained the large majority of his supporters throughout the early primaries, and won handily when the campaign finally reached the states dominated by conservative Republicans. Had Ford maintained his streak through the early weeks of May, Reagan supporters might have given up hope and reconciled themselves to accepting Ford as their candidate (as they did after the Republican convention). Or had a national crisis occurred, Ford might have been able to rally enough of Reagan's weaker supporters to generate a bandwagon. Or had Reagan committed a major blunder, his support might have evaporated. As things were, however, the strength of his candidacy and the commitment of his followers provided them with an effective shield from persuasion by the outcome of the early primaries.

By the same process, bandwagon effects are limited in nature during a general election. Although a third of the respondents delayed or changed their preferences during the general election, they did not gravitate toward the candidate they felt was leading. Indeed, Carter, who after the summer conventions was thought by most respondents to be ahead, lost votes during the general election. If anything, the fact that Carter appeared likely to win the presidency led voters to examine his candidacy more critically than they previously had. For the most part, changes during the general election reflected people's party, issue, and leadership preferences, influences that rather easily overrode their perceptions of the candidates' chances. Regardless of what they thought about the candidates' prospects, for example, Democrats developed increasingly negative opinions of Ford, and Republicans grew increasingly critical of Carter.

In the general election, people apparently find it easier to believe that their side can win—poll results seem to have less impact on their thinking than primary outcomes and delegate counts. When Carter led by two to one in post-convention polls, Ford's supporters felt Carter was more likely to win, but they hardly conceded him the advantage that opposing Democrats had granted him halfway through the primaries. Shortly before the general election day, when the polls had Carter narrowly in the lead, Ford backers rated Ford's chances as slightly better than Carter's, while Carter backers felt the victory would be a Democratic one. Not surprisingly, then, when a voter was faced with the possibility that his preferred candidate would lose the general election, he was more likely to change his belief about the likely winner than he was to switch candidates.

12

IMAGES OF THE
CANDIDATES

A candidate's image, as Kenneth Boulding has defined it, consists of the subjective impressions that voters have of him.[1] These impressions can be of any type—thoughts about a candidate's political values and campaign success are as much a part of his image as are ideas about his personality and leadership.* As such, voters certainly could be expected to acquire many of their impressions of the candidates from what they see through the media. But what types of impressions do they gain from press coverage of the campaign? When do they develop their images? Do television and the newspaper convey similar or different images? Moreover, the voters' images could not be expected to result solely

---

*Consistent with this definition of a candidate's image, respondents had the opportunity to say whatever they wanted about a candidate and to indicate an overall impression of him. They were asked open-ended, nondirective questions such as "What comes to mind when you think about Jimmy Carter?" This chapter concentrates on people's images of Ford and Carter, since they were in the 1976 race from start to finish and provide the best examples of a campaign's image effects. Also, this chapter combines the Erie and Los Angeles respondents. During the primaries when there were so many candidates in the race, there was not sufficient time during the interviews to ask each respondent about all the candidates—each respondent was asked only about three candidates selected randomly from a list of nine candidates. Consequently, in the February, April, and June interviews, only a third of the respondents were questioned about Ford and a third about Carter, too few in each case to analyze separately the Erie and Los Angeles respondents. In August and October all respondents were questioned about Ford and Carter, and there were no significant differences between people in the two locations.

from exposure to election messages. What part does partisanship play in the impressions that voters develop? Do voters see what they want to see in the candidates? These are the questions that this chapter addresses.

STYLISTIC AND POLITICAL IMPRESSIONS

Impressions acquired during the 1976 campaign tended to be stylistic, associated with the candidates' mannerisms and campaign performance. These included thoughts about the candidates' personalities, campaign success and style, and personal backgrounds. People were much less likely to form political impressions, those concerning the candidates' governing capacities and actions, such as their leadership abilities, political backgrounds, and issue positions.[2]

The tendency to form stylistic rather than political impressions was extremely apparent in the public's view of Carter. The large majority of voters had acquired an image of him by April, and their impressions were predominantly stylistic (see Table 12.1). His personality, campaign performance, and personal background accounted for 67 percent of the ideas that voters expressed about him.[3] Such impressions, moreover, were uppermost in people's minds throughout the campaign. Although political impressions of Carter increased slightly during the general election, matters of style still accounted for 60 percent of the respondents' thoughts in October.

News coverage of Carter undoubtedly contributed heavily to the structure of his image. No exact coefficient can be attached to the relationship, but there was a remarkable parallel between the themes of Carter's news coverage and the impressions that people developed. During the primaries, print and television news coverage of Carter was devoted to his campaign performance, personality, and personal background three times as often as it concerned his political positions, political background, and leadership capacities.[4] It was not until after the conventions, when Carter's politics accounted for a more substantial portion of his news coverage, that people's impressions of him became proportionately more political.

An example from the convention period further illustrates the interaction between Carter's news coverage and his image. Carter spent much of the time immediately before and after the Democratic convention in his hometown of Plains, Georgia. Although some of the news from Plains was political in nature, much of it was purely stylistic, as was the coverage of his softball games with the press and other leisure activities. Similarly, 42 percent of the respondents cited an aspect of Carter's personal background, often his hometown life, in the August interviews. This was the highest concentration of specific impressions about any candidate at any time during the 1976 campaign.

The development of Ford's image is a much less dramatic example of the stylistic impact of election news. In February, before the first primary, Ford's image was primarily political—69 percent of the voters' impressions focused on his presidential tenure, leadership, and policy actions. As the campaign progressed, the number of impressions of this type declined while stylistic impressions, particularly of his personality, increased. Despite the fact that most of Ford's coverage during the election pertained to his style, however, corresponding impressions of him did not increase substantially. In October over 60 percent of the thoughts that people expressed about Ford were political.

Once a candidate's image has been developed, it is unlikely to be altered significantly by new information. The developed image will limit the impact of subsequent news about the candidate. When Ford entered the race he was presenting himself as a candidate for the first time, but he had already established himself in the role of the presidency and had developed a political image that persisted throughout the campaign. Indeed, Ford had been stereotyped as a political figure, and once voters have stereotyped a candidate, they are likely to project this image to whatever they see and hear about the candidate in future coverage.[5] In this regard the best predictor of a voter's image of Ford at any time during the campaign was his previous image of Ford. The voters' existing images undoubtedly were also reinforced by continued, politically oriented news about his presidential actions during his candidacy. In any case, the heavily stylistic news communicated about Ford in the campaign made only a slight change in the political focus of people's impressions of Ford.

Carter's image also remained fairly stable. As in the case of Ford's image, the impact of new information on people's impressions of Carter was limited by the image he developed in the primaries. Carter projected an image that was more substantially modified than Ford's, but in general, respondents' impressions of him from interview to interview grew progressively more similar. The establishment of Carter's primary election image apparently reduced the impact of media coverage on the later development of his image. In the general election, increases in news messages about his politics were not matched proportionately by increases in people's impressions of his politics.

Obviously critical to the structure of a candidate's image is the role he fills when the image begins to develop. Ford entered the public view as the new president and, in his role of leader and policymaker, the news about him at that time focused on his political performance. On the other hand, when Carter began to attract attention as a new candidate, most of the news about him pertained to his style. Correspondingly, citizens learned generally to think of Ford in political terms and of Carter in stylistic terms. Perhaps impressions of Carter would have focused more on politics if election news emphasized substance and the candidates' representative roles. Election news, however, stresses the game and the candidates' individuality, and stylistic impressions are the principal results.

As a candidate's image develops, a final noteworthy pattern emerges as part of its structure: people's impressions of the candidate become progressively more general. In the final six months of the 1976 election, specific impressions of Carter (such as, "He's a peanut farmer," "He smiles a lot")

TABLE 12.1 Structure of Images at Various Times during the Campaign (percent)

Image Component	Ford's Image					Carter's Image				
	Feb.	Apr.	Jun.	Aug.	Oct.	Feb.	Apr.	Jun.	Aug.	Oct.
General evaluation	54	45	44	48	47	8	23	27	29	30
Personality										
Sincerity	21	14	19	17	26	6	16	26	35	36
Likability	9	13	13	13	15	3	24	22	22	24
Personal background	12	13	7	12	7	11	23	33	42	22
Campaign performance										
Success	1	4	4	4	2	6	15	17	9	4
Style	0	1	0	2	3	1	13	14	13	12

Stylistic impressions

Political impressions

Leadership										
Strength/Charisma	23	18	28	20	19	4	14	18	14	17
Ability	11	12	15	11	10	1	6	5	8	9
Political positions										
Values	14	10	9	12	13	6	14	12	12	18
Policies	13	10	8	13	15	1	4	3	8	11
Political background										
Experience	18	23	23	20	20	3	4	5	11	9
Performance	18	20	14	12	16	2	2	4	3	3
No impressions	3	4	4	3	1	75	17	8	4	2
Total	197	187	188	187	194	127	175	194	210	197

Note: Figures total more than 100 percent since up to three responses per respondent were coded. Figures based on replies of about 300 respondents in February, April, and June, and 750 respondents in August and October.

decreased in number while general impressions (such as, "He's honest," "He's incapable") increased 50 percent. Even as impressions became more general, however, the overall focus of those impressions remained constant. Early in the campaign specific stylistic impressions of Carter easily outnumbered specific political impressions of him. At the end of the campaign, general stylistic impressions easily outnumbered general impressions that were political—in October, people were twice as likely to mention Carter's personality (such as "He's likeable," "He's insincere") as they were to mention his leadership (such as, "He's capable," "He's weak").

Thus abstract opinions that develop are more likely to concern a candidate's personality than his leadership if voters are primarily exposed to and informed about his style. Presumably, if the news about a candidate were geared so as to involve messages about his political positions, values, and so on, voters would form more impressions of his leadership. This supposition gains support from the development of Ford's image. News coverage of Ford in the two years before the campaign was dominated by political messages; in February 1976 people had more impressions of Ford's leadership than of his personality. In October 1976, however, after exposure to election news that was mostly about his style, people had more thoughts about his personality than about his leadership.

The patterns found to be part of the image development of Ford and Carter also were evident among other candidates in 1976. The news coverage of each was dominated by stylistic messages and the image of each became more stylistic as the campaign progressed. The extent to which voters' impressions concerned a candidate's style, however, depended on how well formed his image was before the campaign began. For newcomers like Udall and Harris, stylistic impressions eventually accounted for most of the thoughts that people had. The information received about these candidates during the campaign formed the basis for their images. For previously familiar politicians like Reagan and Wallace, such impressions merely increased in proportion; older thoughts were not substantially overriden.

FAVORABLE AND UNFAVORABLE IMPRESSIONS

Thus far the observations made about the image of a presidential candidate apply only to its structure. Also to be considered is its direction—the extent to which people's impressions of the candidate are favorable or unfavorable. Of special concern are how the voters' impressions of the 1976 candidates changed during the campaign and how press coverage of the candidates influenced these changes.

Ford's image, for example, changed direction as the campaign wore on, becoming progressively more favorable (see Table 12.2). In February only 35 percent of the respondents' impressions were favorable. Collectively, voters admired his sincerity, but they saw him as a poor leader and opposed his political values and policies. In October, though, respondents felt more positively about Ford's personality and less critical of his leadership; 50 percent of their impressions were favorable.

The change in the public's view of Ford is clear, but the role of press coverage in this case is not. The favorable turn in the direction of his image is perhaps explained in part by consistently favorable references made by the media to Ford's style. Even so, direct statements about his personality were uncommon. Similarly, if news messages about his leadership ability contributed to the change, they did so only indirectly. Throughout the campaign, Ford's opponents charged him with ineffective leadership while he and his supporters argued that he was an able leader, making for news that was rather evenly divided between favorable and unfavorable messages. Ford's image, then, underwent a change in direction whose relationship to press coverage is unclear.

A study of the developing direction of Carter's image, however, readily indicates the effect of news coverage. Initially news messages about Carter's style, which dominated early coverage of him, were extremely favorable—from the opening primary until the final moment of the conventions, there were more than two favorable news messages about Carter for each unfavorable one. Correspondingly, Carter's early image was extremely positive. In April voters' impressions of him were highly favorable—69 percent of their thoughts were positive. There was little change in the convention period—in August 67 percent of people's thoughts about Carter were favorable. Throughout this time people were particularly likely to think highly of his personality, campaign success, and personal background. His personal background particularly was viewed favorably in August, after his life in Plains had received heavy pre- and postconvention coverage.

Carter's image during the general election, however, was suddenly less positive. The proportion of people favorably impressed had fallen to 56 percent by October. This time the precise nature of the media's influence is less easily discerned, for while the change clearly correlates with a significant drop in favorable stylistic messages, especially in messages about his campaign success, there is less correlation with political news about Carter. Unfavorable news messages about his political experience and positions increased substantially, but voters' impressions about these aspects of his candidacy became only slightly more negative.

The most significant change in Carter's image during the general election involved criticisms of his sincerity. In August 21 percent of the respondents had praised his sincerity and only 14 percent had questioned it. By October the proportions had reversed: only 13 percent expressed confidence in his sincerity, while 22 percent were doubtful. The change seemed linked to a charge made by the media that had followed him through the campaign—the allegation that he was deliberately obscuring his positions on the issues (see Chapter 4). The resulting perception among voters that Carter was fuzzy on the issues was the most frequently expressed unfavorable impression of him in the campaign's early months; as time passed and the news persisted with this allegation, this thought

TABLE 12.2 Direction of Images at Various Times during the Campaign

| | Ford's Image | | | | | | | | | | Carter's Image | | | | | | | | | |
| | Positive Impressions | | | | | Negative Impressions | | | | | Positive Impressions | | | | | Negative Impressions | | | | |
	Feb.	Apr.	Jun.	Aug.	Oct.	Feb.	Apr.	Jun.	Aug.	Oct.	Feb.	Apr.	Jun.	Aug.	Oct.	Feb.	Apr.	Jun.	Aug.	Oct.
General evaluation	17	11	17	20	20	17	16	13	14	14	5	14	16	17	14	2	4	7	6	8
Personality																				
Sincerity	15	10	16	14	21	5	4	3	3	5	3	8	9	21	13	3	8	17	14	22
Likability	5	9	8	8	10	1	2	3	3	2	1	14	10	11	14	0	1	0	2	3
Personal background	4	6	3	5	3	1	1	0	0	0	5	12	16	19	10	1	1	1	0	1
Campaign performance _(Stylistic Impressions)_																				
Success	0	2	2	2	1	1	2	2	2	1	3	11	14	7	2	1	1	2	1	1
Style	0	0	0	0	0	0	1	0	0	2	0	0	0	0	0	1	12	12	12	10

140

Political Impressions

Leadership																				
Strength/Charisma	2	3	5	5	6	21	15	21	13	11	4	10	13	9	10	0	2	4	4	5
Ability	1	2	5	5	3	10	10	11	8	9	0	5	4	6	5	1	1	1	2	4
Political positions																				
Values	2	2	1	1	2	8	6	4	5	4	2	7	6	6	10	1	3	3	2	5
Policies	2	3	1	3	4	9	6	6	9	10	1	2	2	3	7	0	0	0	2	2
Political background																				
Experience	0	1	2	3	3	0	1	1	0	0	0	0	0	0	0	0	2	2	2	5
Performance	1	1	1	1	1	17	19	13	13	15	0	0	0	0	0	2	2	4	3	3
Total	49	50	61	67	74	90	83	77	70	73	24	83	90	99	85	12	37	54	50	69

Note: Figures include as many as three responses per respondent. The figures in this table do not total to those in Table 12.1 since neutral responses are omitted.

developed into the general impression that Carter was insincere. Those voters who, early in the campaign, thought Carter was avoiding the issues were particularly likely later to form the opinion that he was insincere.

As with the structure of image, the ability of news messages to influence the direction of image depends on how well formed a candidate's image is prior to the campaign. For Ford, whose image was established before the campaign, the impact of the news was less evident than in the case of Carter, who was new to the national electorate. The same was generally true for the rest of the candidates in 1976. The direction of images of well-known politicians like Reagan and Wallace was only marginally affected by press coverage. Candidates like Jackson and Harris, on the other hand, received mostly unfavorable coverage, focused primarily on their campaign performance. Their images became increasingly negative over the course of their campaigns, due primarily to unfavorable stylistic impressions.

Given the nature of election news, the images of successful and unsuccessful candidates may be expected to change in opposing directions, especially in the early primaries. A winning candidate can expect a favorable balance of news coverage, centered primarily on his performance but extending into other areas as well. A successful newcomer's personal background, for example, is an obvious source of human interest stories for the press. A losing candidate, however, can count upon negative news about his campaign effort and is likely to find that journalists have little interest in his background.

IMAGE STRUCTURE AND NEWS HABITS

Images are rather easily acquired by voters. For example, about 80 percent had an image of Carter by April 1976. For many, this image was nothing more than the impression that Carter was conducting a highly successful nominating campaign. Nevertheless, most people—those who followed the news closely and those who did not—had gained an impression of him. The number and type of impressions that people acquired, however, were somewhat associated with their news habits.

Newspaper reading particularly contributes to the fullness of people's images (see Table 12.3). Throughout the campaign, heavier readers were more likely to acquire additional impressions of Ford and Carter. Television viewing, in contrast, was associated with these increases only in the early primaries. After this period, infrequent viewers were as likely as regular viewers to acquire additional impressions of the candidates.

The newspaper, then, is more instrumental in the formation of images. Underlying this is the fact that impressions are created mainly by words rather than pictures. To be sure, some of the voters' impressions are derived from television's pictures. Particularly during the early primaries, people spoke frequently of how Carter looked or appeared, referring obviously to his televised image. These picture-derived images undoubtedly explain the strong relationship between Carter's early image and people's television exposure. They also may explain the very early formation of images. In general, however, voter's impressions are gained primarily through words. Their thoughts about a candidate's primary victories or his political record, for example, depend mostly on verbal communication, and in this the newspaper excels.

Many observers, however, argue that even though television is not as successful in conveying hard information, it is important because of the general impressions its pictures leave with the audience. "In large part," writes James Q. Wilson, voters judge a presidential candidate "on their sense of [his] character, especially as revealed by television." This argument finds its reasoning in the opinion of some that the term image should apply not to those impressions that may perhaps be regarded as items of information, such as thoughts about a candidate's performance, but only to people's general thoughts about a candidate's personality and leadership. These general impressions, so it is claimed, depend heavily on how a candidate looks and acts on television.[6]

Indeed, when only the voters' impressions about the candidates' personalities and leadership capacities are considered, television's impact is more apparent (see Table 12.3).* During the early primaries, regular viewing of the evening newscasts was strongly associated with the formation of impressions of Carter's personality. Heavier viewers were especially likely to describe Carter as likable and personally appealing. Throughout the campaign frequent viewers also were more likely than infrequent viewers to develop impressions of Ford and Carter's leadership traits. Importantly, though, newspaper reading was more strongly and consistently related than television viewing to developing impressions of the candidates' leadership and personalities.

The newspaper's greater impact reflects the process by which most voters reach conclusions about a candidate's leadership or personality. Typically, voters make such judgments after they feel they have some understanding of the candidate. Some develop this feeling early in the campaign, but for most, as indicated previously, general impressions—abstract thoughts about a candidate's leadership and personality—tend to develop later and are, to a degree, a function of their specific impressions. Therefore voters who acquire more specific information about a candidate are more likely to form general impressions of his

---

*Given the method of measurement, the evidence is even more impressive than might first appear. Respondents were given complete freedom to say what they wanted to say about the candidates. They were not asked, for example, to rate the candidates on a common dimension, such as their personality. Thus when their answers, which included on average two impressions of the candidates, are divided among six specific components, a large number of respondents will be at the 0-point for each specific component. This reduces the variation considerably, thus depressing the correlations.

TABLE 12.3 Relationship of Network Newscast Exposure, Newspaper Exposure, and Party Identification to Changes in Structure of Images

Candidate and Component	Feb. to Apr.			Apr. to June			June to Aug.			Aug. to Oct.		
	TV	NP	PI	TV	NP	PI	TV	NP	PI	TV	NP	PI
Ford's image												
All components	+.07	+.12*	+.21*	-.06	+.16*	+.04	+.04	+.14*	+.10*	-.06	+.08	+.14*
Personality	-.12	+.20*	+.11*	-.02	-.01	+.08	-.01	+.15*	+.04	+.01	+.08	+.18*
Personal Background	+.03	+.13*	-.08	-.08	-.09	+.09*	+.07	-.01	+.06	-.02	+.02	+.07
Campaign performance	+.04	+.06	+.02	+.03	-.12	-.08	+.01	+.08	+.15*	-.09	+.05	.00
Leadership	+.19*	+.15*	-.05	+.04	+.12*	+.12*	+.06	+.08	+.01	+.03	+.07	-.01
Political positions	-.02	+.11*	+.14*	-.03	+.17*	+.05	+.06	+.02	+.06	-.07	+.02	+.02
Political background	-.05	-.20	+.01	-.05	-.09	-.13	-.14	+.10*	-.03	.00	-.09	-.02

144

Carter's image

All components	+.13*	+.11*	-.06	-.04	+.14*	+.01	-.06	+.13*	-.11	+.01	+.06	+.01
Personality	+.16*	+.14*	-.16	-.02	-.03	-.13	-.07	+.18*	-.05	+.03	+.03	-.15
Personal background	+.01	+.16*	-.05	+.16*	+.21*	+.12*	-.01	-.06	+.12*	-.07	+.03	+.03
Campaign performance	-.03	+.20*	+.16*	+.12*	-.04	+.02	-.05	+.12*	-.08	-.07	+.06	-.08
Leadership	-.04	+.02	-.06	+.11*	+.08	-.02	+.09	+.12*	+.04	+.11*	+.02	+.02
Political positions	-.08	+.07	-.11	+.15*	-.08	+.08	-.01	+.03	-.01	-.03	+.05	+.13*
Political background	+.02	-.05	-.03	+.02	-.13	-.21	+.01	-.07	-.15	-.03	+.01	-.07

*Relationship significant at 0.5 level.

Note: Figures are beta coefficients from regression equations in which the dependent variable was the number of impressions of the specific type (for example, personal background) that respondents expressed at the time of the second interview. The independent variables were their evening newscast exposure (TV), their newspaper exposure (NP), and their party identification (PI), and the number of impressions of this type at the time of the first interview. For the Carter equations, the party identification index assigned a higher number to Democrats than Republicans. For the Ford equations, the Republicans were assigned a higher number. Thus a positive coefficient for the party identification indicates that a candidate's image changed more for voters of his party, while a negative coefficient indicates that his image changed more among voters of the opposing party. For a discussion of the use of regression analysis in situations of this type, see the note to Table 9.2.

145

leadership and personality. As the more effective transmitter of information, the newspaper contributes more heavily to what people know about a candidate and, hence, to their images.

This is not to say that television's impact on image formation is insignificant. Its influence in this area, in fact, is greater than in most others. While television's pictures lack any capacity to enlighten voters about the candidates' policy positions, they certainly contribute to the development of people's images of the candidates. Furthermore, television's limited news space is not an overly severe restriction in the area of image formation. It appears that continued exposure to a candidate, whether on television or the newspaper, encourages the voter to make judgments about a candidate's character. Frequent exposure may provide a sense of familiarity and lead gradually to the formation of ideas about the candidate's personality and leadership. Finally, since early images affect the development of later ones, the concentration of television's impact in the early stages of the campaign adds significance to its contribution. Nevertheless, the number and type of impressions voters develop are determined primarily by the specific information they acquire, and the newspaper is the superior transmitter of information.

IMAGE DIRECTION AND NEWS HABITS

Voters' impressions of the candidates are not determined completely by the messages that flow through the media. Voters often have a biased view of what they see when exposed to presidential candidates. Most voters are political loyalists of one kind or another, especially to a political party, and can be expected to perceive the candidates selectively.

Voters' partisan loyalties, however, have little impact on the structure of their images of the candidates. As Table 12.3 indicated, partisanship related only slightly to the number of impressions voters gained. Although theories of selective exposure predict that partisans will develop more impressions of a candidate of their party, Republicans actually acquired more ideas about both Carter and Ford.[7] The types of impressions held were also independent of people's partisanship. Republicans, independents, and Democrats alike had mostly stylistic impressions of Carter and mostly political impressions of Ford.

In the direction of images, however, partisanship was a more important influence than news exposure. The favorable primary coverage of Carter provided close followers of the news with more favorable impressions of him during the primaries, but no obvious relationship between the level of people's news exposure and their evaluations of the candidates was otherwise evident (see Table 12.4). Partisan differences, on the other hand, related clearly to people's feelings about the candidates. Ford's image was more positive to Republicans than to Democrats, and Carter's image was more favorable to Democrats than to Republicans.

Nevertheless, partisanship had an inconstant influence on people's images. Not until the convention and general election periods was partisanship a powerful influence. During the primaries, party loyalty was only modestly related to increasingly favorable and unfavorable impressions of Ford and Carter. In part, this is because competition during the primaries occurs within each party. A voter's commitment to one candidate can affect his response to his party's other candidates. For example, Republicans backing Reagan were more likely than those supporting Ford to develop unfavorable impressions of Ford. In the early part of the campaign, party loyalty also is a less imposing obstacle to favorable impressions of a candidate of the opposing party. Republicans were more likely during the primaries to develop positive thoughts about Carter, and Democrats were more likely to gain favorable ideas about Ford. Apparently, partisanship is not as strong a psychological defense in the primaries—election day is still months away, and voters' partisan biases are not fully mobilized.

The declining strength of partisanship over the past two decades probably contributes to this tendency. One effect of weakened partisanship is a delay in the voting decision. Usually it is not until voters have chosen a candidate that they begin to rationalize heavily, exaggerating the virtues of their candidate and the faults of his opponent. Since most voting decisions are still made along party lines eventually, the delay diminishes the early correlation between images and partisanship.

The nature of election news in the early stages of the campaign also delays partisan reactions. The large bulk of the information reaching the voters during the primaries is politically neutral. As was evidenced in Chapter 8, news about the status and strategies of the nominating races is unlikely to evoke political bias. Party loyalties are likely to be mobilized instead by the candidates' advocacy of policies traditionally associated with one or the other party, their use of party symbols, their alignment with certain groups, and similar things. Yet these are not significantly represented in the flow of daily election information until the nominating process is concluded and, even then, are not dominant.

The tempering effect of election news on party loyalties in image formation can be inferred from the data in Table 12.4. Partisan reactions to the candidates were least evident in the area that was the focus of news content, namely, style. Only one stylistic component—the candidates' personalities—involved sharp partisan differences, largely because of divided opinions about the candidates' trustworthiness. Partisanship was much more decisive in people's political impressions—their reactions to the candidates' leadership, political backgrounds, and political values and policies—than in their stylistic impressions. Even late in the campaign, voters' impressions of the campaign performances and personal backgrounds of Ford and Carter depended less than any other impressions on whether they were Republicans or Democrats.

The effect of this was to minimize the influence of party loyalty in the primary period, for impressions of the candidates' campaign performances and personal backgrounds tended to be among the first ones that the voters formed.

TABLE 12.4 Relationship of Network Newscast Exposure, Newspaper Exposure, and Party Identification to Changes in Direction of Images

Candidate and Component	Feb. to Apr.			Apr. to June			June to Aug.			Aug. to Oct.		
	TV	NP	PI	TV	NP	PI	TV	NP	PI	TV	NP	PI
Ford's image												
All components	-.05	-.14	+.09*	-.06	-.04	+.06	+.05	+.08	+.20*	-.01	.00	+.28*
Personal traits	-.04	-.11	+.26*	-.14	+.14*	+.03	+.09*	+.13*	-.03	+.01	+.08	+.20*
Personal background	+.03	-.02	+.01	-.01	+.05	-.01	+.07	+.02	.00	+.01	+.04	.00
Campaign performance	+.13*	+.06	+.02	+.06	-.01	+.02	+.03	-.02	-.02	+.05	-.10	+.06
Political traits	.00	-.21	+.25*	-.05	-.03	-.09	-.03	+.02	+.20*	-.05	-.01	+.15*
Political tendencies	-.25	+.06	-.08	-.15	-.05	-.04	-.05	+.02	+.06	-.03	+.01	+.18*
Political background	+.03	+.09	+.01	-.06	-.02	-.01	-.03	+.01	+.10*	-.01	-.04	+.11*

Carter's image

All components	+.09	-.03	+.05	+.04	+.10*	+.02	-.02	-.04	+.16*	+.04	+.01	+.29*
Personal traits	+.22*	+.04	-.14	+.17*	-.17	+.23*	-.04	-.06	+.21*	.00	-.01	+.23*
Personal background	+.07	-.06	+.05	-.08	+.17*	+.02	+.05	.00	-.13	-.01	+.02	+.06
Campaign performance	+.05	-.05	+.16*	-.09	+.12*	+.05	+.02	-.09	+.03	+.07	+.01	+.12*
Political traits	-.17	+.19*	+.04	+.12*	+.01	-.05	+.04	+.13*	+.06	+.01	+.05	+.16*
Political tendencies	+.01	-.11	+.07	-.05	-.10	+.18*	-.11	+.08	+.06	+.04	+.01	+.18*
Political background	-.04	-.01	+.06	+.05	+.11*	+.21*	-.08	-.06	+.12*	+.01	-.02	+.10*

*Relationship significant at .05 level.

Note: Figures are beta coefficients from regression equations in which the dependent variable was the number of impressions of the specific type (for example, personal background) that respondents expressed at the time of the second interview. The independent variables were their evening newscast exposure (TV), their newspaper exposure (NP), and their party identification (PI), and the number of impressions of this type at the time of the first interview. For the Carter equations, the party identification index assigned a higher number to Democrats than Republicans. For the Ford equations, the Republicans were assigned a higher number. Thus a positive coefficient for party identification indicates that a candidate's image changed more for voters of his party, while a negative coefficient indicates that his image changed more among voters of the opposing party.

In Carter's case, these two components alone accounted for nearly 40 percent of all the distinct impressions people had in April. In October, however, they accounted for less than 25 percent of the thoughts about Carter; impressions of his leadership, political background, personality, and political positions were more likely to be acquired in the campaign's later stages. Thus the characteristic response to primary election news are the impressions that are least subject to partisan distortion.

The weakened partisanship and neutral media communication of the primary period appear to dampen partisan response in other dimensions as well. Democrats were more likely to form favorable impressions of Ford's politics and leadership in the primaries than they were later in the campaign, while Republicans were more likely to develop favorable thoughts about Carter's policies and personality.

Importantly, even in the campaign's final stages, the more intense partisanship and the more overtly partisan media communication did not completely override these early impressions. First, the voters' initial specific impressions about the candidates' personal and political backgrounds influenced their later ideas about the candidates' leadership and personalities. People who before the conventions were impressed with Carter's personal background, for example, were more likely after the conventions to form favorable opinions of his personality. Similarly, those who had positive reactions to Ford's political background before the conventions were more likely afterward to develop favorable impressions of his leadership. Although the way people viewed the candidates' personalities and leadership during the general election was influenced by partisanship, so was it affected by their earlier and specific thoughts about the candidates. Thus partisanship competed with previous impressions, formed largely independent of party loyalties, for influence on the voters' eventual impressions of the candidates.

Second, impressions that people acquired tended to last throughout the campaign (see Table 12.5). In 80 percent of the cases, any single impression of a candidate held during the general election related more closely to earlier impressions of him than to partisanship.* Those people who thought favorably of a candidate's background, personality, leadership, or positions before the conventions, also thought favorably about him in this area after the conventions,

---

*This finding has particular significance because of the method of measuring images. For early impressions to be related to later ones, respondents not only had to feel the same way in the later interview as in the earlier one, but they had to express the same feelings in response to an open-ended question. Either a change in their thoughts or the expression of different thoughts reduced the correlation between early and late images. If respondents had been asked a forced-choice question each time, their answers would have been on the same dimension each time, and the correlation between early and late images would have been higher.

TABLE 12.5 Relationship of Party Identification and Earlier Images to Later Images

| | Ford's Image | | | | Carter's Image | | | |
| | June to Aug. | | Aug. to Oct. | | June to Aug. | | Aug. to Oct. | |
Component	Party Ident.	Prior Image	Party Ident.	Prior Image	Party Ident.	Prior Image	Party Ident.	Prior Image
Personal traits	-.03	+.18*	+.20*	+.31*	+.21*	+.22*	+.23*	+.24*
Personal background	.00	+.15*	.00	+.13*	-.13	+.22*	+.06	+.19*
Campaign performance	-.02	-.01	+.06	-.03	+.03	+.17*	+.12*	+.14*
Political traits	+.20*	+.23*	+.15*	+.26*	+.06	+.23*	+.16*	+.14*
Political tendencies	+.06	+.16*	+.18*	+.20*	+.06	+.10	+.18*	+.11
Political background	+.10	+.20*	+.11*	+.16*	+.12*	+.12*	+.10	+.05

*Relationship significant at the .05 level.

Note: Figures involve same calculations as those for Table 12.4. People's prior impressions (June in the first instance and August in the second) of each type are included in this table, however.

regardless of their partisan leanings. Again, party loyalty competes with, rather than supplants, early images for influence on later ones.

In short, though election news in the campaign's early stages is largely neutral in its content, it is not neutral in its effects. Early impressions, many of which have no obvious political significance, affect later ones, and provide resistance to partisan leanings. Partisanship remains an obviously powerful influence on people's candidate evaluations, but today it has competition from news messages, particularly those that do not directly challenge partisan stereotypes.

13

INFORMATION ABOUT
THE ISSUES

Among the most vital of all information available to voters during a presidential campaign is that concerning the candidates' issue positions. Recent research by Norman Nie, Gerald Pomper, David RePass, and others indicates that issues have become increasingly important to the voters.[1] To make an intelligent choice based on their issue preferences, however, the voters first must be aware of the candidates' policy leanings. Without this information they cannot know what policy differences are represented in the choice of one candidate over another. But how much do voters learn about the issues during a presidential campaign, when do they learn it, and what accounts for what they learn or fail to learn? The purpose of this chapter is to explore these questions.

ISSUE AWARENESS DURING THE CAMPAIGN

Before the 1976 campaign got under way, the voters' issue information was fairly limited (see Table 13.1). Ford's positions were somewhat familiar to the voters; still, on every issue his position was unknown to the majority of voters. Reagan's positions, although recognized in part by many active Republicans, were unknown to most other voters. The electorate knew even less about the policies of the Democratic candidates. Jackson was one of the better known Democrats before the primaries, yet few respondents could say where he stood on an issue; for example, despite his prominence in Senate debates on national defense, only 5 percent knew his position on defense spending. Less than 5

TABLE 13.1 Awareness of the Candidates' Issue Positions at Different Times during the Campaign

	Percent Accurately Perceiving Candidate's Position on:							
	Public Works Jobs		Defense Spending		Welfare Spending		Tax Burden	
Candidate	Early	Late	Early	Late	Early	Late	Early	Late
Brown (Erie)	2	7	3	5	0	4	3	12
Brown (L.A.)	18	20	10	15	10	26	18	20
Carter	4	54	0	29	5	22	5	40
Ford	12	35	38	57	33	43	10	22
Harris	3	3	2	2	3	3	4	3
Jackson	6	12	5	9	0	1	5	10
Reagan (Erie)	11	11	10	30	19	21	10	11
Reagan (L.A.)	30	32	32	50	45	37	28	35
Udall	11	12	6	10	6	11	10	13

Note: Early denotes the first interview in which respondents were asked to identify the respective candidates' issue position. This was the February interview for all candidates except Brown and Udall, where the early interview was the one conducted in April. Late denotes the last interview in which respondents were asked about the respective candidate's positions. For Harris and Jackson, who dropped from the race halfway through the primaries, this was the April interview; for Udall, Reagan, and Brown, this was the June interview; and for Ford and Carter, this was the October interview. The respondents' perception of the candidates' position were measured on seven-point scales that had an alternative position on each end, for example, on defense spending, one alternative was "no increase in military spending is necessary," and the other was "spend much more on military defense." The position toward which a candidate leaned was determined from a content analysis of his campaign speeches, for example, Reagan stated that he supported increases in military spending. Respondents were considered to be accurate in their perceptions if they placed a candidate on any one of the three positions on the appropriate side of the scale; respondents also were considered to have an accurate perception if they placed a candidate at the scale's midpoint if his statements indicated qualified rather than full support for the position. The table proportions include a correction for guessing.[2]

percent of the respondents had an accurate perception of Carter's position on any given issue.

Issue awareness increased during the campaign, but the amount of learning varied considerably by candidate. The policies advocated by Udall, Jackson, Harris, and Brown were only slightly more evident to voters after the primaries had been held. Fewer than one in 15 voters gained awareness during the primaries of the typical issue position of one of these candidates. Except on one issue, the public also did not learn much about Reagan's stands. The exception was his defense spending position—about 20 percent more of the voters could identify his stand on this issue in June than could do so in February. Overall, however, the present campaign apparently has little capacity to inform voters about the platforms of candidates who do not survive the primaries. The policy infomation about these candidates that voters bring to the campaign is nearly the sum of the information they will possess.

The voters' awareness of Carter and Ford's positions, however, measurably increased during the campaign. Over a third of the voters could identify Carter's position on the typical issue at the end of the campaign, compared with less than one in 20 before the primaries began. Carter's stand on taxes, for example, was known to only 5 percent in February, but to 40 percent in October. The largest increase in people's understanding of Carter's policies occurred during the general election, but the primary and convention periods also were accompanied by gains, as can be seen by the increases from one time to the next in the proportion of respondents identifying each of his stands (figures are percents):

	Jobs	Defense	Welfare	Taxes
Early primaries (Feb.-Apr.)	+17	-6	+9	+6
Late primaries (Apr.-June)	-1	+5	+15	+6
Conventions (June-Aug.)	+15	+11	-17	+10
General election (Aug.-Oct.)	+19	+19	+10	+13

The public's awareness of Ford's policy leanings increased less than did its awareness of Carter's, primarily because voters were more informed about Ford's stands before the campaign started. Nevertheless, people's information about his policies did rise. Those aware of his position on public works jobs, for example, increased from 12 percent to 35 percent during the campaign. Most of the voters' information about Ford was gained during the last half of the campaign (figures are percents):

	Jobs	Defense	Welfare	Taxes
Early primaries (Feb.-Apr.)	+1	+2	+2	+6
Late primaries (Apr.-June)	+2	+9	+8	-2
Conventions (June-Aug.)	+6	+1	0	+8
General election (Aug.-Oct.)	+14	+7	0	0

These changes in the public's information about Ford and Carter reveal both the extent and limit of the campaign's ability to inform. People knew almost nothing about Carter's policies before the campaign, but were almost as well informed about his stands as they were of Ford's by the campaign conclusion. In the case of both candidates, however, the voters' awareness even at its peak fell far short of perfection. As the November election day approached, there were, on average, more voters who did not know where Ford or Carter stood on an issue as could place him.

INCREASED ISSUE AWARENESS AND NEWS EXPOSURE

The public's increased issue awareness during a presidential campaign usually is credited to information received from television and the newspaper. Yet while the newspaper makes a substantial contribution, television actually does not add significantly to what people learn.

In 1976 heavier viewers of the evening news, while somewhat better informed before the campaign began, learned not much more than lighter viewers about Ford and Carter's positions during the campaign.* For more than 90 percent of the issue positions studied, no significant relationship was found between heavier viewing and increased issue awareness from one interview to the next. Such a relationship did appear among newspaper readers. It is true that regular readers were better informed about the issues prior to the 1976 campaign, and thus had less to learn during the campaign. Nevertheless, the

---

*The analysis for the rest of this chapter will concentrate on changes in voters' awareness of Ford and Carter's positions, since people's information about the other candidates did not change significantly during the campaign. (An analysis was conducted for the other candidates, however, and the results parallel those for Ford and Carter—the same variables were important.) The four issues that are the basis for analysis are neither narrow nor technical in their nature and they cover a fairly wide spectrum of policy. Consequently, the respondents' ability to locate Ford and Carter on these issues should provide a reasonably accurate test of the campaign's impact. The following are the alternatives that respondents were given on each of the four issues and the positions of Ford and Carter on these issues: on public works jobs, whether a candidate favored public works jobs (as did Carter) or opposed them (as did Ford) as a major means of dealing with the unemployment situation; whether a candidate preferred to maintain military spending at roughly its current level (as did Carter) or advocated a significant increase in military spending (as did Ford); on social welfare spending, whether a candidate supported the current level of spending on social welfare programs (as did Carter) or advocated a decrease (as did Ford); and on tax reduction, whether a candidate favored a tax cut that would help mostly modest and low income groups (as did Carter) or would benefit all income groups about the same (as did Ford). When the candidate's position was one of qualified support for the position, the midpoint on the scale (as well as the three positions on the correct side of the scale) was taken to represent an accurate perception.

newspaper's campaign coverage had its effect. On the large majority of issues, heavier readers learned more than lighter readers after the campaign began. On 60 percent of all issues, in fact, they learned significantly more (at the .05 level) from one interview to the next.

During the primaries, newspaper reading was significantly related to increased awareness of 75 percent of Carter's positions and 63 percent of Ford's (see Table 13.2). When only the issues given relatively more coverage by the press during the primaries are considered, the proportion of significant relationships for newspaper readers was even slightly higher, reaching 75 percent for both Ford and Carter. On the other hand, frequent viewers gained substantially higher awareness than infrequent viewers of only 13 percent of Carter's positions and none of Ford's.

Newspaper reading continued its strong relationship to heightened awareness during the convention period (see Table 13.3). At this time heavier readers gained significantly greater awareness of 63 percent of Carter's positions and 87 percent of Ford's. Television news viewing, in contrast, was completely unrelated to heightened awareness of Carter's policies and significantly related to increased awareness of only 25 percent of Ford's. Another form of television viewing, however, was associated with issue learning at this time. Those people who watched the televised national conventions became more informed than those who did not watch. Heavier convention viewers became significantly better informed about 63 percent of Carter's positions and 25 percent of Ford's.

The general election period resembled the convention period in these respects, as Table 13.3 indicates. Heavier newspaper reading continued to be associated with heightened awareness, particularly of heavily reported issues, while evening newscast viewing remained unrelated. Exposure to the televised presidential debates, however, contributed to people's issue information. Debate viewing was significantly related to higher awareness of 50 percent of Carter and Ford's policies.

In conveying issue-related information to the public, then, the daily newspaper is far superior to daily television. Although issues are not the newspaper's main focus, its greater news space enables it to cover the issues more frequently and more substantially than television. Issues are communicated with words, and in 1976 the newspaper communicated each of the candidates' issue positions in from three to 15 times as many words as the television did.[3] Of course, many readers do little more than glance at the headlines and read a lead paragraph or two, thus exposing themselves to only a portion of the issue information that the newspaper provides. Nevertheless, the newspaper's depth of coverage enables it to impart issue information on its users.

Television's issue content is too sparse and fragmented to benefit viewers. News of the issues is a small part of election news, which in turn is only a part of all news that must be covered in the 30-minute span of an evening newscast. As a result, most election issues are mentioned so infrequently that viewers could not be expected to learn very much—in 1976 the typical candidate position

TABLE 13.2 Relationship of Network Newscast Exposure, Daily Newspaper Exposure, and Political Party Information to Increases in Awareness of Candidates' Issue Positions during the Primaries

Issue	Carter's Positions			Ford's Positions		
	Network Exposure	Newspaper Exposure	Party Info.	Network Exposure	Newspaper Exposure	Party Info.
Jobs						
Erie	-.01	+.11[b]	+.11[b]	+.02	+.09[b]	+.17[a]
L.A.	+.09[b]	+.09[b]	+.23[a]	+.08	+.09[b]	+.25[a]
Defense						
Erie	+.02	+.04	+.14[a]	+.06	+.08	+.24[a]
L.A.	-.03	+.12[b]	+.16[a]	.00	+.23[a]	+.23[a]
Welfare						
Erie	-.06	+.09[b]	+.20[a]	-.04	+.17[a]	+.06
L.A.	-.08	+.13[a]	+.07	-.05	+.16[a]	+.09
Taxes						
Erie	-.02	+.17[a]	+.22[a]	-.01	+.07	+.22[a]
L.A.	-.05	+.07	+.26[a]	+.04	+.02	+.10[b]

[a]Relationship significant at .01 level.
[b]Relationship significant at .05 level.

Note: Figures are beta coefficients in which awareness of the candidate's position in the June interview is the dependent variable and network exposure, newspaper, party information, and awareness of the candidate's position in the February interview are the independent variables. The party information variable is explained in a later section. Underlined values are those for issues receiving relatively heavier news coverage during the period.

was mentioned between two or three times a month on the evening news. Moreover, most issue references on telecasts are so fleeting that they hardly could be expected to impress their audience—in 1976 a majority of the candidates' issues were covered in news segments of 20 seconds or less, and many of these lasted only a few seconds. Minimal issue awareness is the certain consequence of infrequent, embedded, and fleeting references to the issues.

Television's live coverage of major events, however, has some capacity to inform viewers about policy issues. The effect of exposure to the national conventions and presidential debates was not as substantial as daily newspaper reading, largely because episodic exposure to political messages is less impactful than multiple exposures. People usually acquire and retain detailed political information through repeated exposure.[4] Nevertheless, the issues that are transmitted during these broadcasts are presented at some length and often are the center of attention, and many viewers obviously acquire a better understanding of the candidates' policies from what is said.

ELECTION INTEREST, NEWS USE, AND ISSUE AWARENESS

So thin is daily television's issue coverage that newscast viewing did not contribute even to the awareness of highly interested voters (see Table 13.4). Whether these individuals frequently or rarely watched television news figured not at all in how much they learned about issues during the 1976 campaign. Highly interested voters who ignored the nightly newscasts learned as much as those who watched regularly. Although high interest viewers undoubtedly are somewhat more attentive than other viewers to television news, its very limited issue content does not substantially benefit even them.

The newspaper's capacity to inform, however, was uniformly evident. The frequency with which people read a daily paper's news sections, regardless of how interested they were in politics, was related to how much they learned about the issues. Newspaper use, however, did not have precisely the same impact on each type of voter.

First, high interest voters obtained more benefit from their newspaper exposure. For 50 percent of the issue positions studied, high interest voters who were heavier readers gained significantly higher awareness than those who were lighter readers. Among moderate and low interest voters, newspaper exposure was significantly related to heightened awareness of about 30 percent of the issues.

Second, the amount of newspaper coverage received by an issue was important in whether newspaper exposure resulted in higher issue awareness for low and moderate interest voters—a significant relationship existed for about 38 percent of heavily reported issues but only 25 percent of lightly reported ones. Among high interest voters, however, the proportions of significant relationships were the same—50 percent for heavily reported and lightly

TABLE 13.3 Relationship of Network Newscast Exposure, Daily Newspaper Exposure, and Political Party Information to Increases in Awareness of Candidates' Issue Positions during the Conventions and General Election Periods

Carter's Positions

Candidate	Conventions (June - Aug.)				General Election (Aug. - Oct.)			
	Net. Expo.	Paper Expo.	Conv. Expo.	Party Info.	Net. Expo.	Paper Expo.	Debate Expo.	Party Info.
Jobs								
Erie	-.02	+.08[b]	+.12[a]	+.15[a]	+.04	+.12[a]	+.13[a]	+.14[a]
L.A.	-.08	+.18[a]	+.07	+.30[a]	-.13[a]	+.04	+.04	+.09
Defense								
Erie	-.01	+.08[a]	+.09[b]	+.16[a]	+.04	-.03	+.11[a]	+.12[a]
L.A.	-.02	+.10[a]	+.06	+.26[a]	.00	+.09[b]	+.03	+.16[a]
Welfare								
Erie	.00	+.02	+.09[b]	+.16[a]	-.08	+.19[a]	+.02	+.19[a]
L.A.	-.07	+.08	+.13[b]	+.16[a]	+.05	+.14[a]	-.05	+.09
Taxes								
Erie	+.05	+.07	+.08[b]	+.21[a]	-.02	-.04	+.14[a]	+.11[a]
L.A.	-.06	+.08[a]	+.09	+.22[a]	+.01	-.05	+.12[b]	+.19[a]

				Ford's Positions				
Jobs								
Erie	+.01	+.11[a]	+.05	+.25[a]	+.06	+.05	+.14[a]	+.20[a]
L.A.	+.09[b]	+.10[b]	-.02	+.28[a]	-.04	+.04	+.08	+.13[a]
Defense								
Erie	+.06	+.09[b]	+.07	+.05	-.01	+.05	+.08[b]	+.22[a]
L.A.	.00	+.13[a]	+.05	+.12[b]	+.05	+.09[b]	+.08	+.21[a]
Welfare								
Erie	+.08[b]	+.12[a]	+.11[a]	+.17[a]	-.11	+.21[a]	.00	+.05
L.A.	-.05	+.24[a]	+.01	+.05	-.10	+.12[b]	-.05	+.04
Taxes								
Erie	+.04	+.10[b]	+.01	+.09[b]	-.03	+.03	+.12[a]	+.09[b]
L.A.	+.01	+.07	+.16[a]	+.15[a]	+.03	-.02	+.13[b]	+.19[a]

[a]Relationship significant at .01 level.

[b]Relationship significant at .05 level.

Note: Figures here are similar to those in Table 13.2, except that televised convention exposure (conv. expo.) and televised debate exposure (debate expo.) have been included as independent variables. Underlined values are those for issues receiving relatively heavier news coverage during the period.

TABLE 13.4 Relationship of High, Moderate, and Low Interest Voters' News Exposure and Party Information to Increases in Issue Awareness

Candidate and Time Period	High Interest			Mod. Interest			Low Interest		
	T.V. Expo.	Paper Expo	Party Info.	T.V. Expo.	Paper Expo	Party Info.	T.V. Expo.	Paper Expo	Party Info.
Carter's Positions									
Primaries (Feb.-June)									
Median coefficient	-.06	+.13	+.15	-.01	+.12	+.21	+.06	+.02	+.15
Significant (.10)	13	63	63	0	63	75	25	13	50
General (June-Oct.)									
Median coefficient	+.04	+.09	+.14	-.10	+.06	+.18	+.03	+.11	+.21
Significant (.10)	13	63	63	25	13	88	13	38	75
Ford's Positions									
Primaries (Feb.-June)									
Median coefficient	.00	+.07	+.18	-.02	+.03	+.15	-.02	+.12	+.21
Significant (.10)	0	38	50	0	13	63	0	50	75
General (June-Oct.)									
Median coefficient	-.03	+.09	+.07	-.08	+.05	+.04	+.01	+.07	+.14
Significant (.10)	13	38	38	0	25	13	25	50	63

Note: Figures here are based on same procedures described in Table 13.2, except that separate analysis were conducted for high, moderate, and low interest voters. Figures in significant rows are percent.

reported ones.* High interest voters tend to be more careful readers and, consequently, whether an issue receives more or less news coverage is not overly significant. The frequent readers among them are likely to learn more than infrequent readers about each type of issue.

The emphasis an issue receives has more effect on moderate and low interest voters. The frequent readers among them gain less advantage over infrequent readers in learning about lightly reported issues because they do not take full advantage of the information the medium provides. Most of them merely skim the news, bypassing less prominent news items.

For similar reasons, the type of newspaper available to less interested voters is not of great importance. Because they do not immerse themselves in the newspaper's political content, whether their newspaper provides extensive or limited coverage is rather inconsequential. Among less interested voters, exposure to the Erie newspapers was as closely related to heightened issue awareness as was exposure to the *Los Angeles Times*. High interest voters, benefit from comprehensive newspaper coverage. Among Los Angeles respondents of high interest, frequent exposure to the *Times* was associated with increased awareness of 56 percent of the candidates' positions; among their Erie counterparts, the proportion was 44 percent.†

Exposure to television's coverage of the conventions and debates also had differing effects but, unlike newspaper exposure, there was an inverse relationship between interest and learning (see Table 13.5). High interest voters who were heavily exposed to these telecasts did not learn appreciably more than those who were lightly exposed. Moderate interest voters, however, became moderately better informed from their exposure, and low interest voters became

---

*It should not be inferred that high interest readers learned as much about lightly reported issues as they did of heavily reported ones. In fact, they gained more information about heavily reported ones. The statistical relationships being discussed involve relative differences—whether, on a given issue, frequent readers learned more than infrequent readers. Thus significant relationships might be found in the case of an issue where frequent readers had a 10 percent gain in awareness while infrequent readers had a 2 percent gain, as well as in the case of an issue where frequent readers had a 20 percent gain while infrequent readers had a 12 percent gain.

†It might be noted that the impact of newspaper exposure on issue awareness is somewhat different than its impact on candidate awareness. On issues, its effect is more similar on low and moderate interest voters than on those of high interest. On candidates, its effect is more similar on high and moderate interest voters than on those of low interest. The relative prominence of issues and candidates in the news would account for this difference. The candidates are the central focus of election news, and moderate interest voters, though not overly careful readers, see many news references to the candidates. Issues usually are peripheral news items, however, and moderate interest readers fail to see most issue references.

TABLE 13.5 Relationship of High, Moderate, and Low Interest Voters' Convention and Debate Exposure to Increases in Issue Awareness

Candidate	High Interest		Mod. Interest		Low Interest	
	Conv. Expo.	Debate Expo.	Conv. Expo.	Debate Expo.	Conv. Expo.	Debate Expo.
			Carter's Positions			
Median coefficient	+.04	-.01	+.06	+.06	+.09	+.12
Significant (.10)	13	13	25	25	38	50
			Ford's Positions			
Median coefficient	-.01	-.01	+.03	+.05	+.09	+.14
Significant (.10)	13	13	25	25	38	63

Note: Figures here are based on same procedures described in Table 13.2, except that separate analysis were conducted for high, moderate, and low interest voters. Figures in significant rows are percent.

appreciably more aware of the issues if they watched the conventions or debates.

The contribution of these telecasts, it would appear, depends on whether the issue information they provide is already possessed by the voter or is likely to be obtained from another source. High interest voters were more highly informed about the candidates' positions before the conventions and debates, and most of them followed a newspaper regularly; consequently, these telecasts' information was somewhat redundant. For less-informed citizens of moderate and low interest, the conventions and debates provided new information. Thus the claim of some writers that television provides otherwise ungained issue information to less-informed voters is a valid one.[5] The major source of this information, however, is television's special broadcasts and not its evening newscasts.

CONTRIBUTION OF POLITICAL PARTY INFORMATION

Although newspaper reading was important to people's issue awareness, it was not the most significant influence. People's familiarity with the policy tendencies of the Democratic and Republican parties was more closely associated with heightened awareness of the candidates' positions. Some voters brought to the campaign an understanding of the policies advocated by the two parties (see Table 13.6). Almost 40 percent of the respondents, for example, saw the Democratic party as the stronger advocate of social welfare programs while seeing the Republican party as more concerned with the costs of such programs. The Democratic party also was perceived as more likely to advocate public works jobs, to favor lower income groups in tax reform, and to be less supportive of defense spending.

TABLE 13.6 Awareness of the Policy Tendencies of the Republican and Democratic Parties

Party	Percent Accurately Perceiving Party's Position on:			
	Public Works Jobs	Defense Spending	Welfare Spending	Tax Burden
Republican	34	35	38	37
Democratic	43	23	36	30

Note: Party awareness was measured on seven-point scales similar to those used in measuring awareness of the candidates' issue positions. Party positions were determined from an analysis of party platforms and statements. The figures in this table are based on the February interviews and these precampaign measures were used in all calculations.

These impressions were highly related to what people learned during the campaign (see Tables 13.2-13.4). For instance, respondents who felt before the campaign that the Democratic party was more committed to social welfare spending were more likely during the campaign to gain awareness of a Democratic candidate's position on this issue. For 80 percent of the issue positions studied, increases in awareness from one interview to the next were significantly related to people's prior knowledge of the parties' positions, a proportion considerably higher than that associated with newspaper exposure.

The contribution of party information to issue awareness was partly a logical one. People sometimes assumed that a candidate supported his party's position on an issue. When they became aware of Carter during the primaries, for example, some voters thought his positions were like those of other Democrats, even though they had no specific information to this effect.* Party information also anchored people's judgments. Those who were aware of the party's policy were a third more likely, once having assessed accurately a candidate's position, to retain this perception. They possessed a reference point that aided memory.

Party information also enabled voters to make more efficient use of information. Party knowledgeables were disproportionately likely to gain awareness of lightly reported issues, suggesting they have a greater capacity for interpreting information. Of course, the citizens who are informed about the parties also are more likely to be knowledgeable about politics generally and, as a result, more astute in judging the candidates' positions. But the way in which issues are reported increases the importance of a voter's prior understanding. Issue coverage is not a series of precise statements about the candidates' positions, but instead is a flow of fragmented and frequently indirect references. These messages often have little meaning to people who do not already possess some understanding of the issues. "The value of information is often cumulative," note Robert Lane and David Sears. "Within a given field of knowledge, each new 'bit' gives added value to related 'bits.' "[6]

---

*Only those respondents who indicated they knew the candidate were asked to locate his issue positions. This procedure eliminated guessing about the positions of candidates who were unknown to respondents, thus permitting a comparison of the relative impacts of news exposure and party information once a candidate had come to a voter's attention. Although this chapter has concentrated on Ford and Carter, the importance of party information is best seen when examining candidates such as Jackson, Udall, and Brown. In these cases, only about 20 percent of the newspaper relationships were significant while about 60 percent of the party relationships were significant. Almost no information about the policies of these candidates was provided by the media during the primaries, and news exposure was not an important factor. The increases in the proportion of respondents who could identify the policies of these candidates owed almost entirely to party knowledgeables.

Party information, however, is much more than a translator of the media's messages.* An understanding of party differences, as Table 3.4 indicated, was more important to heightened issue awareness among low and moderate interest voters than among high interest voters. These lesser involved citizens usually are neither political sophisticates nor regular consumers of the news. For them, knowledge of party contributes directly to their understanding of candidate policies. Indeed, were it not for the party information that is sprinkled throughout the electorate, the public's issue awareness during a presidential campaign would be substantially lower than it is.

LIMITING FACTORS

It is the exceptional issue position that is widely recognized by the voters. Perhaps no more than a half-dozen positions have achieved that status in the past 35 years, an example being McGovern's position on Vietnam, which in a 1972 election survey was correctly identified by 88 percent of the voters.

Several influences combine to make this example the exception. One is the candidates' preference for diffuse positions, which are often vague or conflicting in their implications. In 1976 Carter spoke both of his desire to trim the waste from the federal budget and of his commitment to society's underprivileged and disadvantaged. Some voters found this a confusing combination, and only 22 percent—less than half who could identify his clear-cut position on public works jobs—accurately positioned him on social welfare spending.

Even if the candidates' positions were straightforward, the marginal political involvement of most citizens, their casual use of the media, and the limits of their cognitive skills would be significant obstacles to their understanding of the policy choice they face in a presidential campaign. If they were more highly motivated and alert, they would learn more. The amount of issue information possessed by the most attentive third of the electorate is twice that held by the least attentive third.

To these two traditional reasons for low levels of issue information, there needs to be added another: the press's focus on the game. The dominant themes of news coverage are the ones most likely to be impressed on the public, and policy issues are not placed highly in the news. An indication of the effect that heavier issue coverage might have on the voters' awareness is provided by

---

*In the case of the news exposure variables and the party information variable (as well as the other tests discussed in this book), regression equations were run that included only one of the independent variables in addition to the prior measure of the dependent variable. The size and significance of the beta coefficient for an independent variable in these simpler equations was almost always in the same general range as the coefficient for that variable when it was included in equations with several other independent variables.

the Republican race in 1976. Reagan and Ford's positions on national defense became an important news story after being seen by reporters as instrumental in altering the course of the Republican race. The issue was for the press a continuing news item from late March through early June, and for Reagan and Ford the only policy to receive truly substantial coverage. For the voters it became the most familiar position on the Reagan and Ford platforms. During the primaries an additional 19 percent of the public came to know Reagan's position on national defense; an average of only 1 percent gained awareness of his other positions (see Table 13.1). Similarly, 9 percent came to know Ford's stand on this issue during the late primaries, compared with an average of only 2 percent for his other policies.

During the whole of the campaign, in fact, there was no policy issue that became as quickly and widely known to the public as several campaign issues did. Eastern Europe was in the headlines for more than a week and in the minds of about three out of four citizens by the end of that period. The content and emphasis of election news clearly affect what voters came to know during the campaign.

The changes in presidential campaigns since the 1940s make a dubious contribution to the voters' issue awareness. In their 1948 election study, Berelson, Lazarsfeld, and McPhee found that in August, two months before election day, 37 percent of the voters knew three fourths or more of the candidates' positions on major issues. About a third knew one fourth or fewer of the candidates' positions.[7] In October 1976, two weeks before election day, 33 percent of the voters knew three fourths or more of the candidates' positions and 21 percent knew one fourth or less, despite the benefit of a campaign that was four months longer and included television.*

Today's lengthier campaign does not make the added contribution that it might because very little actual learning occurs during the first four months. Issue material is but a rivulet in the news flow during the primaries, and what is there is almost completely diluted by information about the race. The gains in issue awareness that were posted during the 1976 campaign's early months can be traced primarily to people's party information, knowledge that they brought with them to the campaign.* The news media's major contribution to voters' issue awareness came during the convention and general election periods, when

---

*Berelson and his colleagues did not measure issue awareness in the interview they conducted just before election day, but commented that if they had, the amount of awareness "almost certainly" would have been higher. Still, awareness in 1948 compared favorably with awareness in 1976. Such comparisons are somewhat problematic since issues vary from campaign to campaign. The Berelson figures are not corrected for guessing, so the 1976 figures presented also have not been corrected. The corrected figures for 1976 are these: 17 percent of the respondents knew three fourths or more of the candidates' positions and 56 percent knew one fourth or less.

substance was placed more highly on the agenda. It was not until this time that truly substantial increases occurred in the public's understanding of Carter's policies and, to a lesser extent, of Ford's stands. Daily news coverage was not the only source of this information. The televised conventions and debates, as well as the candidates' televised political advertising, were also significant contributors.[8]

Although daily television news has become the candidates' medium, its introduction into the campaign apparently has not added much to the voters' issue awareness. Paradoxically, since its contribution is less than the newspaper's, daily television's ability to inform voters is probably affected less than the newspaper's by the game orientation of today's election news. The newspaper is a relatively spacious, word-centered medium, and its issue coverage is limited less by the nature of the medium than by the interests of reporters and editors. If issues were placed more frequently and prominently in the newspaper, its contribution to an informed electorate undoubtedly would be greater than it is. On the other hand, television communication is not well suited to issue reporting. A few words often are insufficient to state a candidate's position adequately, and for each candidate there are many positions to report. Since people usually acquire this information through repeated exposure, a candidate's position must be reported again and again before it will be impressed on a significant proportion of the news audience. Given the limits of its news space and the difficulty of impressing words on an audience oriented to its pictures, television news may not be capable of adding significantly to the voters' understanding of election issues, even if its news was not consumed by the game.

---

*The importance of party knowledge during the primaries is not fully evidenced in the earlier tables. The cross-lagged coefficients are not always good indicators of absolute differences. It is necessary to examine raw percentages to estimate actual increases in awareness. A cross-tabulation of people's issue awareness in February and in June with their party knowledge and news exposure revealed that the heaviest concentration of acquired information was among the party knowledgeables.

PART V

CONCLUSION

14

THE IMPORTANCE OF POLITICAL INSTITUTIONS

My conclusion is that public opinions must be organized for the
press if they are to be sound, not by the press as is the case today.
Walter Lippmann, 1921

In today's presidential campaign the press is expected by critics and apolo-
gists alike to organize the choices facing the voters. Reporters often claim they
can fill this role. Even if journalists did not want the responsibility, it is theirs
by virtue of an electoral system built upon numerous primaries, self-generated
candidacies, and weak party leaders. The burden on the press is particularly
severe during the nominating phase of the campaign. Communicating with each
voter for a few minutes daily, the press may be asked to create an electorate that
can understand what a half-dozen previously unfamiliar candidates represent and
that can calculate the possible outcomes of a multiple-candidate race, in which
one or two aspirants are backed by intense minorites while the other contenders
divide the majority's support.

It is an unworkable arrangement. If the press is neither so trivial nor so
self-interested as critics suggest, it is much less adequate as a linking mechanism
than is commonly assumed. The problem is that the press is not a political
institution and has no stake in organizing public opinion. Wrote Walter Lippmann:

The press is no substitute for institutions. It is like the beam of a
searchlight that moves restlessly about, bringing one episode and
then another out of darkness into vision. Men cannot do the work

173

of the world by this light alone. They cannot govern society by episodes, incidents, and interruptions.[1]

Although the press and the political party both serve to link candidates with voters, these two intermediaries are very different in kind. The parties have an incentive to identify and represent those interests that are making demands for symbolic and policy representation. The parties do not create these interests but, as Everett Carll Ladd emphasizes, they "are constantly at work ordering and arranging these interests, seeking out positions on which to build majority support."[2]

The press has no such incentive. It is in the news business, and its inadequacy as a linking mechanism becomes obvious once the nature of election reporting is understood. Election news carries scenes of action, not observations on the values represented by these scenes. Election news emphasizes what is different about events of the previous 24 hours rather than everyday political topics. Election news concentrates on competition and controversy instead of basic policy and leadership questions. This is not to say that election news is unimportant. It enlists voters' interest in the campaign, keeps them abreast of election activity, and makes them aware of facts that might otherwise be hidden. But the news is not an adequate guide to political choice. The candidates' agendas are not readily evident in press coverage of the campaign.

The public's attention to politics also is an obstacle to the soundness of press-mediated elections. Most citizens do not have the great amounts of time and energy that are necessary to become well-informed about the candidates. Casual daily news exposure does not produce informed voters. It results only in a partial awareness of those subjects that repeatedly appear at the top of the news. Voters consequently are more conversant about the candidates' campaign styles and successes than about their platforms and leadership skills.

DISORGANIZED POLITICS

It is wishful thinking to believe that self-governing people are masters of every task their democracy sets before them. The electorate of today is better educated and more self-reliant than its predecessors, but as Nie, Verba, and Petrocik noted, it is still dependent on coherent political structures.[3]

Disorganization, however, is the hallmark of the present electoral system. The primaries are waged between entrepreneuring candidates interested mainly in selling themselves, and their backing comes from groups and elites joined together solely for the election. There is no continuing name associated with these factions, no continuing core of supporters, and typically the appeals that dominate one campaign are unlike those emphasized in the previous campaign. The result is an extraordinary burden on voters, one that Key identified in his classic study of one-party politics in the South:

> Under the system of fluid factions, the voters' task is not simplified
> by the existence of continuously competing parties with fairly well-
> organized general policy orientations. . . . The voter is confronted
> with new faces, new choices, and must function in a sort of state
> of nature.[4]

Today's general election also places heavy demands on voters. When party
leaders controlled nominations, the nominee was linked to the party's traditional
constituencies and policies, and a line of responsibility was established between
the nominee and his party's performance in office. Voters thus could reward or
punish the nominee for the conduct of his party and had some assurance about
the nature of his politics. Today's nominee cannot be measured so easily. Every
nominee has some enduring ties, including those to party, but the fact that the
candidate now organizes his campaign increases his independence. Moreover,
there is little that prevents a candidate from disclaiming responsibility for the
actions of any preceding administration and, indeed, he actually may campaign
against many of the policies of his party, as did McGovern in 1972.

It is this chaotic electoral system that the press is expected by citizens and
politicians alike to make intelligible. But the press has neither the means nor the
incentive to correct the system's weaknesses. Indeed, the press is likely to
magnify the defects. The news media, said Lippmann, "necessarily and inevitably
reflect, and therefore, in greater or lesser measure, intensify, the defective organization of public opinion."[5]

The truth of Lippmann's proposition seems evident. The present nominating system naturally gives added influence to voters in states holding early
contests, a bias magnified by the press's extraordinary build-up of these contests,
and its determination to call and cover the winners. These tendencies can fuel a
bandwagon such as the one that carried Carter to the Democratic nomination in
1976. They also contribute to a presidential selection system that permits the
nomination and election of unknown and untried politicians who campaign
for months in the states holding early contests.

The nature of election news also combines with the length and structure
of today's campaign to divert the public's attention from the performance of the
in-party. It is one thing to focus on the record of the incumbent administration
when the campaign is a few months long and waged primarily between the
parties, and another thing to do so when the campaign lasts a year and centers
mostly on conflict within the parties. The press contributes to an election that
de-emphasizes the incumbent's performance by finding significance primarily
in the campaign's contests, activities, and episodes. The public's response to this
type of election news is predictable. As the 1976 campaign progressed, the
electorate's concern with the policies and leadership of the Ford administration
declined, replaced by a heightened interest in Ford's campaign style, electoral

success, and tactical mistakes.

In general, the nature of election news acts to diminish the public's concern with the candidate's programs and leadership. Although changes in the campaign have increased the voters' need for information about the candidates' politics, election news now contains proportionately less information of this kind. In studies of 1940s reporting, Lazarsfeld and Berelson found that national policy and leadership were the major subjects of election news.[6] But in 1976 the coverage centered on the race. The principal subjects were the status of the contest and the candidates' strategies and campaign efforts. Moreover, the issues that the news emphasized in 1976 were not the ones stressed by the candidates. Although the candidates concentrated on general and coalition appeals, journalists preferred lively, controversial issues. Increasingly, election news has come to reflect journalistic values rather than political ones.

The press's added influence in setting the agenda increases the probability that the candidate who "naturally" would be elected because of the political conditions of the moment will, in fact, not be elected. As Seymour-Ure has noted, the press's biases introduce into the campaign an element of random partisanship in the sense that prevailing news subjects and themes may coincidentally favor one candidate or another.[7] The publicity advantage that accompanies the winning of an opening contest, the adverse news that follows upon a candidate's inconsequential gaffe, or the emphasis on issues that have journalistic appeal can affect the candidates' chances of gaining nomination or election.*

TINKERING WITH THE SYSTEM

For the most part the problem of today's campaign lies deeper than the press. As long as disorganization characterizes the structure of the campaign, it will characterize the news of the campaign. The press might recognize more fully how it exaggerates the system's weakness and try to limit some of its practices. Must the candidates' small mistakes be among the major news stories of the campaign? Must the first primary be enlarged beyond all reasonable proportion? But the press is guided by its own values, conventions, and organizational imperatives, and these are certain to dominate its news decisions. The political problems facing the country will tend not to be the subjects that prevail in election news. The messages that flow from the media will note the candidates' fates and maneuvers and not the values at stake. The press cannot be

---

*When journalists are criticized for unduly influencing an election, they are inclined, notes Paul Weaver, to fall back on their professionalism and fair treatment of the candidates, meaning that they handle events in much the same way regardless of which candidate is involved. But the news obviously can be completely fair in this journalistic sense and still be biased in its impact.

expected to organize political information in a meaningful way.

Candidate-controlled communication comes closer to providing voters with useful information. It was the presidential debates, the convention speeches, and the candidates' televised political advertising in 1976 that gave voters the clearest idea of their choices. The campaign probably would serve the voters' needs more fully if the candidates had additional opportunities to communicate directly with voters. But the solution for disorganized polities is not to be found in modes of communication; the messages of the campaign are unlikely to be more sensible than the campaign itself.

What changes in the presidential campaign would enable it, and thus the information about it, to better serve the public? Or realistically, what desirable changes are also feasible? Presidential primaries, for example, seem certain to continue as the principal means of delegate selection, even though their great number results in a campaign that is unwieldy and contestual.

A provision to limit substantially the campaign's length would improve presidential elections. The usual argument against a lengthy campaign is that it disrupts the policy process and discourages the candidacies of responsible officeholders. On the other hand, it has been claimed that a lengthy campaign enables the voters to learn more about the choices they face. The evidence, however, provides no support for this contention. The public acquires very little information about the candidates' politics during the primary months and, over the course of a long campaign, the public gets distracted from its concern with presidential performance. A lengthy campaign also makes it difficult for the candidates to establish their platforms; their pledges quickly become "old" news, resulting in an agenda dominated by secondary matters. Ironically, today's year-long campaign actually makes the candidates' politics less intelligible to voters than would a shorter campaign.

The parties have it within their power to shorten the campaign. The Democratic party, for example, will not certify selection processes that begin before the calendar year of the convention, and it could advance the acceptable starting date by several months. The electorate probably would respond favorably to a reduced campaign. Today's election obviously tests the voters' endurance; their interest in 1976 peaked several months before the November balloting despite the closeness of the Ford-Carter race and the staging of the presidential debates. Moreover, when asked at the end of the campaign for their thoughts about the 1976 election, people's major objection was that it was too long and immaterial.

The electoral system also could be altered in ways that would give more weight to the opinions of the full electorate. The rush to judgment by press and politicians following the initial state contests places far too much weight on the preferences of a small proportion of the nation's voters. As long as state contests are scheduled in serial, this bias will exist.

It would seem advisable to group state contests. If several states held their nominating contests on the same day the candidates would be less able to concentrate their time, money, and organizations, thus reducing the impact that the small arts of electioneering have on presidential choice. The press's influence also would be tempered. If one candidate won nearly all of the contests on the first Tuesday, the press's declaration of a clear winner and front-runner would be more sensible than when it follows from a first-place finish in a single state. On the other hand, if several candidates each won a contest or two, or if two candidates split those held, the press's interpretation likely would reflect the candidates' divided support. At present, divided support in a single state usually is reported as an unqualified victory for one candidate.

The suggestion that state contests be grouped is not a new one. National and regional primaries were proposed previously. Regional primaries have been criticized (as can the present system) for providing an advantage to candidates from the region that begins the process. A national primary, particularly with a runoff provision, has been criticized as posing even a greater threat to political parties than does the present system.*

A clustering of state contests might be achieved simply by advancing the acceptable starting date of the nominating process. If states could not begin their selection procedures until two months before the conventions, for example, they would be compelled to group their contests. Or, state contests could be aggregated by providing each state the option of holding its contest on any one of a limited number of dates. If there were four such dates, for example, each cluster probably would include states of diverse location and population, thus providing an outcome more reflective of national sentiment than do the results from a single state. In such an arrangement, it might be helpful to separate the contest dates by more than a single week. The added time would enable candidates to make appearances in most of the states in the next grouping; would provide the press with more space in which to report the candidates' views, since each Tuesday would not bring contests that the press felt compelled to forecast, report, and analyze; and would give voters more time to consider their options—in 1976, each week was so filled with news of the latest and upcoming races that voters thought and talked about almost nothing but the candidates' success in the primaries.

---

*Without a runoff provision, however, a national primary might enhance party influence. First, the present system enables candidates to depend on a few key operatives who can be moved from state to state as the primaries unfold. A national primary would encourage candidates to develop national organizations, and this would lead them to depend heavily on party leaders in the 50 states. Secondly, a national primary without a runoff provision would be more likely than the present system to lead to a deliberative national convention, because one candidate would be less likely to gain enough delegates to win outright nomination. Such a convention would assign party leaders a more influential role than they have had in recent conventions. It is hard to imagine any system more destructive of political parties than the present one.

Like all other arrangements, a system that clustered state contests would have its biases. Nationally-known and admired politicians would have a greater advantage than they have in the present system. Even if their current responsibilities prohibited heavy campaigning, they would be contending in a system where campaign effort mattered less. Some observers have been critical of clustered systems for this very reason, suggesting that the nominations would be decided simply by the candidates' recognition. But this criticism actually applies more to the present system. The dynamics of it enable a candidate of unknown politics to win nomination in large part through a recognition advantage gained in early state contests. Moreover, there is the question of the importance that campaign effort should play in presidential selection. Should a politician's willingness to spend a year or two on the campaign trail rank near the top of presidential qualifications? Although proponents extol the present system precisely because it forces the candidates to mingle with the voters, the relevance of electioneering is exaggerated. First, intense personal campaigning typifies only those few states holding early contests, and most candidate-voter contacts are so superficial that they are meaningless. Second, skill at electioneering does not indicate a hopeful's ability to handle the presidency. The halls of government, and not television studios and shopping malls, are the appropriate testing grounds for would-be presidents.

A clustered system would have the additional advantage of making it more difficult for a candidate of the minority to gain nomination. Because of the momentum that a candidate can gain, the present system, even when the field of contenders is large, has a high probability of producing a first-ballot nominee. A candidate who appeals only to an intense minority within the party is not excepted from this tendency, because the race in effect may be over before the majority coalesces around a single candidate. In the proposed system, momentum would be harder to generate because divided support would be more apparent. Unless a very strong contender was in the race, no candidate would be likely to gain enough delegates to win outright nomination. In the deliberative convention that would result, the tendency would be to select a nominee acceptable to the majority.

THE INSTITUTIONAL CHALLENGE

A clustered system of primaries does not meet the institutional challenge set down by Lippmann. It still assumes that a mass public, on the basis of messages received from the media, can gain the information and make the calculations necessary to settle the claims of a large field of candidates, most of whom were unknown to the voters before the campaign began.

The real weakness of today's campaign is that it was built upon the dismantling of the political party, which in Everett Carll Ladd's words, is "the one institution able to practice political planning."[8] Although individual voters cannot readily discover the politics of several contenders for the party's nomination, party leaders can make this determination because politics is their specialty. Moreover, judging from the most recent campaigns, party leaders are more adept than the voters themselves at selecting nominees who can gain the voters'acceptance. Parties have a very good reason, the desire to win election, for selecting nominees who appeal to a majority. "The parties," wrote E. E. Schattschneider, "do not need laws to make them sensitive to the wishes of the voters any more than we need laws compelling merchants to please their customers."[9]

That the people cannot fully bear the nominating decisions does not mean that democracy is unworkable. A great mischief results from viewing democracy as a system in which the people make every decision. The problem of democracy, as Schattschneider stated it, "is not how 180 million Aristotles can run" the government, "but how we can organize a community of 180 million ordinary people so that it remains sensitive to their needs." This is not a matter of an outpouring at the grass-roots but of a system that offers the people a choice between meaningful alternatives. To this day, competitive political parties are democracy's best solution to this problem. [10]

In addition to the parties' superior ability to provide acceptable nominees, other advantages would follow an increase in the party's influence. The fact that candidates now organize their own campaigns encourages them to emphasize personality appeals and ephemeral issues, making it more difficult for voters to determine what their choice is. Party influence would assist voters in this determination, since the nominees more or less would represent the parties' general policy orientations. Second, the recent changes in campaigns have widened the gap between the electoral and governing processes. Party influence would link the two more closely, since the line of responsibility between the nominees and the performance of preceding administrations would be more clearly drawn. Finally, the entrepreneurial character of the present campaign has weakened the tie between Congress and the Presidency. Actual and would-be presidents now court "public opinion" more assiduously than they do Congress. Party influence would link more closely the executive and legislative branches because members of Congress would have considerable influence on the selection of the nominees.

Public and elite opinion would not sanction a nominating process completely controlled by party leaders. But the time has come to find ways to increase the party's role in a nominating system that blends popular participation and party influence. The national parties could, for example, establish rules for delegate selection that would encourage more states to rely on caucuses. Another possibility, similar to a proposal made to the Democrats' Winograd Commission, is to make voting delegates to the national convention of the party's most recent nominees for gubernatorial and congressional office. These 600 delegates would not comprise a majority of the convention delegates but they would represent a broad spectrum of party opinion, would be free of the immediate pressures of the state nominating contests, and would hold the balance of power in a divided convention.

A foolproof electoral system is beyond reach. And it is easy to exaggerate the merits of a party-based system. Writing in 1893, James Bryce identified shortsighted party leaders as a reason "why great men are not chosen presidents." [11] But alternative ways of selecting presidents are more or less prone to error. A workable system must take into account what the people, the parties, and the press can and cannot do. However appealing the image of the omnicompetent public and however attractive the idea of the press as the corrective for defective political institutions, these beliefs are not the basis for a sound electoral system.

CHAPTER NOTES

PREFACE

1. V. O. Key, *Public Opinion and American Democracy* (New York: Knopf, 1961), p. 392. The mirror analogy was more popular among journalists than social scientists. See, for example, Sig Michelson, *The Electric Mirror* (New York: Dodd, Mead, 1972).

2. In recent years, however, several excellent studies of news organizations have appeared. See, for example, Chris Argyris, *Behind the Front Page* (San Francisco: Jossey-Bass, 1974); Leon V. Sigal, *Reporters and Officials* (Lexington, Mass: D. C. Heath, 1973); Edward Jay Epstein, *News from Nowhere* (New York: Random House, 1973).

3. For reference to the hypodermic model and its origins, see Sidney Kraus and Dennis Davis, *The Effects of Mass Communication on Political Behavior* (University Park, Penn.: Pennsylvania State University Press, 1976).

4. Paul Lazarsfeld, Bernard Berelson, and Hazel Gaudet, *The People's Choice*, 3d ed. (New York: Columbia University Press, 1968), published originally by Duell, Sloan, and Pearce in 1944; Bernard Berelson, Paul Lazarsfeld, and William McPhee, *Voting* (Chicago: University of Chicago Press, 1954).

5. The best summary of what was believed about political communication during the 1950s is Joseph T. Klapper, *The Effects of Mass Communication* (New York: Free Press, 1960), chaps. 1-5.

6. Angus Campbell, Phillip Converse, Warren Miller, and Donald Stokes, *The American Voter* (New York: Wiley, 1960); Norman H. Nie, Sidney Verba, and John R. Petrocik, *The Changing American Voter* (Cambridge, Mass: Harvard University Press, 1976).

7. A few examples of this research are Campbell et al., *The American Voter*; Nie et al., *The Changing American Voter*; Warren E. Miller and Teresa E. Levitan, *Leadership and Change* (Cambridge, Mass.: Winthrop, 1976); Gerald Pomper, *Voters' Choice* (New York: Dodd, Mead, 1975). A full listing of writings based on the questions and data of this tradition would include a score of books and hundreds of journal articles, professional papers, and Ph.D. dissertations.

8. Harold Mendelsohn and Garrett O'Keefe, *The People Choose a President* (New York: Praeger, 1976); Richard Hofstetter, *Bias in the News* (Columbus: Ohio State University Press, 1976); Thomas E. Patterson and Robert D. McClure, *The Unseeing Eye* (New York: Putnam, 1976).

9. Most of the work in the late 1960s and early 1970s in the United States was conducted by scholars in schools of journalism and mass communication rather than in departments of political science. Kraus and Davis's book (*Effects of Mass Communication*) summarizes much of this literature. For a book-length study, see Donald L. Shaw and Maxwell McCombs, *The Emergence of American Political Issues* (St. Paul: West Publishing, 1977). The forerunner to much of this work was a British Election study: Jay G. Blummer and Denis McQuail, *Television in Politics* (Chicago: University of Chicago Press, 1969).

10. Many of the 1976 studies centered on the presidential debates, and some of the better ones can be found in Sidney Kraus, ed., *The Great Debates* (Bloomington, Ind.:

Indiana University Press, 1979). An excellent study of media politics in 1976, though not about voters, is James David Barber, ed., *Race for the Presidency* (Englewood Cliffs, N.J.: Prentice-Hall, 1978).

CHAPTER 1. A BRIEF ON THE MASS MEDIA ELECTION

1. V. O. Key, *Politics, Parties, and Pressure Groups*, 5th ed. (New York: Crowell, 1964), p. 342.

2. See, for example, William R. Keech and Donald R. Matthews, *The Party's Choice* (Washington, D.C.: Brookings Institution, 1976), p. 238.

3. For a summary of the changes in delegate selection, see Austin Ranney, *Participation in American Presidential Nominations* (Washington, D.C.: American Enterprise Institute, 1977).

4. Richard Rubin, *Press, Party, and President* (New York: W.W. Norton, 1980), chap. 7.

5. See, for example, F. Christopher Arterton, "Campaign Organizations Confront the Media-Political Environment," in *Race for the Presidency*, ed. James David Barber, pp. 3-24 (Englewood Cliffs, N.J.: Prentice-Hall, 1978).

6. Frank Sorauf, *Political Parties in American Democracy* (Boston: Little, Brown, 1964), pp. 38-39.

7. Richard Jensen, "American Election Campaign," paper delivered at the 1968 Midwest Political Science Association Meetings, Chicago, May 1968.

8. For a discussion of early television newscasts, see Martin Mayer, *About Television* (New York: Harper & Row, 1972), pp. 203-5; Robert Sobel, *The Manipulators* (Garden City, N.Y.: Anchor Press, Doubleday, 1976) chap. 11.

9. Richard Rubin and Douglas Rivers, "The Mass Media and Critical Elections," paper presented at 1978 Meeting of Northwestern Political Science Association, Tarrytown, New York, November, 1978.

10. Michael Robinson, "Television and American Politics 1956-1976," *Public Interest*, Summer 1977, p. 14. What this change meant to presidential candidates is illustrated by comments made a few years apart by John and Robert Kennedy. Despite television's role in his 1960 campaign, John Kennedy stated shortly after his election that *Time* magazine was the news source with the greatest influence on public attitudes. Later in the decade, Robert Kennedy expressed his belief that the network evening news was the most influencial source.

11. See, for example, Barber, *Race for the Presidency*; Robert MacNeil, *The People Machine* (New York: Harper & Row, 1968).

12. Ben H. Bagdikian, "Newspaper Mergers–The Final Phase," *Columbia Journalism Review*, March-April 1977, p. 18.

13. David Broder, *The Party's Over* (New York: Harper & Row, 1972), p. 239.

14. See, for example, Robinson, "Television and American Politics," p. 17. The 1964 campaign was the breakthrough for advertising. From what it had been in 1960, advertising spending increased 300 percent in 1964. Of the slightly more than $20 million provided each nominee in federal funds in 1976, almost half was spent on the production and purchasing of televised political advertising.

15. Campbell et al., *American Voter*, chap. 6.

16. Nie et al., *Changing American Voter*, chap. 4.

17. See, for example, Rubin, *Press, Party, and President*.

18. Walter Dean Burnham, *Critical Elections and the Mainsprings of American Politics* (New York: W.W. Norton, 1970), chaps. 4, 5.

19. James L. Sundquist, *Dynamics of the Party System* (Washington, D.C.: Brookings Institution, 1973), chap. 15.

20. Phillip E. Converse, "Information Flow and the Stability of Partisan Attitudes," in *Elections and the Political Order*, ed. Angus Campbell, Phillip Converse, Warren Miller, and Donald Stokes (New York: Wiley, 1966), pp. 136-57.

21. See, for example, Lazarsfeld et al., *People's Choice*, chap. 6; Berelson et al., *Voting*, chap. 2.

22. Walter Lippmann, *Public Opinion* (New York: Free Press, 1965), p. 223. Original publication year was 1922.

23. For a discussion of the development and tenets of objective journalism, see Theodore Peterson, "The Social Responsibility Theory of the Press," in *Four Theories of the Press*, ed. Fred Siebert, Theodore Peterson, and Wilbur Schramm (Urbana, Ill.: University of Illinois Press, 1956). In the nineteenth century, of course, the press was partisan and the candidates received anything but equal treatment in their news coverage.

24. See, for example, Key, *Public Opinion in American Democracy*, p. 392. This is not to say, of course, that all newspapers neatly balanced their coverage of the candidates. In their study of the 1948 campaign, Lazarsfeld, Berelson, and McPhee reported that the Republican-managed newspapers of Elmira (New York), while confining most of their support for Dewey to editorials and columns, did work in an edge for him in straight news coverage—about 60 percent of their news reports were favorable to him and about 40 percent were favorable to Truman.

25. In the working outline to her study of candidates and the media, Mary Ellen Leary stated: "A few journalists feel they ought to transmit as faithfully as possible . . . what the candidate projects. All feel they should do this at least some of the time."

26. Timothy Crouse, *The Boys on the Bus* (New York: Ballantine, 1973), pp. 323-24.

27. Lippmann, *Public Opinion*, p. 221.

28. Daniel Boorstin, *The Image* (New York: Atheneum, 1972), p. 11.

29. Keech and Matthews, *Party's Choice*, pp. 223-25: Donald R. Matthews, "Winnowing," in *Race for the Presidency*, chap. 3.

30. James David Barber, "Characters in the Campaign: The Literary Problem," in *Race for the Presidency*, p. 114. For a more general discussion of the values involved in news selection, see Steven H. Chaffee and Michael J. Petrick, *Using the Mass Media* (New York: McGraw-Hill, 1975), pp. 32-42.

31. Paul H. Weaver, "The New Journalism and the Old—Thoughts after Watergate," *Public Interest*, Spring 1974, p. 67.

32. See, for example, Max Kampelman, "The Power of the Press," *Policy Review*, Fall 1978, pp. 11-14; Irving Kristol, "Crisis over Journalism," in *Press, Politics, and Popular Government*, ed. George Will (Washington, D.C.: American Enterprise Institute, 1972), p. 50.

33. Kampelman, "Power of the Press," p. 13.

CHAPTER 2. TOPICS AND EVIDENCE

1. Colin Seymour-Ure, *The Political Impact of Mass Media* (Beverly Hills, Calif.: Sage, 1974), p. 38.

2. There were 1,001 respondents who were eligible for the five personal interviews. Of these, 53 percent were interviewed all five times; 14 percent were interviewed four times (two thirds of whom missed either the October or August wave); 10 percent were interviewed three times (the majority missing the October and August waves); 8 percent were interviewed twice (two thirds of whom missed the October, August, and June waves); and 16 percent were interviewed once (only in February). The 16 percent loss between the first and second interviews corresponds almost exactly to the attrition between the SRC's

pre- and postelection interviews. There were 126 respondents added to the panel in the April wave. Of these, 46 percent were interviewed in all four waves for which they were eligible, 15 percent in all but one wave, 14 percent in two waves, and 25 percent only in April. Finally, there were 109 respondents added to the panel in the June wave. Of these, 65 percent were interviewed in all three waves for which they were eligible, 18 percent in two waves, and 17 percent only in June.

     3.   Lazarsfeld et al., *People's Choice*; Berelson et al., *Voting*; Mendelsohn and O'Keefe, *People Choose a President*; Patterson and McClure, *Unseeing Eye*. The Lazarsfeld and Berelson 1940 election study was conducted in Erie county, Ohio, and their 1948 election study in Elmira, New York. Later studies also have been based on single communities, for example, the Mendelsohn and O'Keefe 1972 study was based on Summit County, Ohio, and Patterson and McClure's 1972 study on Syracuse, New York.

     4.   See, for example, Klapper, *Effects of Mass Communication*; Kraus and Davis, *Effects of Mass Communication on Political Behavior*.

CHAPTER 3. PRESS COVERAGE OF THE CAMPAIGN

     1.   Lippmann, *Public Opinion*, pp. 221, 226.

     2.   Paul Weaver, "Is Television News Biased?," *Public Interest*, Spring 1972, p. 69.

     3.   Tom Wicker, "The Role of the Media — Informing or Influencing the Electorate?," paper presented at NBC Forum, March 1977, Washington D.C., pp. 1-2.

     4.   Hal Wolsky, "On any Given Sunday: A Content Analysis of 'Issues and Answers,' 'Meet the Press,' and 'Face the Nation,' " unpublished paper, 1976, Syracuse, New York. Newspapers vary, of course, in the opinion columns they carry. For the columns contained in the four newspapers studied, however, about 35 percent of the content pertained to the game.

     5.   Neither of the two coding systems described in Chapter 2 measured the complete content of election news stories. Consequently, Table 3.1 is based on a separate content analysis in which the coders were instructed to divide the news content of campaign stories into the categories shown in the table. A sampling of almost 20 percent of election stories was conducted. The following are examples of the kind of news references placed in each category: winning and losing included statements about the candidates' chances for victory, opinion polls indicating the voters' candidate preferences, vote projections and returns, delegate counts, et cetera; strategy and logistics include references to the candidates' strategies, tactics, finances, organizational strength, et cetera; appearances and crowds included references to crowds, the candidates' comings and goings on the campaign trail, their rallies and motorcades, et cetera; issues and policies included statements about the candidates' issue stands, their policy preferences, their ideologies, references to the party platforms, conditions underlying the election's issues, et cetera; candidates' traits and records included references to the candidates' leadership capacities, personal traits, public records, personal history, et cetera; endorsements included references to group support for candidates, the candidates' group preferences, et cetera. All news references that could not be fitted into one of the above categories were placed in the other category.

     6.   Barber, "Characters: The Literary Problem," p. 117.

     7.   Weaver, "Is Television News Biased?," pp. 67-68.

     8.   Lazarsfeld, et al., *People's Choice*, pp. 115-19; Berelson, et al., *Voting*, p. 240.

     9.   The candidates' advertising and other unfiltered communication are discussed again in Chapters 4 and 14.

     10.   See, for example, Theodore White, *The Making of the President 1972* (New York: Bantam, 1973). White wrote inside accounts of each of the four presidential campaigns from 1960 to 1972.

     11.   See, for example, Epstein, *News from Nowhere*, p. 30.

CHAPTER 4. REPORTING THE ISSUES

1. Seymour-Ure, *Political Impact of Media*, p. 223.
2. Barber, "Characters: The Literary Problem," pp. 114-15.
3. Seymour-Ure, *Political Impact of Media*, p. 219.
4. Ibid.
5. Gerald Pomper, *Elections in America* (New York: Dodd, Mead, 1968), p. 194.
6. David E. Butler and Michael Pinto-Duschinskey, *The British General Election of 1970* (London: Macmillan, 1971), p. 137
7. Benjamin I. Page, *Choices and Echoes in Presidential Elections* (Chicago: University of Chicago Press, 1978), chap. 6.
8. Percentages based on a 5 percent sampling of election news stories; original content analysis did not include this categorization.
9. William E. Bicker, "Network Television News and the 1976 Presidential Primaries," in *Race for the Presidency*, p. 105.
10. One edition of the *Times* for the week immediately following the second debate was unavailable; consequently, these are the headlines for six days rather than seven.
11. Examples of campaign issues include Carter's ethnic purity statement, the charge that Senator Jackson had Communists on his staff, Carter's *Playboy* interview, the policy of Carter's hometown church toward black members, Ford's Eastern Europe statement, and allegations that some of Carter's workers had pocketed campaign money. Whether a campaign issue was heavily reported depended primarily on two things. First, it mattered which candidate was involved—an issue received more coverage if a major candidate (for example, Carter) rather than a minor candidate (for example, Jackson) was involved. Second, it mattered how intimately involved a candidate was, receiving more coverage if the candidate was directly responsible (for example, Ford's Eastern Europe statement) and less coverage if the candidate was indirectly responsible (for example, the pocketing of money by Carter workers). Policy issues involved such matters as the candidates' positions on unemployment, inflation, abortion, busing, national defense, crime, public transportation, public housing, and energy.
12. See, for example, Chaffee and Petrick, *Using Media*, chap. 3.
13. Cited in Barber, "Characters: The Literary Problem," p. 117.
14. F. Christopher Arterton, "The Media Politics of Presidential Campaigns," in *Race for The Presidency*, pp. 48-51.
15. Carl Leubsdorf, "The Reporter and the Presidential Candidate," *ANNALS*, September 1976, p. 6.
16. Weaver, "Is Television News Biased?," p. 69.
17. Matthews, "Winnowing," p. 67.
18. The term "weary distaste" is from Seymour-Ure, *Political Impact of Media*, p. 220.
19. Berelson et al., *Voting*, p. 236.

CHAPTER 5. PRESENTING THE CANDIDATES

1. For many weeks of the campaign, there was only a single primary contest, and the order of finish in that primary determined the candidates' placement. On weeks when more than one contest was scheduled, the order of finish was determined by overall performance and the emphasis placed on each contest. For example, the Massachusetts and Vermont primaries were held on the same day, but Massachusetts was greatly more publicized, and its winner (Jackson) was considered the first-place finisher for the week. On weeks in which more than four candidates actively campaigned, the fourth-place finishers'

coverage was considered to be the combined coverage of all candidates placing fourth or less.

2.   Brown's position as California's governor is the reason why he received comparatively more coverage from the Los Angeles newspapers than from the other news outlets, as shown in Table 5.2.

3.   Jules Witcover, *Marathon* (New York: Viking, 1977), p. 202.

4.   Michael J. Robinson and Karen A. McPherson, "For Better or Worse, News Content Can Make a Difference," unpublished paper, 1976.

5.   Arterton, "Campaign Organizations," p. 21.

6.   There was about a 5 percent difference in the coverage received during winning and losing weeks by Ford and Reagan. The balance of campaign coverage between these candidates fluctuated considerably, however, depending on whether Ford spent most of his time on the campaign trail or at the White House.

7.   In 1964 Goldwater lost Florida to an unpledged slate; lost New Hampshire's primary to write-in candidate Henry Cabot Lodge; and did not contest Rockefeller in West Virginia's primary. Goldwater dominated only Kentucky, where in 1976 Ford edged Reagan by 51-49 percent in the primary. In 1964 Goldwater received 100 percent of the delegates in the states of North Carolina, Indiana, Idaho, and Nebraska.

8.   Wicker, "Role of the Media," pp. 1-2.

CHAPTER 6. THE AUDIENCE FOR NATIONAL NEWS

1.   James David Barber, "Characters in the Campaign: The Educational Challenge," in *Race for the Presidency,* p. 185.

2.   Kevin P. Phillips, *Mediacracy* (Garden City, N.Y.: Doubleday, 1975), p. 28.

3.   Robinson, "Television and American Politics," p. 15.

4.   Dan Nimmo, *The Political Persuaders* (Englewood Cliffs, N.J.: Prentice-Hall, 1970), pp. 114-15.

5.   Robinson, "Television and American Politics," p. 15.

6.   These figures undoubtedly overestimate people's actual news exposure. Research has shown that people usually overstate their use of news sources.

7.   Ralph L. Lowenstein, "Why Network TV News is Criticized," Freedom of Information Center Report no. 0012, School of Journalism, University of Missouri at Columbia, May 1971, p. 2.

8.   Patterson and McClure, *Unseeing Eye,* p. 87.

9.   Ibid., chaps. 2,4.

10.   Marshall McLuhan, *Understanding Media* (New York: McGraw-Hill, 1964), chap. 31.

11.   Barber, "Characters: The Educational Challenge," p. 178.

12.   Lazarsfeld et al., *People's Choice,* p. 151. Lazarsfeld and Berelson's evidence was insufficient to support their conclusion. They asked people whether they had tried to persuade others. Respondents who indicated they had were categorized as opinion leaders, while the others were labeled as opinion followers. They found that opinion leaders were more likely to use the media regularly and concluded that opinion leaders passed along their information to those who did not follow the media closely. It should be noted, however, that they had no confirmation that opinion followers relied on opinion leaders for this information. They did not ask those respondents who were classified as opinion followers whether they had regular contact with opinion leaders, since they shared a greater interest in politics and in news coverage, and were otherwise more similar in their backgrounds.

13.   Key, *Public Opinion in American Democracy,* p. 359.

14.   Blumler and McQuail, *Television and Politics,* p. 206.

CHAPTER 7. INTEREST IN THE CAMPAIGN

1.   Interest was measured by having respondents locate themselves on a seven-point scale based on the statement "I have a lot of interest in this year's presidential campaign." Those indicating strongly agree were placed in the strongly interested category; those indicating somewhat agree or slightly agree were placed in the moderately interested category; and those giving any of the other four responses (not sure, slightly disagree, somewhat disagree, strongly disagree) were placed in the not interested category. The assignment of each of the seven scale points to one of the three categories was not done arbitrarily. The 1976 SRC Election Survey included a three-point interest question, and the response distribution obtained in the October interviews by the assignments just mentioned most closely approximates the response distribution to the SRC's question in its general election interviews. In the regression analysis presented later in this chapter, the full seven-point scales are used since they provide more variation and are more sensitive to the interest changes that occurred during the campaign. As a final note, the percentages shown in Table 7.1 are based only on respondents who participated in at least three interviews; this was done in order to minimize change due to changes in which respondents were interviewed from one time to the next.

2.   Lazarsfeld et al., *People's Choice*, p. 77; Berelson et al., *Voting*, pp. 28-30. In their 1940 study, the proportion expressing strong interest was 28 percent in May, 31 percent in August, and 38 percent in October. In their 1948 study, the proportion expressing strong interest remained constant at about 30 percent through all of their interviews.

3.   Ibid.

4.   Lazarsfeld et al., *People's Choice*, p. 77.

5.   Proportion based on an analysis of *New York Times* election coverage in the first week of the months of January through June in 1948 and 1975.

6.   Although the 1952 campaign is regarded as the first televised election, there was limited televised coverage of the 1948 campaign in a few cities.

7.   Christopher Achen, "Measuring Representation: Perils of the Correlation Coefficient," *American Journal of Political Science*, November 1977, pp. 805-15; Donald T. Campbell, "From Description to Experimentation," in *Problems in Measuring Change*, ed. C. W. Harris (Madison, Wis.: University of Wisconsin Press, 1962), pp. 212-42; David Heise, "Separating Reliability and Stability in Test-Retest Correlation," *American Sociological Review*, February 1979, pp. 93-101; Donald C. Pelz and Frank M. Andrews, "Detecting Causal Priorities in Panel Study Data," *American Sociological Review*, December 1964, pp. 836-48; Malcolm E. Turner and Charles D. Stevens, "The Regression Analysis of Causal Paths," *Biometrics*, Summer 1959, pp. 236-58. The most common use of panel data involves cross-lagged analysis, most easily illustrated by discussing the relationship between two variables (X,Y) measured at two points in time (1,2). The telling clues to the nature of the causal sequence between the two variables depends on the magnitude of the relationships from X1 to Y2, and from Y1 to X2. If the magnitude of the former is the larger, the researcher can reasonably infer that X is more of a cause than an effect of Y. But if the latter is larger, Y is more a cause than an effect of X. Campbell initially suggested using cross-lagged simple corrections to test for the predominance of X or Y. The most obvious difficulty with cross-lagged correlations, however, is their failure to account for autocorrelation, for example, the effect of X1 on X2. Consequently, Pelz and Andrews suggested using cross-lagged partial correlations (for example, the correlation between Y1 and X2 controlling for X1) to control for autocorrelation. This works fine when only a single relationship is being examined. When comparisons are being made, as Achen and others have indicated, correlations are not advised because they are dramatically affected by differences in variances. In this case, which is the situation here, regression analysis, as Heise as others have suggested, is the preferred method.

8.   The convention-interest relationship even would have been stronger had it been possible to conduct all of the interviews immediately after the last convention. The interviewing stretched for a couple of weeks past this time, and those interviewed earlier in the period had higher interest levels than those interviewed later.

9.   See, for example, Campbell et al., *American Voter*, pp. 143-45.

10.   Television news viewing, as might be expected, was more closely correlated than newspaper reading with convention and debate viewing.

11.   Most communications research has found that the newspaper's impact is steadier than television's. See, for example, Shaw and McCombs, *Emergence of Political Issues.*

CHAPTER 8. THE VOTERS' CONTROL OF INFORMATION

1.   Lazarsfeld et al., *People's Choice*, p. 76.

2.   See, for example, Leo Bogart, *Strategy in Advertising* (New York: Harcourt, Brace, and World, 1967), p. 139; Patterson and McClure, *Unseeing Eye*, p. 110.

3.   David Sears and Jonathan Freedman, "Selective Exposure to Information: A Critical Review," *Public Opinion Quarterly*, Summer 1967, pp. 194-213.

4.   Blumler and McQuail, *Television and Politics*; see also the articles in Jay G. Blumler and Elihu Katz, *The Uses of Mass Communication* (Beverly Hills, Calif.: Sage, 1974).

5.   See for example, Patterson and McClure, *Unseeing Eye*, chap. 3.

6.   See, for example, Lazarsfeld et al., *People's Choice*, chap. 9; Berelson et al., *Voting*, chap. 10.

7.   Lazarsfeld et al., *People's Choice*, p. 76.

CHAPTER 9. THE VOTERS' AGENDA

1.   See Lazarsfeld et al., *People's Choice*; Berelson et al., *Voting*; see also the interpretation of these studies contained in Klapper, *Effects of Mass Communication.*

2.   The correlation between people's partisanship (measured on a seven-point scale) in one interview and in the next interview was about + .85.

3.   Jacques Ellul, *Propaganda* (New York: Vintage Books, 1965), p. 19.

4.   V. O. Key, *The Responsible Electorate* (Cambridge, Mass.: Belknap Press, 1966); Page, *Choices and Echoes.*

5.   White, *Making of President, 1972*, p. 327.

6.   John Aldrich and Charles Cnudde, "Probling the Bounds of Conventional Wisdom: A Comparison of Regression, Probit, and Discriminant Analysis," *American Journal of Political Science*, August 1975, pp. 571-608; L. A. Goodman, "The Relationship between Modified and Usual Multiple Regression Approaches to the Analysis of the Dichotomous Variables," in *Sociological Methodology*, ed. David Heise (San Francisco: Jossey-Bass, 1976), pp. 241-56; Eric A. Hanushek and John E. Jackson, *Statistical Methods for Social Scientists* (New York: Academic Press, 1977), chap. 7; Gregory B. Markus, *Analyzing Panel Data* (Beverly Hills, Calif.: Sage, 1979), pp. 36-37. Probit analysis often is suggested instead of regression analysis when a dummy dependent variable is involved, particularly when the dummy variable's distribution is quite uneven. Aldrich and Cnudde, Hanushek and Jackson, and others have discovered, however, that though the coefficients will vary in magnitude when using probit or regression analysis (with the regression coefficients invariably being smaller), the order of magnitude of the coefficients within the equation remains the same. Consequently, for the sake of continuity, regression analysis is used in this table and two similar ones in Chapter 12. The evidence in these tables con-

forms with the other findings of this study, adding confidence to the statistical results. The author urges some caution with this evidence, particularly when the dummy variable involves an extreme split. It might be noted, however, that Goodman and others suggest that extreme splits have little effect up to 25 percent/75 percent and that even 10 percent/90 percent splits often are not a problem.

7.   Shaw and McCombs, *Emergence of Political Issues*, chaps. 3, 6, 7, 9.
8.   Patterson and McClure, *Unseeing Eye*, p. 87.
9.   Berelson et al., *Voting*, p. 106.

CHAPTER 10. AWARENESS OF THE CANDIDATES

1.   Based on rank-order correlations in which the news sources respondents used were taken into account.
2.   Robert Agranoff, *The New Style in Election Campaigns* (Boston: Holbrook Press, 1972), p. 258.
3.   A separate analysis of newspaper readers confirmed that exposure to the *L.A. Times* had the highest relationship to increased candidate awareness.
4.   Austin Ranney, "Turnout and Representation in American Presidential Elections," *American Political Science Review*, March 1972, pp. 21-37.
5.   Wallace and Harris were also on the ballot in Pennsylvania, but they were essentially out of the race by this time and are not included in the analysis.

CHAPTER 11. VIEWS OF WINNERS AND LOSERS

1.   Herbert Krugman, "The Impact of Televised Advertising," *Public Opinion Quarterly*, Fall 1965, pp. 349-65; Carolyn W. Sherif, Muzafer Sherif, and Roger E. Nebergall, *Attitude and Attitude Change* (Philadelphia: W. C. Saunders, 1965), chap. 1; Muzafer Sherif and Carl Hovland, *Social Judgment* (New Haven, Conn.: Yale University Press, 1961).
2.   Ellul, *Propaganda*, pp. 112-16.

CHAPTER 12. IMAGES OF THE CANDIDATES

1.   Kenneth Boulding, *The Image* (Ann Arbor, Mich.: University of Michigan Press, 1956).
2.   The terms stylistic and political are from Dan Nimmo and Robert L. Savage, *Candidates and Their Images* (Pacific Palisades, Calif.: Goodyear, 1976).
3.   In calculating this percentage, responses that fell in the general evaluation category are not included, since these cannot be classified as either political or stylistic. The general evaluation category includes responses such as "I don't like him" and "He's the candidate I'm backing."
4.   Most of this coverage, of course, related to Carter's electoral success.
5.   See, for example, Patterson and McClure, *Unseeing Eye*, chaps. 3,6.
6.   James Q. Wilson, "In Politics the Media can Make the Loser the Winner," *U.S. News and World Report*, December 3, 1979, p. 42; MacNeil, *People Machine*; Boorstin, *Image*; Gene Wykoff, *The Image Candidates* (New York: Macmillan, 1968); Joe McGinniss, *The Selling of the President, 1968* (New York: Trident Press, 1969); Joseph Napolitan, *The Election Game* (Garden City, N.Y.: Doubleday, 1972); Herbert I. Shiller, *The Mind Managers* (Boston: Beacon Press, 1973).

7.   That Republicans developed more impressions of Ford than of Carter, however, suggests that some selectivity was occurring.

CHAPTER 13. INFORMATION ABOUT THE ISSUES

1.   Nie et al., *Changing American Voter*; Pomper, *Voters' Choice*; David E. Repass, "Issues Salience and Party Choice," *American Political Science Review*, June 1971, pp. 389-400.
2.   The seven-point scales had alternative positions on each end. Respondents were instructed that the midpoint on the scale was to be used when the candidate's position involved a mix of the alternatives. The midpoint was never used in correcting for guessing. For the correction, only the proportion of respondents who located the candidate in any of the three positions on the wrong end of the scale was subtracted from the proportion placing the candidate in one of the three or four right positions.
3.   The differences in television and newspaper coverage were more pronounced for the *Los Angeles Times* than for the other newspapers that were studied.
4.   See Patterson and McClure, *Unseeing Eye*, chaps. 2, 4, 6; for a more general discussion of the importance of message repetition; see Krugman, "Impact of Television Advertising," pp. 349-65.
5.   See, for example, Robinson, "Television and Amerian Politics."
6.   Robert Lane and David Sears, *Public Opinion* (Englewood Cliffs, N.J.: Prentice-Hall, 1964), p. 69
7.   Berelson et al., *Voting*, pp. 227-28.
8.   For evidence on the impact of televised political advertising, see Patterson and McClure, *Unseeing Eye*, chapters 5-7. A full analysis of advertising's impact was not conducted for the present book, but the author's partial analysis confirms the general findings presented in *Unseeing Eye*.

CHAPTERS 14. THE IMPORTANCE
OF POLITICAL INSTITUTIONS'

1.   Lippmann, *Public Opinion*, p. 228. The student of Lippmann will notice a close and intentional resemblance between the arguments and style of this chapter and Lippmann's chapters 1, 23, 24.
2.   Everett Carll Ladd, *American Political Parties* (New York: Norton, 1970), p. 2.
3.   Nie et al., *Changing American Voter*, pp. 352-56.
4.   V. O. Key, *Southern Politics* (New York: Vintage, 1949), p. 303.
5.   Lippmann, *Public Opinion*, p. 19.
6.   Lazarsfeld et al., *People's Choice*, pp. 115-19; Berelson et al., *Voting*, p. 240.
7.   Seymour-Ure, *Political Impact of Media*, chapter 8.
8.   Everett Carll Ladd, *Where Have All the Voters Gone?* (New York: Norton, 1978), p. 72.
9.   E. E. Schattschneider, *Party Government* (New York: Holt, Rinehart and Winston, 1942), p. 60.
10.   E. E. Schattschneider, *The Semi-Sovereign People* (New York: Holt, Rinehart and Winston, 1960), pp. 138-41.
11.   James Bryce, *The American Commonwealth* (New York: Macmillan, 1893), p. 78.

BIBLIOGRAPHY

Achen, Christopher. "Measuring Representation: Perils of the Correlation Coefficient." *American Journal of Political Science* (November 1977): 805-15.

Agranoff, Robert. *The New Style in Election Campaigns.* Boston: Holbrook Press, 1972.

Aldrich, John, And Cnudde, Charles. "Probing the Bounds of Conventional Wisdom: A Comparison of Regression, Probit, and Discriminant Analysis." *American Journal of Political Science* (August 1975) :571-608.

Argyris, Chris. *Behind the Front Page.* San Francisco: Jossey-Bass, 1974.

Arterton, F. Christopher. "Campaign Organizations Confront the Media-Political Environment." In *Race for the Presidency*, edited by James David Barber, pp. 3-24. Englewood Cliffs, N.J.: Prentice-Hall, 1978.

_____. "The Media Politics of Presidential Campaigns." In *Race for the Presidency*, edited by James David Barber, pp. 25-54. Englewood Cliffs, N.J.: Prentice-Hall, 1978.

Bagdikian, Ben H. "Newspaper Mergers — The Final Phase." *Columbia Journalism Review* (March-April 1977) :17-22.

Barber, James David, ed. *Race for the Presidency.* Englewood Cliffs, N.J.: Prentice-Hall, 1978.

_____. "Characters in the Campaign: The Educational Challenge." In *Race for the Presidency*, edited by James David Barber, pp. 173-98. Englewood Cliffs, N.J.: Prentice-Hall, 1978.

_____. "Characters in the Campaign: The Literary Problem." In *Race for the Presidency*, edited by James David Barber, pp. 111-46. Englewood Cliffs, N.J.: Prentice-Hall, 1978.

Berelson, Bernard; Lazarsfeld, Paul; McPhee, William. *Voting.* Chicago: University of Chicago Press, 1954.

Bicker, William E. "Network Television News and the 1976 Presidential Primaries." In *Race for the Presidency*, edited by James David Barber, pp. 79-110. Englewood Cliffs, N.J.: Prentice-Hall, 1978.

Blumler, Jay G., and Katz, Elihu. *The Uses of Mass Communication.* Beverly Hills, Calif.: Sage, 1974.

Blumler, Jay G., and McQuail, Denis. *Television in Politics.* Chicago: University of Chicago Press, 1969.

Bogart, Leo. *Strategy in Advertising.* New York: Harcourt, Brace, and World, 1967.

Boorstin, Daniel. *The Image.* New York: Atheneum, 1972.

Boulding, Kenneth. *The Image.* Ann Arbor, Mich.: University of Michigan Press, 1956.

Broder, David. *The Party's Over.* New York: Harper & Row, 1972.

Bryce, James. *The American Commonwealth.* New York: Macmillan, 1893.

Burnham, Walter Dean. *Critical Elections and the Mainsprings of American Politics.* New York: W. W. Norton, 1970.

Butler, David E., and Pinto-Duschinskey, Michael. *The British General Election of 1970.* London: Macmillan, 1971.

Campbell, Angus; Converse, Phillip; Miller, Warren; and Stokes, Donald. *The American Voter.* New York: Wiley, 1960.

Campbell, Donald T. "From Description to Experimentation." In *Problems of Measuring Change*, edited by C. W. Harris, pp. 212-42. Madison, Wis.: University of Wisconsin Press, 1962.

Chaffee, Steven H., and Petrick, Michael J. *Using the Mass Media.* New York: McGraw-Hill, 1975.

Converse, Phillip E. "Information Flow and the Stability of Partisan Attitudes." In *Elections and the Political Order*, edited by Angus Campbell, Phillip Converse, Warren Miller, and Donald Stokes. New York: Wiley, 1966.

Crouse, Timothy. *The Boys on the Bus.* New York: Ballantine, 1973.

Ellul, Jacques. *Propaganda.* New York: Vintage Books, 1965.

Epstein, Edward Jay. *News from Nowhere.* New York: Random House, 1973.

Goodman, L. A. "The Relationship between Modified and Usual Multiple Regression Approaches to the Analysis of the Dichotomous Variables." In *Sociological Methodology*, edited by David Heise, pp. 241-56. San Francisco: Jossey-Bass, 1976.

Hanushek, Eric A., and Jackson, John E. *Statistical Methods for Social Scientists*. New York: Academic Press, 1977.

Heise, David R. "Separating Reliability and Stability in Test-Retest Correlation." *American Sociological Review* (February 1969): 93-101.

Hofstetter, Richard. *Bias in the News*. Columbus: Ohio State University Press, 1976.

Jensen, Richard. "American Election Campaigns." Paper delivered at the 1968 Midwest Political Science Association Meetings, Chicago, May 1968.

Kampelman, Max. "The Power of the Press." *Policy Review* (Fall 1978) :11-14.

Keech, William R., and Matthews, Donald R. *The Party's Choice*. Washington, D.C.: Brookings Institution, 1976.

Key, V. O. *Politics, Parties and Pressure Groups*. 5th ed. New York: Crowell, 1964.

_____. *Public Opinion and American Democracy*. New York: Knopf, 1961.

_____. *The Responsible Electorate*. Cambridge, Mass.: Belknap Press, 1966.

_____. *Southern Politics*. New York: Vintage, 1949.

Klapper, Joseph T. *The Effects of Mass Communication*. New York: Free Press, 1960.

Kraus, Sidney, ed. *The Great Debates*. Bloomington, Ind.: Indiana University Press, 1974.

Kraus, Sidney, and Davis, Dennis. *The Effects of Mass Communication on Political Behavior*. University Park, Penn.: Pennsylvania State University Press, 1976.

Kristol, Irving. "Crisis over Journalism." In *Press, Politics, and Popular Government*, edited by George Will. Washington, D.C.: American Enterprise Institute, 1972.

Krugman, Herbert. "The Impact of Televised Advertising." *Public Opinion Quarterly* (Fall 1965) :349-65.

Krugman, Herbert. "The Impact of Televised Advertising." *Public Opinion Quarterly* (Fall 1965) :349-65.

Ladd, Everett Carll. *American Political Parties.* New York: Norton, 1970.

_____. *Where Have All the Voters Gone?* New York: Norton, 1978.

Lane, Robert, and Sears, David. *Public Opinion.* Englewood Cliffs, N.J.: Prentice-Hall, 1964.

Lazarsfeld, Paul; Berleson, Bernard; and Gaudet, Hazel. *The People's Choice.* 3d ed. New York: Columbia University Press, 1968.

Leubsdorf, Carl. "The Reporter and the Presidential Candidate." *Annals* (September 1976) :1-11.

Lippmann, Walter. *Public Opinion.* New York: Free Press, 1965.

Lowenstein, Ralph L. "Why Network TV News is Criticized." Freedom of Information Center Report no. 0012, School of Journalism, University of Missouri at Columbia, May 1971.

MacNeil, Robert. *The People Machine.* New York: Harper & Row, 1968.

Markus, Gregory B. *Analyzing Panel Data.* Beverly Hills, Calif.: Sage, 1979.

Matthews, Donald R. "Winnowing." In *Race for the Presidency,* edited by James David Barber, pp. 55-78. Englewood Cliffs, N.J.: Prentice-Hall, 1978.

Mayer, Martin. *About Television.* New York: Harper & Row, 1972.

McGinniss, Joe. *The Selling of the President, 1968.* New York: Trident Press, 1969.

McLuhan, Marshall. *Understanding Media.* New York: McGraw-Hill, 1964.

Mendelsohn, Harold, and O'Keefe, Garrett. *The People Choose a President.* New York: Praeger, 1976.

Michelson, Sig. *The Electric Mirror.* New York: Dodd, Mead, 1972.

Miller, Warren E., and Levitan, Teresa E. *Leadership and Change.* Cambridge, Mass.: Winthrop, 1976.

Napolitan, Joseph. *The Electric Game.* Garden City, N.Y.: Doubleday, 1972.

Nie, Norman H.; Verba, Sidney; and Petrocik, John R. *The Changing American Voter.* Cambridge, Mass.: Harvard University Press, 1976.

Nimmo, Dan. *The Political Persuaders*. Englewood Cliffs, N.J.: Prentice-Hall, 1970.

Nimmo, Dan, and Savage, Robert L. *Candidates and Their Images*. Pacific Palisades, Calif.: Goodyear, 1976.

Page, Benjamin I. *Choices and Echoes in Presidential Elections*. Chicago: University of Chicago Press, 1978.

Patterson, Thomas E., and McClure, Robert D. *The Unseeing Eye*. New York: Putnam, 1976.

Pelz, Donald C., and Andrews, Frank M. "Detecting Causal Priorities in Panel Study Data." *American Sociological Review* (December 1964) :836-48.

Peterson, Theodore. "The Social Responsibility Theory of the Press." In *Four Theories of the Press*, edited by Fred Siebert, Theodore Peterson, and Wilbur Schramm. Urbana, Ill.: University of Illinois Press, 1956.

Phillips, Kevin P. *Mediacracy*. Garden City, N.Y.: Doubleday, 1975.

Pomper, Gerald. *Elections in America*. New York: Dodd, Mead, 1968.

_____. *Voter's Choice*. New York: Dodd, Mead, 1975.

Ranney, Austin. *Participation in American Presidential Nominations*. Washington, D.C.: American Enterprise Institute, 1977.

_____. "Turnout and Representation in American Presidential Elections." *American Political Science Review* (March 1972) :21-37.

RePass, David E. "Issue Salience and Party Choice." *American Political Science Review* (June 1971) :389-400.

Robinson, Michael. "Television and American Politics 1956-1976." *The Public Interest* (Summer 1977) :64-90.

Robinson, Michael J., and McPherson, Karen A. "For Better or Worse News Content Can Make a Difference." Unpublished paper, 1976.

Rubin, Richard. *Press, Party, and President*. New York: W. W. Norton, 1980.

Rubin, Richard, and Rivers, Douglas. "The Mass Media and Critical Elections." Paper presented at 1978 meeting of Northeastern Political Science Association, Tarrytown, New York, November 1978.

Schattschneider, E. E. *Party Government*. New York: Holt, Rinehart and Winston, 1942.

_____, *The Semi-Sovereign People*. New York: Holt, Rinehart and Winston, 1960.

Sears, David, and Freedman, Jonathan. "Selective Exposure to Information: A Critical Review." *Public Opinion Quarterly* (Summer 1967) :194-213.

Seymour-Ure, Colin. *The Political Impact of Mass Media*. Beverly Hills, Calif.: Sage, 1974.

Shaw, Donald L., and McCombs, Maxwell. *The Emergence of American Political Issues*. St. Paul: West Publishing, 1977.

Sherif, Carolyn W.; Sherif, Muzafer; and Nebergall, Roger E. *Attitude and Attitude Change*. Philadelphia: W. C. Saunders, 1965.

Sherif, Muzafer, and Hovland, Carl. *Social Judgment*. New Haven, Conn.: Yale University Press, 1961.

Shiller, Herbert I. *The Mind Managers*. Boston: Beacon Press, 1973.

Sigal, Leon V. *Reporters and Officials*. Lexington, Mass.: D. C. Heath, 1973.

Sobel, Robert. *The Manipulators*. Garden City, N.Y.: Anchor Press, 1976.

Sorauf, Frank. *Political Parties in American Democracy*. Boston: Little, Brown, 1964.

Sundquist, James L. *Dynamics of the Party System*. Washington, D.C.: Brookings Institution, 1973.

Turner, Malcolm E., and Stevens, Charles D. "The Regression Analysis of Causal Paths." *Biometrics* (Spring 1959) :236-58.

Weaver, Paul H. "The New Journalism and the Old—Thoughts after Watergate." *Public Interest* (Spring 1974) :67-88.

_____. "Is Television News Biased?" *Public Interest* (Winter 1972) :57-74.

White, Theodore. *The Making of the President 1972*. New York: Bantam, 1973.

Wicker, Tom. "The Role of the Media—Informing or Influencing the Electorate?" Paper presented at NBC Forum, March 1977, Washington D.C.

Wilson, James Q. "In Politics, the Media Can Make the Loser the Winner." *U.S. New and World Report*, December 3, 1979, p. 42.

Witcover, Jules. *Marathon*. New York: Viking, 1977.

Wolsky, Hal. "On Any Given Sunday: A Content Analysis of 'Issues and Answers', 'Meet the Press', and 'Face the Nation'." Unpublished paper, 1976, Syracuse, New York.

Wykoff, Gene. *The Image Candidates*. New York: Macmillan, 1968.

INDEX

ABOUT THE AUTHOR

THOMAS E. PATTERSON is a member of the political science faculty at Syracuse University's Maxwell School of Citizenship and Public Affairs. In 1980 he became chairperson of his department.

Dr. Patterson is the author of numerous articles on politics and the mass media. He co-authored *The Unseeing Eye*, a book about the impact on television news and advertising on presidential campaigns.

Dr. Patterson has received grants from the National Science Foundation and the John and Mary R. Markle Foundation for his research on political communication. Since 1975 he has been a member of the Social Science Research Council's Committee on Mass Communication and Political Behavior.

Professor Patterson graduated with highest honors from South Dakota State University. He served in the U.S. Army in Vietnam during 1966, and attended the University of Minnesota where he received his M.A. in 1969 and his Ph.D. in 1971.